BECOMING A SKILLED READER

Becoming a
Skilled Reader

JANE OAKHILL

AND

ALAN GARNHAM

Basil Blackwell

Copyright © Jane Oakhill and Alan Garnham 1988

First published 1988
Reprinted 1994

Blackwell Publishers, the publishing imprint of
Basil Blackwell Ltd
108 Cowley Road,
Oxford OX4 1JF, UK

Basil Blackwell Inc.
238 Main Street
Cambridge, Massachusetts 02142,
USA

British Library Cataloguing in Publication Data
A CIP catalogue record is available from the British Library.

Library of Congress Cataloging in Publication Data
Oakhill, Jane.
  Becoming a skilled reader.
  Bibliography: p.
  Includes indexes.
  1. Reading. 2. Reading comprehension.
  3. Learning, Psychology of. I. Garnham, Alan.
  1954– , II. Title.
  LB1050.018 1988   372.4   87–35529
  ISBN 0–631–15244–X
  ISBN 0–631–15776–X (pbk.)

Typeset in 10 on 11pt Times
by Columns of Reading
Printed and bound by Athenæum Press Ltd.,
Gateshead, Tyne & Wear.

This book is printed on acid-free paper

To our parents:
Trudy, Jack and Harry

Contents

Preface

In writing this book our main aim has been to provide a summary of the psychological research on children's reading comprehension – to give an account of what it is to become a *skilled* reader. Despite increasing interest in comprehension in recent years, the emphasis in reading research has been on word identification and decoding skills, so the topics we highlight have not been given a central place in recent textbooks on the psychology of reading. Neither have they been at the forefront of teacher training. We believe that both psychologists and educationalists need an accessible introduction to the acquisition of reading skills beyond the level of decoding. All too often it is assumed that children who can 'say the words' have mastered the skills of reading. The further skills that fluent readers possess have received little attention. As a result, children who have difficulty with them are either not identified or, if they are, they are not given the extra training that could help them considerably.

In our own experience about 10 per cent of children with normal decoding skills have a significant comprehension deficit. We hope that in bringing attention to 'higher-level' reading skills we can offer some hope that these children will be identified and will receive the remediation they need.

We are both experimental psychologists, and it is our intention that the book should be included on reading lists for undergraduate psychology courses such as Psychology of Reading and Language Development. However, research on children's reading comprehension has obvious educational implications, which have not received the attention they deserve. We have attempted, therefore, to write in a way that will be both comprehensible and useful to those involved either directly or indirectly in education – in particular, educationalists, educational psychologists and teachers. We have tried to avoid jargon and to explain clearly those technical terms we have inevitably had to introduce. However, we have not oversimplified our arguments or suggested pat solutions to what are often very difficult problems. Because of the complexities of our subject matter, our book should not be thought of as an 'easy read'.

We have many people to thank for help in the efforts that eventually led to this book. Much of our discussion of less-skilled comprehenders stems from our own investigations of these children. This work began with Jane Oakhill's D.Phil research at the Laboratory of Experimental Psychology, Sussex University, which was supervised by Phil Johnson-Laird. It continued under a grant from the Economic and Social Research Council (to Alan Parkin), for which we are very grateful. This research was set out in a proposal prepared by Jane Oakhill but was carried out mainly by Nicola Yuill, who took up the position of research fellow on the grant and whose contribution we gratefully acknowledge. Much of chapter 3 was written while we were Visiting Fellows at the Max-Planck-Institut für Psycholinguistik, at Nijmegen, The Netherlands. We would like to thank the staff there for making our stay such a pleasant one and for providing a congenial working environment. We would also like to thank Margaret Harris for comments on chapter 3, Jane Brocklehurst for reading and commenting on chapter 4 from the point of view of a teacher, and Nicola Yuill for her comments on chapters 5 and 6.

At Basil Blackwell, Philip Carpenter saw the project through its initial stages and made some useful suggestions about how to make the book more accessible to our intended audience. The latter stages of production were ably supervised by Harriet Barry, Rosemary Roberts and Mary Robinson, with the assistance of Connie Wilsack.

Jane Oakhill
Alan Garnham

CHAPTER 1

Introduction

Almost everyone knows, or has heard of, children who have reading problems. Take Warren, for example. He is 8 years and 4 months. Here is his attempt to read a simple story from a standard reading test (the Neale Analysis of Reading Ability). Two dots (. .) indicate places where he could not finish a word. Words in square brackets were supplied by the person administering the test.

> John and – is it John? [yes] – John and Ann were fishing. Su . . s . . [suddenly] they heard a sp . . [splash]. A wooden [woodman] woodman had found [fallen] fallen into the lake. He called [could] could not swim for he was h . . [hurt] hurt. The children tried to pull him a . . as . . as hoar [ashore] ashore. He was too heavy. Then John had um [held] held the man's hand [head] head head! [held the man's head] head er [above] above water and Ann ran for help.

Warren has difficulty reading words such as *suddenly, splash, could, hurt, ashore, held, head* and *above*. Indeed his reading accuracy age is 7 years and 5 months, nearly a year below his real age. He has, if only to a minor degree, a problem that many children share, and one that is widely recognized by teachers, educationalists and research psychologists alike.

Nicola is just 8 years, and her reading accuracy age is 1 month above this. She reads the story about the woodman much more successfully.

> John and Ann were fishing. Suddenly they heard a splash. A woodman has found [fallen] fallen into the lake. He could not swim for he was hurt. The children tried to pull him a. . .shore. He was too heavy. Then John heard [held] held the man's head above the water and Ann ran for help.

After reading the story each child was asked eight simple questions about it:

1. What were John and Ann doing at the lake?
2. What noise did they hear?
3. What had happened?
4. Why could the man not swim ashore?
5. What did the children try to do?

6. Why were they unable to pull him ashore?
7. How did John help the man?
8. How did Ann help?

Here are their answers. Can you tell which child is which?

A1. Fishing
A2. Splash
A4. The man a na the woodman fell into the water
A4. Because he hurt hisself
A5. Tried to pull him out
A6. Because he was too heavy
A7. By holding his hand and keeping his head above water
A8. By running to running to get help

B1. Fishing
B2. Erm . . a . . [remember?] no
B4. Em they were fishing and em the man come along and they em [the man came along. Did anything else happen?] er they . . they . . he put the man's head in the water above the water
B4. Because . . em . . can't remember
B5. They tried to ran and catch him [they tried to run and catch him]
B6. Because . . em . . he was too heavy
B7. Because . . em . . John tried to get him out but he couldn't [John tried to get him out but he couldn't. Did he do anything else to help or was that all?] No that's all.
B8. Well . . em . . Ann helped by em . . she tried to help him get out but she couldn't because she was em . . they was trying to run and catch him but he was in the water before they got there.

Your first impression is probably that Nicola, the 'better reader', gave the first set of answers and Warren, the 'poorer reader', gave the second. But answer A7 contains a clue that shows this first impression to be wrong. It includes the word *hand*. The children's renderings of the stories show that it was Warren who misread *head* as *hand*, and he still 'remembers' John doing something to the woodman's hand. Nevertheless, Warren's answers all count as correct according to the criteria for scoring the Neale test. Furthermore, despite his relatively poor reading of words, Warren's overall comprehension score on the Neale test, based on this and other stories, is a little above the average for his age. Nicola on the other hand, only gave satisfactory answers to questions 1 and 6; her comprehension age is 16 months below her chronological age and 17 months below her reading accuracy age.

Although Warren's problem is widely recognized, Nicola's is not. It is all too easy to assume that a child who reads stories fluently understands them. Yet this may not be so. Indeed, in some ways, Nicola's is the more serious problem, first, because it is more difficult to spot and, second, because most of the time the *point of reading* is to understand what is written. Adults do not usually read so that they can recite the words on the page, and identifying the words is only a step towards extracting the message that the author is trying to get across. We are not, of course, denying that it is a crucial step, whether it is achieved by direct visual identification or by 'sounding out'. We are simply pointing out that word identification is not an end in itself. Neither are we suggesting that because word identification problems are widely recognized they are unimportant or easy to solve. Indeed, more severe cases in children of normal intelligence, who are sometimes labelled *dyslexic*, are very difficult both to understand – as witnessed by the many controversies surrounding dyslexia – and to remediate. However, we shall have comparatively little to say about them.

A major theme of this book is that there are *two* principal aspects to becoming a skilled reader. The first is acquiring the decoding skills in which Warren is slightly deficient. The second is to learn to go beyond the decoded words and to extract the author's message – something Nicola has problems with.

One of the authors (Jane Oakhill) was first alerted to the problems of children like Nicola when she was working as a teacher. Listening to 8-year-olds reading she noticed that some seemingly proficient readers, who were able to articulate individual words, had very little idea of the content of stories they had just 'read'. Tests such as the Neale Analysis quantify this discrepancy between ability to read individual words and ability to understand text by providing separate, age-related measures of word recognition and comprehension ability.

Comprehension problems such as Nicola's may not be immediately obvious to educationalists and teachers, since reading development is generally monitored by listening to children read aloud and by administering tests that involve no more than the recognition of isolated words. Indeed, such methods of assessment may be part of the problem. They may lead young readers to regard the whole enterprise as one of 'getting the words right', and those children may fail to connect this activity with the communication of information. This problem is made worse by the nature of many children's reading books. 'Stories' in such books often bear little resemblance to the lively and interesting ones that the teacher reads to the class. Reading books are getting better but, even so, graded reading schemes stop just where real reading – reading for pleasure and information – starts.

The lack of emphasis on teaching comprehension skills is underlined by the fact that once children have got over the initial hurdles of word recognition and can articulate enough long and obscure words to get through the hardest books in a reading scheme, they are deemed to be fluent readers. Thereafter, little attention is given to their reading progress. Obviously, the children's vocabulary and world knowledge continues to improve with or without coaching, and they may be taught skills such as selective reading and the use of an index, but they are rarely given any guidelines for improving their understanding of text. Fortunately, however, *most* children do develop adequate reading comprehension skills.

As with the teaching of reading, reading research has, in the main, focused on word identification and not on how to develop reading beyond the initial stages. Furthermore, those studies that have investigated reading comprehension have not always produced clear results. Perhaps the most influential way of studying reading has been the so-called 'factor analytic' approach, which attempts to identify a small number of factors that contribute to comprehension skill or, strictly speaking, to scores on tests of comprehension. The results of factor analysis depend, in part, on the tests used, which is one reason why those results are not consistent. However, the studies do agree that knowledge of word meanings is a separate and necessary factor, and one that, not surprisingly, makes a major contribution to the ability to comprehend. It must be noted, however, that many comprehension tests, unlike the Neale Analysis, do not provide independent word identification and comprehension scores.

There are two further problems with factor analysis. First, it picks out trends in the scores from large numbers of children, making it difficult to identify smaller groups of readers – poor comprehenders like Nicola, for example – who differ from the norm. Second, it does not identify the processes that underlie comprehension, such as those discussed in chapter 2. It is much easier to suggest remediation schemes for poor comprehenders if these processes are understood (see chapter 6).

As we have already remarked, research into children's reading comprehension often takes as its starting point the idea that reading requires only the ability to decode written words plus a general ability to understand language (e.g. Perfetti and Hogaboam, 1975a). There are two assumptions underlying this idea. The first is that, apart from a large number of vocabulary items, the only thing that beginning readers lack compared with skilled readers is the ability to identify written words. The second is that understanding written language is much the same as understanding spoken language, so children who are proficient in the latter skill should have no problems with reading once they have acquired the appropriate decoding skills. Unfortunately neither of these assumptions is true, as we show in the later chapters of this book. On the one hand, as chapter 3 documents, children's knowledge of syntax (the structure of sentences) continues to increase well beyond the age at which they start learning to read (e.g. Chomsky, 1969). So there may be types of sentence in both spoken and written language that children up to 12 years do not understand. On the other hand, children cannot necessarily understand a written sentence that they would understand if it were spoken. The interpretation of spoken language may be guided by factors such as tone of voice, stress and intonation, which are not available in written language. For example, stress can signal that something is being referred to for the first time, and it can indicate who or what a pronoun refers to. Intonation can indicate whether an utterance, of say *he says I should open the window* is a statement ('normal' intonation) or a question (pitch rises at the end). Text uses punctuation marks to convey some of the information carried by pausing, stress and intonation in speech, but young readers do not have a good grasp of the way punctuation works.

Another problem that is often ignored in research on reading comprehension is that language understanding makes heavy use of very short-term memory stores. For example, the comprehension of sentences with complex structures depends not only on understanding the structure itself, but also on being able to store the bits of structure until they can be put together. Furthermore, if the immediately preceding text cannot be remembered, it may be difficult to link together the information from different sentences and to work out the overall message carried by a text. Short-term memory limitations could therefore be a source of comprehension problems. Indeed, the use of these stores may vary both between good and poor comprehenders and between reading and listening. As discussed in chapter 6, good and poor comprehenders differ on some tests of short-term memory, particularly those that test what is called 'working' memory. Furthermore, short-term memory for sounds is better than short-term memory for visual patterns, a fact that may make understanding spoken language easier than understanding written language. It might be argued, against this idea, that words do not 'disappear' in the way sounds do, so readers should not have to hold words in a short-term memory. However, skilled readers do hold words in memory. They do not constantly look back to what they have just read.

Even if poor comprehenders can *remember* what they have previously read, they may not know how to link it to information in the current sentence. Texts contain many *cohesive* devices, such as pronouns and ellipses, that allow complex ideas to be expressed succinctly. If children do not understand how these devices operate (and many of them are used differently in spoken and written language) texts may appear to them to lack any clear 'flow of ideas' or overall structure. The inability to integrate the ideas in a text can lead to further memory problems since unconnected bits of information are much harder to remember than connected ones. We shall discuss children's understanding of cohesive links in chapter 3.

Skilled readers expect texts to be coherent. Indeed, they supply their own links between sentences if those links are not explicitly signalled in the text. The ability to draw inferences that go beyond the explicit linguistic message is a very important one, and one that plays a variety of roles in understanding. To cite just one example, inferences are often needed to provide the correct interpretation of sentences in context. John Bransford and Nancy McCarrell (1975) present some simple yet striking illustrations of the fact that the meaning of a sentence as a whole may be unclear, even when the meanings of the words in it and its structure are perfectly straightforward. Sentences such as:

> The notes were sour because the bag split.
> The haystack was important because the cloth ripped

make very little sense upon first reading. However, given the contexts 'bagpipes' and 'parachute' the interpretation of the sentences immediately becomes clear because we can infer the links between the words in the sentences and the contexts.

Authors expect their readers to make such inferences, and readers often have to make considerable use of knowledge about the sorts of events in the text to do so. Texts would be tediously long if even the inferences needed to make minimal sense of them were made explicit by the author. In chapter 2 we elaborate on the role of inference in text comprehension and in chapter 6 we argue that one of the major differences between good and poor comprehenders is that poor comprehenders do not *spontaneously* make inferences.

In this brief introduction we have sketched some possible sources of comprehension problems. The list is not intended to be complete, and it should be clear that poor comprehension may be the result of one or more of a number of deficits. We shall have more to say about poor comprehenders later in the book, particularly in chapters 5 and 6.

We end this first chapter with a brief outline of the rest of the book. In the next chapter we describe skilled adult reading. This discussion indicates the wide range of skills that children need to become skilled readers and suggests some of the things they may have to learn, over and above how to identify words. In chapter 3 we describe how children's knowledge of language changes beyond the age of 5 and discuss how these changes might affect their reading development. Chapter 4 considers two aspects of how children learn to read words. First we describe the skills that children may need to acquire before they can read words, such as knowing what a word is and how it can be broken up into separate sounds. Second we consider methods of teaching children to read words. In the following chapter we describe work on children's text comprehension. We first outline what, in general, is known about how comprehension develops and then discuss the differences between good and poor comprehenders. In chapter 6 we consider the educational implications of poor comprehension – how poor comprehenders can be identified and how they can be helped.

When describing the results of American research on children's language and reading we often describe the subjects as being at a particular grade level, rather than stating their age. This is because actual ages are not always mentioned in the research papers, and to translate grade levels into ages may be misleading. As a rough guide, grades can be converted to ages by adding 5 years. Thus, first graders are about 6 years old, second graders 7 years old and so on. For American readers, British primary education is from 5 to 11.

CHAPTER 2

The skilled adult reader

This book is called *Becoming a Skilled Reader*, but what is a skilled reader? What is it that children learn when they learn to read? There are no simple answers to these questions, since there is no one thing that skilled readers do when they read. Indeed, one reason for calling readers skilled is that they are able to adjust their reading strategies both to the kind of text they are reading and to the kind of information that they hope to extract from it. On the one hand, a newspaper story, a light novel, an article in a scientific magazine and a set of instructions for a vacuum cleaner demand different styles of reading. On the other hand, reading a newspaper article for its story is a different activity from skimming it to find out the name of the president of Nigeria. Skilled readers are therefore people who can get the information that they want from a text efficiently.

However, despite the variety of skills that skilled readers have, in the more straightforward, and more 'central', cases of reading the reader's goal is to *comprehend* the text, to find out what it describes. To put this another way, when reading through an article or a book the reader is trying to discover what the world is like, or what it would be like if the text was true. In reading a newspaper article, for example, the goal is to find out what the world is like, on the assumption that the article describes, or is intended to be taken as describing, the real world. However, the qualification 'what it would be like' is necessary, because fictional writing describes not the real world but an imaginary one.

This chapter describes the major psychological processes that underlie the ability of skilled adult readers. However, it does not cover general visual processes, which, although necessary for reading, are not specific to it. The biological and psychological mechanisms that enable us to see are highly complex and only partly understood. To explain them would require a book in itself.

The chapter begins with an account of how skilled readers move their eyes over a page of text. It then considers how patterns of strokes, curves and spaces can be identified as occurrences of words that the reader knows about, a skill known as *word recognition* in the psycholinguistic

7

literature but usually referred to as *decoding* in the context of learning to read. After that we discuss how readers group words together into phrases and clauses, how the meanings of those phrases and clauses are derived, and how the meanings of texts are worked out from those of phrases, clauses and sentences. These processes that compute meaning are highly complex. They depend not only on the information that is explicit in the text but also on related background knowledge that the text makes available to the reader. In chapter 5 we argue that an important but relatively neglected cause of reading problems is difficulty in constructing the meaning of a text. We shall, therefore treat the processes responsible for constructing meanings at considerable length. Our discussion will be complicated by the fact that there are many facets to a text's meaning. The chapter closes with a brief review of some general theories about reading in adults.

When reading this chapter one very important point must be kept in mind. The psychological processes described are not ones that we are normally conscious of. In ordinary reading we are not aware, for example, of how our eyes move across the page, or of the fact that we are grouping the words into phrases. All we are aware of is the final product of these processes – our comprehension of the text. For this reason, evidence about how we group words together, for example, can only be indirect. The fact that the words are grouped together is apparent from a detailed analysis of what reading must entail, if it is a skill we can hope to understand scientifically. The exact way in which the grouping of words into phrases is effected must, however, be determined experimentally.

EYE MOVEMENTS

When extracting information from a text, skilled readers view different parts of it in turn. To do so they move their eyes over the text in a series of characteristic movements. However, people do not have good introspective awareness of how their eyes move across a page. If anything, they are inclined to think the movements are smooth. They are not. If you watch a person's eyes as they read you will see that they move in short sharp steps with pauses of about a fifth to a quarter of a second between them. The short movements, which take between a fiftieth and a twentieth of a second, are called *saccades*, and the pauses, *fixations*.

The detailed pattern of these eye movements was first studied in the late 19th century. Edmund Huey (1968/1908) gives a good overview of this early work, which was so thorough that little more was discovered about eye movements in reading until highly sophisticated computer-based experimental systems were developed in the 1970s.

The reason why our eyes have to move across the page when we read is that there is only a small area at the centre of our visual field in which our vision is clear. Again this is something we are not usually aware of, but if you hold your eyes still for a moment, you will soon see that it is true. I only in this central area, which visual scientists call the *fovea*, that letters and words can be distinguished. Not surprisingly, we do our reading during the fixations, when our eyes are still. Indeed, it has been demonstrated that vision is poorer when the eyes are in motion – we are much less sensitive to changes in what we are looking at during the saccades.

Most saccades are in the 'forwards' direction – left to right along the line (for English), and from near the end of one line to near the beginning of the next. However, a surprising number of them are in the 'backwards' direction – *regressive* saccades. Even in fluent reading, where there is a strong subjective impression of forwards movement, 10 per cent of the saccades may be regressive. Saccades are usually described as *ballistic* movements, though there is some recent evidence against this view. A ballistic movement is one that is completely planned before it is executed. Nothing that happens during the movement can affect the mechanism that controls the movement. This means that the location of the next fixation must be determined during the present fixation, so that the next saccade can be programmed. An important question, therefore, is what information about the upcoming text is used to decide where the next fixation point should be? The answer to this question is complicated. However, roughly speaking, information more than fifteen letters or spaces ahead has no effect on the position of the next fixation. Within fifteen characters the pattern of spaces and punctuation, and to some extent the shapes of the words and letters, determine the location of the next fixation point. Fixations tend to fall at points of high information – away from little words like *the*. A typical fixation would be about a third of the way into a long word.

Another important question is how is the information from different fixations is matched, so that no words are missed and no words counted twice. This process is not well understood, but, surprisingly, knowing how far the eye has moved does not seem to be of any help.(see e.g. Mitchell, 1982, pp. 23–7; Underwood, 1985, pp. 46–51).

Some people read more slowly than others, and any particular person reads some texts quickly and others slowly. Both the duration of fixations and the length of saccades vary between fast and slow reading. Shorter saccades mean more fixations per line. Some poor readers, particularly some of those labelled 'dyslexic', show unusual patterns of eye movements. It is not yet clear whether these abnormal eye movements are a cause or an effect of their reading difficulties.

WORD RECOGNITION

As the eye moves along lines of text it is moving across a pattern of (usually) black marks on a white background. However, it is very difficult to see a text in a language you know as simply a visual pattern.

The fact that it *is* such a pattern is obvious if you look at words in an unfamiliar language that does not use the Roman alphabet, say Arabic or Chinese. It is usually assumed, therefore, that the very first stages in extracting the information from written text rely on the same psychological processes that analyse any visual pattern.

Once the visual features of a stretch of text have been extracted, those features are used to recognize (i.e. to determine the identities of) the letters and words on the page. This process, which is highly automatic in literate adults, is one that beginning readers have great difficulty with and perform very slowly. Many poor readers continue to have word identification problems. We discuss some of them in chapter 4.

The problem of word recognition is to decide which (if any) of all the words you know, the current visual pattern is an instance of. Printed text makes this problem easier by standardizing the form of each letter and by making the beginnings and ends of words clear. Ordinary handwriting presents a much more difficult problem. How cursive script is deciphered is not well understood.

Any theory of word recognition must posit a mental store of information about words. This store is called the *mental lexicon* since the information it contains is, in many ways, similar to that found in a dictionary. So, the mental lexicon contains information about how words are pronounced, how they are spelled, whether they are nouns, verbs, adjectives, prepositions or whatever, what they mean, and so on. However, there are two crucial differences between the mental lexicon and a printed dictionary. First, the organization of the two is very different. Printed dictionaries are organized on the alphabetic principle, according to how the words are spelled. The mental lexicon is organized in many different ways at once, something that is not possible in a printed book. For example, from one point of view, it groups words according to how common they are. The most frequently used words need to be the most readily available, since they are encountered most often. From another point of view it groups words according to the number of syllables they have, and which of those syllables are stressed. This type of organization explains why many speech errors result in words that sound like those intended but have very different meanings (e.g. *magician* instead of *musician*).

The second difference between the mental lexicon and a printed dictionary is the use to which they are put. We consult printed dictionaries when we encounter words we do not know or whose meanings we are not sure of. The mental lexicon, on the other hand, is constantly being consulted. Of course, we know the meanings of most of the words we read, but we have to get those meanings out of the mental dictionary to make sense of the current text. We use the visual pattern together with contextual information to decide what word we are looking at. Then we retrieve its meaning from our store of knowledge. This process is similar to consulting a printed dictionary. We first generate a description of the word that does not make reference to its meaning. When looking up a word in a printed dictionary this description is based on the word's spelling. We then locate the word in the dictionary, using the dictionary's alphabetical organization. Similarly, in locating a word in the mental lexicon we make use of its organization. Finally, having located the word, we consult its meaning and use it to make sense of what we are reading.

Two kinds of process have been proposed to explain how the visual properties of words enable us to locate them in the mental lexicon. Most models of word recognition claim that both types of process are used. The first is the use of *word detectors*. A word detector is a device that is always on the look out for a particular word. A word detector model of word recognition holds that a person has a word detector for each word that they know. When they look at a word, each word detector has to decide how likely it is that the word is its word. So, if the word is *dog* then the 'dog' detector should be the most certain that its word has appeared. However, detectors for words like *log* and *fog* also have some evidence that their word has appeared, since these words share some visual features with *dog*. The detector for *elephant*, on the other hand, can be fairly certain that the word is not 'elephant'.

The best known detector model of word recognition is John Morton's (e.g. 1970) *logogen model*. In the original version of this model each detector, or logogen as it was called, had a threshold, and when it reached that threshold – when it had collected enough visual evidence that its word was present – it 'fired'. More common words were assumed to have lower thresholds, since they were found experimentally to be easier to identify. More recent experiments have caused the logogen model to be revised. (see Morton, 1981). In particular, because the recognition of spoken and printed words appear to be independent of one another and independent of the mechanisms responsible for producing words, Morton proposes separate logogen systems for reading, for listening and for speaking and writing. Whether there are separate logogen systems for speaking and for writing is an open question.

A more recent detector model is Jay McClelland and David Rumelhart's (1981) *interactive activation* model. The major difference between the interactive activation model and the logogen model is that the former includes connections between the detectors. The connections between the word detectors are inhibitory ones. The presence of these connections reflects a fact about the world: each letter or cluster of letters on a page can only belong to a single word. So evidence that a letter cluster is the word *dog* is evidence against it being *elephant*, or even the visually similar *fog*. When visual information enters this system, some detectors become active. So, the word *dog* initially activates the 'dog' detector and, to a lesser extent, the detectors for words like *fog* and *log*. The greater activation of the 'dog' detector then actively inhibits that of the 'fog' and 'log' detectors, in order to speed up the positive identification of the word.

The second process proposed to account for how we recognize words is *search*. Search is the detailed looking through a set of *candidates* for the identity of a word. The set of candidates may be derived in a number of ways. A pure search model of word recognition holds that for each word we encounter we derive a visual description and then search through the whole mental lexicon to see which word the description matches. Although no one has proposed quite this model of word recognition, Ken Forster (1976) comes close to it. To account for frequency effects, Forster proposed that the entries in the mental lexicon are searched through in the order of their frequency and that the search stops when a match is found.

The amount of experimental research on word recognition is very large. Models of word recognition make detailed predictions about the effects or word frequency, the repetition of words, the context in which a word occurs, and the quality of the display – whether the word is easy to see. More particularly, they make predictions about what happens when two or more of these factors are varied at the same time. From the point of view of reading research, the most interesting questions are those about context. It is well-established that a word can be identified more quickly when it is preceded by an associated word, as when *butter* follows *bread*. More controversial are questions about the effects of sentence contexts, as opposed to single word contexts, and whether there are 'inappropriate' contexts that make words more difficult to identify.

The results of this research are difficult to account for using a pure detector model or a pure search model. A number of models that use both processes have therefore been proposed, for example Curt Becker's (1979) verification model and Dennis Norris's (1986) checking model. Although these models differ in detail, the idea is that a detector-like process makes available a comparatively small set of words that are compatible with the visual stimulus, perhaps at a stage where it is only partly analysed. A search-like process then has to decide between the candidates.

Whatever the precise mechanism of word identification, it is a highly automated skill in skilled adult readers. For simple texts, reading speeds of 300 words a minute are not unusual. Such speeds imply the recognition of, on average, five words a second.

Orthographic redundancy

One way that words could be identified would be for their component letters to be recognized first. The string of letters would then determine the identity of the word. However, experimental evidence suggests that words are not analysed letter by letter. Briefly presented words are more accurately perceived than other strings of letters, which they should not be if words are simply the sum of their component letters. If subjects are shown either single letters (A or O), whole words (PORT or PART) or non-words (TAPR or TOPR), and are asked to indicate, as quickly as possible, whether they saw an A at a certain position in the display, the fastest responses are for the words. It is easier to see A in PART than when it is presented by itself. This finding is called the *word superiority effect* (Reicher, 1969; Wheeler, 1970). Similarly, the time taken to find a single letter in a series of non-words decreases as the non-words become more word-like.

The obvious explanation of these facts is that words have properties that other strings of letters do not have, and that these properties are used to identify words. In particular, the sequences of letters in words are not random but are, to some extent, predictable. The technical name for this predictability is *orthographic redundancy*. The reason for this name can be clarified by considering the letter sequence 'qu' in English. The presence of a 'q' in an English word means that the next letter must be 'u'. You don't really need to look at the letter, so the time it takes to recognize the word should be reduced. The occurrence of the 'u' is redundant. It provides no information (except about the absence of printing errors) that cannot be deduced from the presence of the 'q' and the rules of English orthography. Similarly, if orthographic constraints reduced the number of possible letters at some position in a word, or make one letter much more likely than others, processing time can be saved.

Ambiguous words

Ambiguous words cause a special problem to the reader because they have more than one meaning. However, in any particular context, only one meaning is intended. How is that meaning selected? Once an ambiguous word has been identified, are all its meanings considered or only the appropriate one? The fact that we very often encounter ambiguous words without noticing any ambiguity suggests that the second hypothesis may be correct. However, although this proposal is attractive in the light of introspective evidence, it is difficult to imagine a mechanism that could ensure that only the correct meaning of an ambiguous word is retrieved from the mental lexicon. On the one hand, if two (or more) meanings have already been retrieved from the lexicon, it should be fairly easy to check which is appropriate in a given context. On the other hand, it is hard to to see how, in the general case, context could suggest what *kind* of meaning a word should have and hence prevent other kinds of meaning from being accessed.

Don MacKay (1966) showed that sentences containing ambiguous words are harder to process than those without them. This result suggests that choosing between the two meanings of ambiguous words takes time. However, only recently has convincing evidence been obtained that both meanings of an ambiguous word become 'active' when that word is read. Dave Swinney (1979) made use of the fact that a word is recognized more quickly after one it is related to. So, for an ambiguous word, such as *bug*, this so-called *priming* should aid the recognition of words such as *ant* when the 'creepy-crawly' sense is activated, and recognition of words like *spy* when the 'espionage' sense is activated. Swinney asked subjects to respond to words (*ant*, *spy*) on a screen while they were listening to a sentence about bugs over headphones. He was able to show that even when *bug* occurred in a context that strongly suggested the creepy-crawly sense, *spy* was primed. This result held just after the subjects had heard *bug*. However, less than a second later only *ant* was recognized more quickly. It therefore appears that initially both meanings of *bug* are accessed, but that once they become available they are checked against the context and only the intended meaning is retained.

Phonological recoding

To identify printed words that they do not recognize, beginning readers often vocalize them. In principle, skilled readers could identify words in the same way, converting the written form into a spoken form and then using the spoken form to access the mental lexicon. However, if such *phonological recoding* is part of skilled reading, it happens much more swiftly and silently than it does for young children.

One piece of evidence suggesting that phonological recoding is important in skilled reading is that we often 'hear' what we are reading in our heads. However, this observation does not establish whether we hear the words before we identify them or only afterwards. In the first case phonological encoding would be a component of word recognition. In the second case the sound of a word would be read out of the mental lexicon *after* the word had been recognized.

Glenn Kleiman (1975) proposed a *dual route* model of word recognition, which has proved extremely popular. Kleiman argued that skilled readers can recognize written words either directly from their visual appearance or by first converting letters to sounds, using rules called *grapheme–phoneme correspondence rules* (see also chapter 4), and then using the sounds to access the mental lexicon, just as if the word had been spoken. Kleiman believed that the direct route was used when reading was easy, and that phonological recoding was more common for difficult passages and for less-skilled readers.

Recently it has been argued that the facts about skilled adult reading that can be explained using the dual route model can also be explained by an alternative *analogy theory*, in which similarities (or analogies) between the sounds of words directly affect the way the mental lexicon is accessed. The dual route model has, however, also received considerable support from the study of language disorders that result from brain damage. It remains to be seen whether an analogy theory can provide satisfactory explanations of these findings as well.

If phonological recoding is not always, and perhaps never, used to *recognize* words, why do we so often hear what we are reading in our heads? The answer to this question is suggested by the results of experiments in which subjects have to subvocalize (i.e. say to themselves) irrelevant material while reading a passage of prose. Subvocalization, because it is a phonological task, is assumed to interfere with the generation of a phonological code from the text. Kleiman and others had found that subvocalization does not affect the comprehension of single words. It does, however, affect the comprehension of connected prose, though Betty Ann Levy (1978) showed that this effect only occurs when precise information about the wording of the text has to be retained. As Huey (1968/1908) suggested, a phonological code is a good way to hold the beginning of a sentence in short-term memory while the end of it is read. It seems, then, that even if phonological codes are not necessary for accessing the mental lexicon they have a function in comprehension.[1]

SYNTACTIC PROCESSING

The branch of linguistics that describes the structure of sentences is called *syntax*. Syntax deals with the grouping of words into phrases, and the grouping of those phrases into larger units – clauses and sentences. Sentences, therefore, have several layers of structure, which can be displayed in hierarchical tree diagrams. For example, a tree diagram showing the structure of:

Jill saw Spot chase a cat

might be:

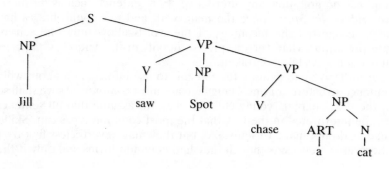

where S = sentence; NP = noun phrase; VP = verb phrase; V = verb; ART = article; N = noun. This diagram illustrates the fact that one phrase can be part of another. For example, the noun phrase *a cat* is part of the verb phrase *chase a cat*.

What is the relevance of syntax to reading? Although we can readily recognize the groups of words in a sentence – we know that *chase a cat* forms a group in a way that *saw Spot chase* does not – grouping words together is not the same as working out the meaning of a sentence. And working out the meaning is the primary goal of reading. However, if recognizing phrases is not working out meaning, it is a necessary preliminary to it. Groups of words are used to refer to the kinds of things that texts are about: people, places, animals, objects, activities, events and so on. So grouping the words in a sentence properly can be a great help in understanding it.

Working out the syntactic structure of a sentence is called *parsing*. Parsing is a component of normal reading, but its place in the reading process is not as straightforward as it might at first appear. Although the meaning of a sentence depends on the way its words are grouped together, there may be other clues to its meaning that allow some of the syntactic clues to be ignored. For example, information about syntax and verb forms is necessary to distinguish between the meanings of:

> The butcher saw Mary
> The butcher was seen by Mary.

It is important not to mistake the first for the second. However, a sentence such as:

> The bicycle was ridden by Mary

which is also a so-called *passive*, is much less likely to be confused with:

> The bicycle rode Mary

since that sentence does not make sense. Given a person, a bicycle and an act of riding, it must be the person that performs the act and the bicycle that gets ridden. The meanings of the main words of the sentence do not allow any alternative. In a sentence such as *the bicycle was ridden by Mary*, once the main verb and the noun phrases have been recognized the meanings of the words allow only one sensible interpretation, whatever the precise details of its syntax. A *full parse* may not always be undertaken.

Another way to avoid a full parse is to use information about which sentence structures of one's language are most common. As we shall see in the next chapter, young children seem to assume that all sentences can be interpreted in the way that the most common types can. Skilled readers do not make this mistake, but they may nevertheless first try to interpret sentences as though they had common forms and only if they fail, or come up with highly implausible interpretations, might they revise their ideas. Tom Bever (1970) describes a set of strategies that interpret sentences in this way. We shall describe just one of them here, one that will be particularly important in the discussion in chapter 3.

The most common form for English sentences is subject followed by verb followed by object:

The tabby cat ate some fish.

The most important word in the phrases describing the subject and the object is almost always a noun, so subject–verb–object is usually reflected in a . . . Noun . . . Verb . . . Noun . . . sequence in the sentence. The usual interpretation of the subject, verb and object is that the subject is the actor, the verb names the action and the object is the thing acted upon. One of Bever's strategies for interpreting sentences therefore states that, other things being equal, an NVN sequence should be interpreted as Actor–Action–Acted Upon. Young children have yet to learn when other things are not equal – as they are not, for example, in passive sentences, such as:

Some fish was eaten by the tabby cat.

In this sentence the *first* noun introduces the Acted Upon and the second the Actor.

There are, however, many cases in which cues to the meaning of a sentence are not available, or in which the sentence has an uncommon form. So it often is necessary to complete a syntactic analysis. The question therefore arises as to what mechanism produces this analysis.

There have been many detailed proposals, though no completely satisfactory model of human parsing has yet been formulated. One of the major issues is which way the tree is built. Is it constructed by starting at the top S and working down towards the words (*top-down* analysis), or from the words up to the S (*bottom-up* analysis)?

A popular parsing method called *augmented transition network* (ATN) *parsing*, borrowed from computer science, uses the top-down method. But this method results in a lot of errors (followed by re-analysis) as the parser has to first 'guess' a structure and then see if the words fit it. It would seem that using a top-down parsing method, many readily understood sentences would be difficult to process.

The amount of psychological research on parsing has been comparatively small. However, some recent experiments have addressed two important questions. The first is: what is the role of the verb in parsing? Verbs are important because particular verbs must be followed by particular types of phrase in their complements and might therefore suggest what the parser should be looking for. For example, *put* must have both a noun phrase as a direct object and a location phrase. You cannot say *John put the cup* or *John put on the table*, it must be *John put the cup on the table.* Furthermore, verbs that can occur in two kinds of sentence may occur more commonly in one of them. For example, both *drive* and *steal* can occur with a direct object (transitive use) and without a direct object (intransitive use). However, *drive* usually occurs without one (e.g. *drove home, drove into town*), whereas steal usually occurs with one (e.g. *stole the money*). These *structural expectations* associated with verbs have been shown to influence the way sentences are parsed. (see e.g. Clifton, Frazier and Connine, 1984; Mitchell and Holmes, 1985).

The second, related, question is how the human parser copes with structural ambiguities. Many unambiguous sentences are *locally ambiguous*. There are short stretches over which it is unclear how the words should be grouped. For example, a sentence that starts:

> After the young man had visited his mother. . .

could continue in two ways:

> . . . had to tidy the whole house.
> . . . she had to tidy the whole house.

His mother could either be the direct object of *visited* or the subject of a new clause. Which it is does not become clear until later in the sentence. These particular sentences are only ambiguous over short stretches but others remain ambiguous for longer, and others have ambiguities that are never (syntactically) resolved. For example,

> I saw the man with the telescope.

has one structure in which *with the telescope* qualifies *man* (the man had a telescope) and one in which it qualifies *saw* (I used the telescope to see him).

There are three accounts of what happens when the human sentence parsing mechanism has to cope with local ambiguities. One is that it makes no decision about the structure of the sentence but waits for further information. The second is that both structures are initially constructed, but one of them is discarded when the rest of the sentence is read. The third is that only one structure is built, perhaps the most common one. If this structure is incompatible with the rest of the sentence, it is discarded and the other one has to be tried out.

Recent experimental work has supported the third hypothesis. However, there are conflicting views about how the favoured analysis is selected. Some work (e.g. Ferreira and Clifton, 1986) has suggested that the most common structure is chosen regardless of its plausibility. Other research (e.g. Crain and Steedman, 1985) suggests that the contextually most plausible reading is chosen. This issue will only be resolved by further research.

THE MEANING OF SENTENCES AND TEXTS

As was mentioned above, there are many aspects of a text's meaning. Some of these are directly related to the structure of the sentences in the text. Others depend on the relation of those sentences to both linguistic and non-linguistic context. We shall first say a little about the structure-dependent aspects of meaning before moving on to those aspects, such as inference making, which we shall later claim that some children have difficulty with (see chapter 5).

The main verb plays a crucial role in determining the literal meaning of a sentence. As was discussed above, each verb has associated with it a specification of the participants in the kind of state, event or process that it describes. It also carries information about where in syntactic structure phrases denoting those participants will occur. To take a simple example, any event of giving requires a giver, a gift and a recipient of the gift. There are a number of types of verb phrase containing the verb *give*. The chief of these are (V = verb, NP = noun phrase):

V NP(gift) [to NP(recipient)]	John gave a book to Mary.
V NP(recipient) NP(gift)	John gave Mary a book.
V(passive) [to NP(recipient)] [by NP(giver)]	A book was given to Mary by John.
(passive) NP(gift) [by NP(giver)]	Mary was given a book by John.

A general rule for interpreting the subject noun phrases of active and passive verbs ensures that the subject noun phrases in these four sentences are correctly interpreted as giver, giver, gift and recipient, respectively. The rule is that the subject NP takes whatever (obligatory) role is left after those in the VP have been assigned. Sometimes the participants in an event remain implicit. It is possible to say, for example:

Mary was given a book.

However, skilled readers recognize immediately that someone must have given the book, even though that person is not mentioned.

The semantic and syntactic information that is part of the entry for a verb in the mental lexicon, together with syntactic analysis of a sentence in which the verb occurs, determine the type of situation that the sentence describes. The obligatory participants in the situation are typically introduced by noun phrases and prepositional phrases, unless they are implicit. Other aspects of the situation, for example where, when and how it occurred, may be mentioned in adverbial phrases of various kinds.

The other major aspect of working out the meaning of a single sentence is deciding what sort of people and things the NPs and PPs describe. Since nouns in NPs can be qualified by relative clauses, as in *the man who broke the window*, which are effectively further sentences, the interpretation of an NP can be fairly complicated.

Working out what sort of situation a sentence describes, although a step towards understanding it, is not understanding itself. We have not really understood a text until we have worked out what particular people it describes, and how the information in its various sentences can be fitted together into a coherent whole. This mental representation of the situation described by a text has been referred to (e.g. Garnham, 1981; and especially Johnson-Laird, 1983) as a *mental model*. However, the information in mental models, or at least the information that can be derived from them, goes well beyond what is explicit in texts. How it does so is a topic that we cover in detail in the next section, since we shall argue in chapter 5 that some poor readers have trouble with the process of elaborating mental models. We close this section with a discussion of the role of short term memory in text understanding.

'Working memory' and text processing

If readers are to combine information from two sentences (or two parts of the same sentence) efficiently in the construction of a mental model, the information from the earlier sentence must be readily available when the second is encountered, and it must be in a form that facilitates such integration. The kind of memory store that is needed to hold and manipulate information for brief periods is referred to as a *working memory*. The capacity of working memory for holding information is known to be strictly limited. Texts that impose heavy demands on working memory might therefore be difficult to understand. Indeed, we argue in chapter 5 that some poor comprehenders suffer from a relatively low working memory capacity.

The most thoroughly developed account of working memory is that of Alan Baddeley and his colleagues (see Baddeley, 1986). In a number of experiments Baddeley has shown that a concurrent working memory load, such as remembering a series of numbers, interferes with performance on comprehension tasks (see Baddeley, 1986, p. 54–6). Furthermore, Walter Kintsch and Teun van Dijk's (1978; van Dijk and Kintsch, 1983) influential model of text comprehension incorporates a limited capacity memory of the kind described by Baddeley to store information that is likely to be useful for interpreting upcoming sentences. However, there are many aspects of text comprehension that Baddeley's experiments did not investigate, and it may be that a more complex notion of working memory is needed to give a complete account of the integration of information from different parts of a text (cf. e.g. Greeno, 1973).

Attempts to discover exactly how working memory is used in text comprehension have not, on the whole, been successful. Meredith

Daneman and Patricia Carpenter (1980, 1983) developed a task that they claimed was particularly suitable for measuring working memory load during text comprehension. The task is to read a series of unrelated sentences and to remember the last word of each. Performance on this task correlated with a number of measures of reading ability. Most interestingly, from the point of view of assessing the role of working memory in specific comprehension processes, it correlated with how easily a pronoun in the final sentence of a passage was understood when the person or thing it referred to had last been explicitly mentioned up to seven sentences back. Baddeley et al. (1985) showed that Daneman and Carpenter's working memory measure correlated with comprehension more strongly than a non-verbal measure. Unfortunately the correlation between the two working memory measures was comparatively low, and a closer consideration of Daneman and Carpenter's task suggests that it may have a comprehension as well as a working memory component. If so, it is not surprising that performance on this task correlates with reading ability!

Finally, when does the integration of the information held in working memory take place? The answer to this question is that different types of integration take place at different times. William Marslen-Wilson (e.g. 1973, 1975) has shown that people repeating back speech played to them over headphones correct mispronunciations (e.g. *compsiny* for *company*) within a few syllables of hearing them, *but only if the corrected word fits with the context*. This finding, which presumably applies also to reading, shows that an integrated representation of the text is being constructed on a word-by-word basis. It also refutes an earlier idea, the *clausal processing hypothesis*, that most syntactic and semantic processing is delayed to clause boundaries. Nevertheless, there are certain aspects of meaning, perhaps mainly those that require information from different sentences to be put together, that are dealt with at the end of each sentence.

INFERENCE

It is not obvious to the skilled reader that to understand a text is to go well beyond the information explicit in it. Neither was it immediately obvious to psycholinguistics in the early 1960s, when the new cognitive approach to the psychology of language was inaugurated. Their attention was focused on the role of syntax in comprehension. However, even simple texts can only be understood by making inferences that, in processing terms, are fairly complex. Consider, for example, the following children's story (Charniak, 1972).

> Jane was invited to Jack's birthday party.
> She wondered if he would like a kite.

> She went to her room and shook her piggy bank.
> It made no sound.

This story can only be understood against a background of knowledge about birthday parties, taking presents to them, saving money and the need for money to buy presents. Someone from a culture that did not have birthday parties, piggy banks or money would find this simple story almost impossible to understand. Consider, more specifically, the second sentence. To understand this sentence correctly, you have to realize that Jane did not simply wonder if Jack would like a kite, she was thinking about buying him one for his birthday. Similarly, the full implication of the lack of sound in the last sentence is far from explicit in the text, however obvious it may be to skilled readers.

In cognitive psychology the importance of inference making in comprehension was stressed by John Bransford and his colleagues (e.g. Bransford, Barclay and Franks, 1972). Bransford attacked the view, popular in the mid-1960s, that a theory of comprehension should be based on ideas from linguistics, and that mental representations of sentences corresponded to linguistic representations of them. Bransford drew attention to two aspects of comprehension that he felt could not be explained by the linguistic properties of texts. Comprehension is *integrative* and it is *constructive*.

To say that comprehension is integrative is to make the point that understanding a text requires the putting together of the ideas from its various sentences. While the point itself is an obvious one, even now it is far from clear how the language processing system performs this integration.

One thing we do know is that integration often requires inferences. Consider, for example, the following short passage.

> Barbara decided to lend Trish her car.
> She was going to take up cycling.

To understand this passage the information in the two sentences must be integrated by identifying *she* in the second with Barbara in the first. But to decide that *she* is Barbara and not Trish requires the use of knowledge about lending and borrowing, and about cars and cycles being alternative forms of transport.

By saying that comprehension is constructive, Bransford was drawing attention to the fact that the information derived from a text is not always explicit in it. Understanding is not just the passive reception of information from a text, but the active putting together of a message, using several types of information. We construct the intended message from what is explicitly stated, together with both general and specific background knowledge. This process was illustrated in the discussion of Charniak's story.

In the following sections we discuss a number of questions about inference that are important for our later discussion of the acquisition of reading (see chapter 5).

Necessary and elaborative inferences

The inferences discussed in connection with the birthday passage are *necessary* for a full interpretation of the text. Someone who does not make those inferences has not understood the text properly. Becoming a skilled reader means learning to make these inferences. However, there are other inferences that can be made from a text which are not necessary for comprehension, inferences that are *merely elaborative*. We will give an example of this type of inference for a very simple, one sentence, text. If someone reads that:

Sue cut into the juicy steak.

they will probably guess that she was using a knife. Certainly if some other instrument was used they would expect to be told about it. However, as the text stands, it is not necessary to make this inference to understand it. It may become so. The next sentence might be:

The knife was blunt and she was having difficulty.

Then it would be necessary to infer that the knife mentioned in this second sentence was the instrument used for the cutting mentioned in the first. Note again that the use of a knife is not explicitly mentioned, only implied, in the first sentence.

This example illustrates an important point about necessary and elaborative inferences. An inference cannot be classified as necessary or elaborative from its content or its form. An inference about an instrument (e.g. a knife for cutting) may be either necessary or elaborative, depending on its discourse context.

Since necessary inferences are needed for a proper understanding of a text, they must typically be made as texts are read. Introspection suggests that this is so. People readily understand texts such as Charniak's story. There is also experimental evidence that such inferences are made 'on-line'. The first, and in many ways the clearest, study demonstrating this point was conducted by Susan Haviland and Herb Clark (1974). They asked people to read simple two-sentence passages, such as:

We took the beer out of the trunk.
The beer was warm.

We checked the picnic supplies.
The beer was warm.

Andrew was especially fond of beer.
The beer was warm.

The second sentence is the same in all three passages. However, Haviland and Clark found that people took longer to read this sentence in the second passage than in the first. The difference between the two is that whereas the beer of the second sentence is explicitly mentioned in the first sentence of the first passage, to understand the second passage it is necessary to infer that there was beer among the picnic supplies. The third passage was included to check that the effect was not simply caused by the repetition or lack of repetition of the word *beer*. The second sentence was read comparatively slowly in this type of passage, despite the repetition of *beer*.

Necessary inferences are, at least very often, made as texts are read, but what about elaborative inferences? For a long time it was thought that at least some inferences of this type were also made during reading. This conclusion came from a series of experiments in which subjects confused explicitly stated information with inferable information. For example, Johnson, Bransford and Solomon (1973) showed that when subjects had heard a sentence such as:

He slipped on a wet spot and dropped the delicate glass pitcher on the floor.

they later claimed that they had heard:

He slipped on a wet spot and broke the delicate glass pitcher when it fell on the floor.

The problem was not simply general forgetfulness, because they did not make the same mistake when they read:

He slipped on a wet spot and just missed the delicate glass pitcher on the floor.

The investigators explained this result by claiming that when people heard the first sentence they used their knowledge about dropping delicate glassware to infer that the pitcher had broken. Furthermore, they suggested that the inferred information *was encoded into the memory representation of the sentence*.

There are two reasons for doubting this interpretation of these results, one conceptual and one empirical. The first is that many elaborative inferences can be made from a text, even if that text contains only a single sentence. Assuming that it takes some cognitive effort to make an elaborative inference, and that most elaborative inferences will not be useful either for understanding subsequent text or for answering questions about it, it is unparsimonious to assume that such inferences are made.

The second reason comes from a study by Albert Corbett and Barbara Dosher (1978) that followed up previous work by Scott Paris and Barbara Lindauer (1976). Paris and Lindauer asked subjects to read a series of sentences and then showed those subjects a set of words. For each word they were asked to write down the sentence of which they were reminded. Paris and Lindauer found for older children and for adults, that *knife* was an equally good cue for the recall of both the following sentences:

> The teacher cut into the juicy steak.
> The teacher cut into the juicy steak with a knife.

Paris and Lindauer gave this result the standard inferential interpretation. They claimed that when subjects read the first sentence, they infer that a knife was used and encode a knife into their memory representation. The representations of the two sentences are therefore similar, and it is not surprising that *knife* is a good cue for both.

However, Corbett and Dosher's findings cast doubt on this interpretation of the results. Corbett and Dosher carried out an extended version of Paris and Lindauer's experiment. They presented three versions of each sentence, for example:

> The grocer dug a hole.
> The grocer dug a hole with a shovel.
> The grocer dug a hole with a pitchfork.

Instead of just including the most plausible instrument (a knife for cutting or a shovel for digging), they also included an implausible instrument (a pitchfork for digging). Likewise, there were three types of cue: *grocer, grocer shovel* and *grocer pitchfork*. The results of this experiment were that *grocer shovel* was the best cue for all three of the sentences. Furthermore, when subjects recalled the third sentence, they did *not* substitute *shovel* for *pitchfork*. So the fact that *shovel* was a good cue for this sentence could not be explained by assuming that a shovel was encoded into its representation. *Shovel* is a good cue for any sentence about digging. Going back to Paris and Lindauer's experiment, it cannot be argued that their findings prove that a knife is encoded into the representation of:

> The teacher cut into the juicy steak.

Knife is a good cue for this sentence simply because it is a sentence about cutting.

We propose the *omission theory* (Garnham, 1982) to explain a wide range of apparently conflicting data on elaborative inferences. The omission theory claims that inferable information, *whether it is implicit or explicit*, is left out of the mental representation of a text. If it can be inferred from the text, it can be inferred from a representation of the text, so it need not be encoded. This theory provides a straightforward explanation of why people confuse explicit and inferable information. The representation is the same in each case, but not because the inferable information is encoded in both cases. The omission theory claims that it is encoded *in neither case*. The identity of the representations also explains why one word can be a good cue for different sentences.

However, there is some evidence that explicit information is more readily available than implicit information in the very short term. The omission theory can explain this fact by appealing to the well-established fact that people construct a representation, usually fairly short-lived, of the verbatim form of a text. Explicit information is more easily recoverable from this representation than implicit information.

Instantiation

In this section we briefly discuss another type of inference, *instantiation*. To instantiate a general term, such as *animal*, is to interpret it more specifically on the basis of contextual information. For example, if an animal is described as running towards a kennel, it is probably, though not necessarily, a dog. Instantiations, like other inferences, may be necessary for comprehension:

> The animal ran toward the kennel
> The dog went inside to shelter from the rain.

or merely elaborative. We discuss instantiation here because a number of the studies described in chapter 5 investigate children's ability to instantiate.

Instantiation was first investigated by Richard Anderson and his colleagues. Anderson and Ortony (1975) asked their subjects to read sentences such as:

> The container held the apples.
> The container held the cola.

Later those subjects were given either *basket* or *bottle* as a memory cue and asked to write down the sentence from the list they had heard that the cue reminded them of. *Basket* was a better cue for the first sentence and *bottle* for the second, suggesting that *container* was interpreted differently in the two sentences.

Anderson et al. (1976) produced further evidence for the instantiation of general nouns. They presented sentences such as:

> The fish attacked the swimmer

and found that of the two words *fish* and *shark*, the instantiation *shark* was a substantially better cue than the word in the sentence, *fish*. Our own work show that verbs are also instantiated (Garnham, 1979). *Strained* is a better cue than *injured* for:

> The sportsman injured a muscle.

Anderson et al. concluded that instantiation is an integral part of sentence comprehension and memory, and that instantiation is the selection of one of many meanings of a word, depending on its context. We believe that a more plausible characterization is that people make inferences about the possible *referent* of a word (the thing in the world that it refers to) according to the context (Garnham, 1979). As Phil Johnson-Laird (1983, p. 238) points out, *shark* would probably be a better cue than *fish* for:

It frightened the swimmer.

Although the probable referent of *it* in this sentence is a shark, *shark* is not a meaning of *it*, neither could it be said to be an instantiation of that word.

Use of knowledge about the world in inference making

How are inferences made? An important part of the answer to this question is that they are made by using a vast store of mundane knowledge. Each of us knows an enormous amount about how things usually happen in both the physical and the social world – that children have parties on their birthdays to which other children take presents, that steaks are cut with knives, and so on. When we read a text about a birthday party, for example, relevant information becomes available from our long-term memory for interpreting that text. This observation raises two questions: how is knowledge organized in long-term memory so that it can be made available for the interpretation of texts, and how does the information in a text indicate what information might be relevant for interpreting it?

The fact that knowledge *is* organized in memory is suggested by a number of observations. For example, when we think of one fact about a particular topic, others tend to come to mind. Work in computer science also suggests that the efficient retrieval of information from large databases – which is essentially what our long-term memories are – depends on that information being sensibly organized. However, although it is fairly obvious which facts are grouped together in our memories, it is hard to propose a suitable way of *representing* that memory organization.

Frederic Bartlett (1932), later Sir Frederic, introduced the idea of a memory *schema*, which he describes as 'an active organisation of past reactions, or past experiences' (p. 201). This definition is somewhat vague, though the claim that the organization is active is an interesting one, and one that has not been pursued in the recent literature. More recent attempts to describe memory organization have been more clearly defined, in the sense that they have used the terminology of computer science. However, they have not imposed strong constraints on psychological theories of memory organization. Although they force one to describe memory structures clearly, they allow both plausible and implausible memory structures to be described. These modern ideas include Roger Schank and Bob Abelson's (1977) theory of *scripts, goals* and *plans*. As the concept of a script was formulated specifically to account for how we understand certain types of text, it will serve as an example of these ideas.

Within any society there are sequences of events that frequently recur. For example, people often eat in restaurants, visit doctors or go on plane flights. When people eat in a restaurant they typically travel to the restaurant, enter it, ask for a table if they do not have a reservation, or ask for their reserved table if they do, and so on. Indeed, these events are so typical of visits to restaurants that people infer that they happen, even if a text provides only the sketchiest account of such a visit. So, given a simple text, such as:

Tanya and Darren went to Luigi's.
They ate pizzas.
On the way home they praised the chef.

people will be quite happy to accept, for example, that Tanya and Darren were shown to a table, that a waiter brought the pizzas to the table, that they paid the bill, and so on. None of this information is explicit in the text, but it can be extracted from the 'restaurant script'. Here is a clear example of information in long-term memory being used to elaborate the explicit content of a text.

Schank (1982) recognizes that there are problems with the notion of a script. In particular, the 'visit to the doctor' script and the 'visit to the dentist' script share many parts, but this fact goes unrecognized on Schank and Abelson's original account. In Schank's more recent formulation, scripts are built out of smaller units called *memory organization packets*, which may be shared between several scripts.

The second question about the use of world knowledge is how does the story about Tanya and Darren activate the restaurant script? Some stories about restaurants contain the word *restaurant* near the beginning, so it is reasonably clear how information about restaurants becomes available for their interpretation. Others contain words such as *waiter* and *menu* that might also be expected to activate knowledge about restaurants. The Tanya and Darren story contains the word *chef*, though by the time it appears it is already apparent that a visit to a restaurant is being described. In general, it is not individual words that indicate what a text is about. For example, the phrase:

The 5-hour journey from London to New York

suggests a plane flight, though none of the individual words do (see Garnham, 1985, p. 167). A theory of how cues in a text access information from memory would be much easier to formulate if it were only single words that acted as cues. As it is, no fully satisfactory theory has yet been proposed.

LOCAL LINKS IN A TEXT

An important part of understanding a text is to link the various parts of it into a coherent whole. Links must be established at both a global and a local level. Deciding that a visit to a restaurant is being described helps to make sense of a whole section of a text – to determine what has been called its *macrostructure*. *Microstructure*, on the other hand, depends to ● large extent on linguistic devices that link items in one sentence to those in nearby sentences. Michael Halliday and Ruqaiya Hasan (1976) refer to these links as *cohesive links*. They are created by what can be broadly termed *anaphoric* devices, though Halliday and Hasan use the term *anaphora* in a more restricted sense.

Anaphoric devices include pronouns, repeated noun phrases and various types of ellipsis. A typical anaphor, the definite pronoun *it*, has little semantic content of its own. So a sentence such as *it was ready* gives almost no clue to what *it* is. However, if the sentence is set in a suitable context, for example:

Bill checked the cake in the oven.
It was ready.

it takes on a more specific meaning. An important part of understanding text is identifying anaphoric expressions and assigning meanings to them. These expressions take their meaning from some other part of the text, usually a preceding part. That other part of the text is called the *antecedent* of the anaphor. In the simplest cases, anaphors have the same meaning as their antecedents. So, in the text above, *it* means the same as *the cake in the oven*. In this case the pronoun refers to the very same cake – it has the same meaning as the previous expression in the sense of having the same reference. Other anaphoric elements have the same meaning as their antecedents in a different sense. For example, the indefinite pronoun *one* refers to another thing of the same kind as one that has previously been mentioned.

My brother has an ice-cream and I want one, too.

Here it is not the same ice-cream I want, but something equivalent to what my brother has. Although anaphoric devices do not usually cause comprehension problems, their interpretation is quite complicated. Pronouns, for example, have so little semantic content that there is usually a range of things that they could refer to. For example, in the passage about the cake, *it* is naturally taken to refer to the cake. However, as far as the word itself is concerned, it could refer to the oven just as well as to the cake, though it could not refer to Bill except in special circumstances because it is neuter, not masculine. However, the predicate of the second sentence *is ready* ensures that *it* will be taken to refer to the cake. Why? Because our knowledge about cooking tells us that cakes are more likely to be checked for readiness than ovens.

This case is typical of pronoun interpretation in general. Some potential antecedents, Bill in this case, can be ruled because of their number or their gender. A decision among the remainder has to be made using knowledge about the world. So world knowledge is used to establish both the global structure of a text and in many cases its local structure as well.

One of our own studies has shown that the use of this knowledge takes time (Garnham and Oakhill, 1985). In a sentence such as:

> Keith (Trisha) lent his (her) jumper to Carol
> because she was feeling cold.

The second clause takes longer to read when the two people in the first clause are both female as it is then only possible to work out who *she* refers to using knowledge about jumpers and how they are useful to people who are feeling cold.

Knowledge about the world is used in a different way to understand another class of anaphoric expressions: definite noun phrases (ones beginning with *the*). Not all definite noun phrases are anaphoric, but many are. Furthermore, the antecedents of such noun phrases can be implicit rather than explicit, as they were in one of the types of passage used by Haviland and Clark. When the first sentence was only about picnic supplies in general, the beer of the second sentence was only implicitly mentioned as part of those supplies. In that case knowledge about the world, the knowledge that there can be beer among picnic supplies, can be used to find an antecedent for *the beer*. This example is one of a variety of cases that Clark (1977) discusses under the head of *bridging inferences*.

TEXT STRUCTURE

We have already seen that knowledge about the world is important in establishing global links between the parts of a text. However, it is often felt that stories have a structure over and above that of a series of episodes, such as a visit to a restaurant. This feeling has resulted in proposals for text grammars (e.g. van Dijk, 1972) and story grammars (e.g. Rumelhart, 1975). These grammars try to describe the structure of stories in the same way that sentence grammars describe the structure of sentences – using hierarchical tree diagrams – But there are a number of problems with these proposals (Black and Wilensky, 1979; Garnham, 1983). We suggest that the structure that story grammarians find in stories, which is mainly a hierarchical structure of goals and subgoals, is simply another case in which knowledge about the world affects the structure of texts and hence is useful for understanding them. The structure of goals is not specific to stories. We also recognize it in the actions of people around us. It is part of our general knowledge that goals are structured, and there is therefore no need to encode that knowledge into a special structure for understanding stories – a story grammar.

APPRECIATING THE OVERALL POINT OF A TEXT

So far we have discussed the meaning of texts primarily in terms of the types of situations they describe, though we have stressed that much of the information conveyed by texts is implicit rather than explicit. However, there are other aspects of meaning that must also be discerned if a text is to be understood fully. Most of these contribute to the *significance* of the text or of part of it. It is to these aspects of meaning that we now turn. Although some of the ideas that we will discuss in this section apply primarily to spoken language, they are relevant to text comprehension since texts, particularly those for young readers, often contain dialogue.

One aspect of the significance of a text is its significance for a particular reader. This aspect of significance depends on the reader's goals. A person may read a text in detail to learn what is in it, or merely skim it for a particular fact. At a more specific level, Richard Anderson and James Pichert (1978, Pichert and Anderson, 1977) have shown that people remember different facts from a text about a house if they read it from the perspective of a home buyer than if they read it from the perspective of a burglar. Home buyers remember things about the house that affect its value as real estate. Burglars are more interested in removable property. These results are explained partly by what happens when the text is read, but partly also by what happens at the time of recall. An instruction to change perspective caused subjects to remember facts that they had not previously recalled.

Two other aspects of the significance of an utterance are the message it is intended to convey, which may be different from its literal meaning, and the *speech act* that it performs. The idea of a speech act is, of course, directly applicable only to spoken language. It applies only indirectly to text.

Paul Grice (1975) discusses the relation between the literal meaning of an utterance and the message it is intended to convey. He argues that conversation is, or at least ought to be, a co-operative enterprise, and that people are entitled to interpret contributions to conversation on the assumption that the speaker is trying to be co-operative. This idea can also be applied to written text. A very simple conversation, adapted from Grice (1975), illustrates his ideas.

A: [trying and failing to start his car] I'm out of petrol.
B: There's a garage round the corner.

Literally, B's statement is a description of the location of a certain business. However, under normal circumstances, it conveys information about where petrol can be bought. B's response would be uncooperative if, for example, he knew that the garage was closed.

To explain how utterances are interpreted, Grice proposes a variety of *maxims* which speakers can be assumed to be following, but which they sometimes play off against one another. These maxims include: say only what you know to be true, be brief and be relevant. Dan Sperber and Deirdre Wilson (1986) have suggested that utterance interpretation is better explained by a single principle of relevance. This principle of relevance is not simply Grice's maxim 'Be relevant!' in a different guise. That maxim is addressed to speakers and writers and is supposed to guide them in choosing what to say. Sperber and Wilson's principle of relevance is intended as a description of how *listeners* (or readers) interpret utterances – they search for the contextually most relevant interpretation of what they hear or read.

The idea of a *speech act* was formulated by John Searle (1969), building on the work of J.L. Austin (1962). Austin and Searle emphasize that much of our language, especially our spoken language, is not descriptive. It comprises questions, requests, commands, promises and so on. To understand a sentence, it is necessary to grasp which of these speech acts it performs, as well as working out the kind of situation that it is about. The form of a sentence usually suggests its function. Declarative sentences tend to be descriptions, for example, and interrogatives usually express questions. However, in many cases, a sentence does not fulfil its normal role.

Can you shut the window?

has the form of a question, but it often has the force of a command. When it is a command, the context usually makes it apparent that its literal meaning as a question would be inappropriate. With normal people and normal windows it is not usually necessary to enquire whether someone can open one. The principle of relevance, therefore, suggests a different interpretation, one in which the question is taken to be a command or a request.

MODELS OF READING

We have seen that a large number of psychological processes contribute to skilled reading. It might therefore be asked: how do these processes operate together? Another way of asking this question is: can we formulate an overall model of reading? The simple answer to this question is that the task is a very difficult one. Indeed, the more that has been discovered about reading, the more apparent it has become that an overall model of reading would be very complex. It is partly this reason that overall models of reading have become less comm. in recent years. Most of the early models did not cover all aspects reading.[2] In particular, many of them did not attempt to describe the control of eye movements or the higher level processes that integrate information from different parts of a text.

An important question in the early literature was whether reading, and more particularly word identification, is chiefly a *top-down* or chiefly a *bottom-up* process. A top-down process, in this sense, is one that makes use primarily of stored information rather than perceptual information. A bottom-up process relies primarily on perceptual information. Kenneth Goodman (1967, 1970) captured the idea of reading as a top-down process by describing it as a 'psycholinguistic guessing game'. He suggested that skilled readers predict ('guess') what the next part of the text will be about and look at it only in sufficient detail to confirm or disconfirm their guesses. However, as we argue more fully in chapter 4, this account of reading more accurately characterizes beginning readers than skilled readers. Phil Gough (1972) provided a largely bottom-up model of the word recognition component of reading, and Dave Rumelhart (1977) developed a model in which top-down and bottom-up information act together – a so-called *interactive* model.

A somewhat different perspective on reading comes from those psycholinguists who have investigated language processing in general rather than reading in particular. They have addressed the question of how lexical, structural and semantic processes fit together in an overall model of what they call the *language processor*.[3] In this research the basic question is whether a model of the language processor should be serial or interactive. A serial model is one in which the lower-level processes are not subject to influences 'from above'. So, for example, in a serial model the lexical subprocessor (i.e. the word identification system) cannot be influenced by the structural or semantic context in which a word occurs. In interactive models it can be. However, deciding between serial and interactive models is more difficult than might be imagined. Although there is much evidence that *decisions* about words are influenced by context, it is easy to construct models in which these decisions are made not by the lexical *processor* but by, say, the semantic processor. For example, the lexical processor might identify an ambiguous word but not make any decision about which meaning is the appropriate one. It can pass both possibilities on to the structural and semantic processors. The decision about which meaning is intended may only be made when the semantic processor tries to integrate each meaning with meaning of the sentence as a whole.

Although it is difficult to find any clear experimental evidence for interaction in the language processing system, it is of course possible to construct interactive models that account for its behaviour. Recently a different argument in favour of interactive models has been put forward.

McClelland and Rumelhart's (1981) *interactive activation* model of word identification, which can account for a wide variety of facts about how words are recognized, comprises a large number of simple processors. Proponents of such models claim that they are successful because their structure mirrors the structure of the human brain, in which the simple processors are the nerve cells or neurons (see e.g. McClelland, Rumelhart and Hinton, 1986).

SUMMARY

Skilled adult readers possess a wide variety of skills, ranging from the ability to scan a text in an appropriate way to the ability to work out its significance. Information is extracted from text in a series of discrete fixations, linked by short sharp eye movements during which little information is absorbed. A limited amount of information about the next few words, extracted from peripheral vision, determines the position of the next fixation. The process of combining visual information from successive fixations is not well understood.

The visual information extracted from the text is used to identify the words on the page. The two main types of model of word identification are word detector models and search models. Recent models combine features of the two kinds. In skilled reading, word identification is aided by some types of contextual information and may sometimes be achieved by phonological recoding. However, the conversion to a phonological code *after* identification appears to be more common. Ambiguous words take longer to process than non-ambiguous words, because all the meanings are made available and a choice has to be made between them.

Once words have been identified, they have to be grouped into phrases and sentences so that the meaning of the text can be discovered. This grouping process is called parsing. In some cases it may not be necessary, if there are strong semantic cues to the meaning of a sentence.

There are many aspects of sentence meaning, ranging from literal meaning to intended message. The literal meaning of a sentence is organized around its main verb, which relates the things denoted by the noun phrases and prepositional phrases. However, much of the information carried by a text is implicit rather than explicit, and must be extracted by using knowledge about the world, stored in long-term memory, to make inferences. These inferences establish both the global structure of the text and local links between sentences. Other inferences simply elaborate on the information in a text, without helping to tie it together. There is increasing evidence that these elaborative inferences are not made automatically but only if they are needed, for example to answer a question. The idea that stories have a special global structure captured by a story grammar is difficult to maintain. The structure that story grammarians find in stories mirrors the structure we perceive in events around us.

Having worked out what situation a text is about, the reader has still to determine the significance of the text. Is it a description, a question or a command? What message is it intended to convey? What information do *I* want to get out of it?

The way the many skills of reading work together can be investigated by attempting to produce a model of reading or, more generally, a model of the *language processor*. However, reading has so many component skills that this task is a daunting one, and one that has not been tackled successfully to date.

Notes

1. For a thorough review of phonological recoding see Perfetti and McCutchen, 1982.
2. Mitchell (1982, ch. 6) provides an overview of some of the most influential models.
3. See Garnham, 1985, ch. 8, for a review of this work.

CHAPTER 3

Language development beyond the age of five

Over the last twenty years or so, there has been a great upsurge of interest, among both psychologists and linguists, in language acquisition. Attention has focused particularly on the language of pre-school children. This bias reflects the fact that language development after the age of 5 is less dramatic than it is in the first few years. For example, by 5, children have a grasp of the basic syntactic structures of their language, and are already competent communicators. Indeed, later language development is less readily noticed. So much so that 5-year-olds were at first thought to have little more to learn about their language, apart, of course, from a lot of vocabulary. However, since Carol Chomsky's (1969) pioneering study, it has been known that acquisition is not as nearly complete by 5 as was previously thought – certain fundamental changes in children's knowledge of language have still to take place. For example, children of 5 still do not know the meaning of certain complex syntactic structures. Neither have they fully mastered apparently simple aspects of language, such as the use of the indefinite and definite articles (*a* and *the*: see Karmiloff-Smith, 1979, 1986).

It is surprising that such developments remained largely unnoticed by child language researchers for so long. Piaget, whose influence on developmental psychology was even stronger in the 1960s than it is now, had long claimed that language development depends on the development of other cognitive abilities. Furthermore, he claimed that many aspects of cognitive development take place after the age of 5. It would seem reasonable, therefore, to expect corresponding changes in linguistic skills beyond this age. Indeed, some Piagetians explicitly discussed language development beyond 5. For example, Sinclair (1967: cited by Karmiloff-Smith, 1986), argued that, although young children use relational terms, such as *longer than* and *bigger than*, they do not understand the true relational meaning of these terms until they have mastered conservation and seriation (at about 7 years).

In this chapter, we provide an overview of some of the more important developments in language comprehension in children of primary-school age. We then consider how these developments might affect the acquisition of reading skills. Our coverage is not intended to be exhaustive. There are numerous recent reviews of specific topics in language acquisition, and we shall only attempt to indicate what primary school children have still to learn about language. Some aspects of language development that are of somewhat tangential relevance to learning to read (e.g. classroom discourse, language and social cognition) are not discussed here, but are are covered in chapters of a recent book by Kevin Durkin (1986).

Several early studies of language development in schoolchildren (e.g. Loban, 1963; Menyuk, 1963, 1964) were based on collections (or *corpora* as they are usually known) of children's spontaneous utterances. However, these studies provide little information other than how often children use various linguistic forms. Such information provides only an indirect indication of children's understanding of those forms. On the one hand, the fact that a sentence form is used does not mean that its meaning is fully understood. On the other hand, the fact that a form is not produced does not mean that children cannot understand it.

The corpus-based method has remained important in studying early language acquisition, largely because of the difficulty of using more controlled techniques with very young children. However with children of school age, the usual way cf investigating language development is in controlled experiments. Such studies will be the focus of the present chapter. The major disadvantage of experimental techniques is that they bring a certain artificiality to the study of children's language. Their major advantage is that they permit systematic comparisons between children of various ages and abilities, since crucial aspects of the experimental procedure and materials can be held constant. Experimental studies typically explore children's comprehension – it is far easier to test understanding of a construction than to try to elicit that construction from children. From the point of view of reading research this bias is a fortunate one, since reading requires the comprehension, rather than the production, of written language.[1]

SYNTACTIC DEVELOPMENT

Five-year-olds understand and use a wide variety of sentence types and cope readily with fairly long sentences. It is therefore easy to think that, allowing for differences in vocabulary, in interests and in attention span, such children's language is very similar to adults'. However, there are more English sentence types than a 5-year-old has mastered. Some constructions are neither used nor understood properly by children of this age. One reason why this fact is not obvious is that the types of sentence children find difficult are not necessary ones that seem difficult to adults. However, they all have one thing in common – an 'irregular' relation between structure and meaning.

Of course, this relation is not really irregular, or it would be difficult if not impossible for anyone to learn. However, it is different from the relation found in the most common types of sentence in adult speech, which correspond quite closely to those that children master first. In the most common English sentence types we find the following basic skeleton: a noun followed by a verb followed (perhaps) by a another noun (. . . N . . . V . . . N . . .). In the simplest cases those are the only words in the sentence:

John saw Mary

but in longer sentences they may be 'hidden' among other words.

In the afternoon, the little *girl* I knew *built* an enormous *sandcastle*.

At a superficial level, the noun, verb and noun are the subject, main verb and object of the sentence, respectively. At a deeper level they are *usually* the deep (or underlying or grammatical) subject, the name of the action, state or process described by the sentence, and the deep object. The deep subject is the person or thing that performs the action named by the verb, has the state named by the verb or undergoes the process named by the verb. The deep object has the action performed on it or, in the case of mental states, it may be what philosophers call the *object* of the state, as Bill is in 'John knows Bill'.

Usually, therefore, an English sentence can be understood by identifying the superficial subject and object, which can be readily identified from the surface features of the sentence, with, respectively, the deep subject and the deep object of the main verb, which is also readily identifiable. However, there are many constructions – for example, *easy to* . . . , passives and relative clauses, which we discuss below – in which these relations are systematically broken. Children have difficulty with these sentences, seemingly because they assume all sentences can be interpreted by identifying superficial and deep subjects and objects. They use an interpretation strategy that would only work properly if that identification were always correct.

In this section we take as our starting point Carol Chomsky's (1969) study. Chomsky investigated the understanding of a number of 'complex' sentence types in children over 5. In particularly, she studied the *easy to see* construction (sometimes referred to as the product of a sentence construction process called *tough* movement), and complement constructions with the verbs *promise, persuade, ask* and *tell*. She also studied children's understanding of pronouns. We discuss Chomsky's experiments in relation to subsequent results that have followed up her findings. We shall then consider the understanding of other types of complex sentence: passives and relative clauses.

Chomsky's experiments

Carol Chomsky (1969) set out to explore children's understanding of constructions that are regularly used by adults but which are not found in the spontaneous speech of children. Some of her experiments required children to act out a sentence with dolls. Others demanded a verbal response, such as an answer to a question. Chomsky found that some of the constructions she tested were difficult even for 10-year-olds. Her work will be described briefly in the sections that follow; those who want a more detailed account can do no better than read her book, which is clearly and engagingly written.

'Easy/eager to see' An important part of understanding a sentence is to work out, of the various people and things mentioned in it, who did what. In English, the most common way of describing an action is to mention first the person or thing that carried out the action (the 'grammatical subject' or 'underlying subject'), then the action itself, then the person or thing that had the action done to it ('the grammatical object' or 'underlying object'). For example, in the sentence

Jim followed Mary

Jim is the subject, the person who did the following, and Mary is the object, the person who was followed. This sentence follows the standard S(ubject)–V(erb)–O(bject) pattern of English. This pattern is very common in children's spontaneous utterances: O'Donnell, Griffin and Norris (1967) found that S–V (e.g. John laughed) and S–V–O forms accounted for nearly four-fifths of the grammatical utterances of 6-year-olds and nearly 90 per cent of 12-year-olds'. However, not all sentences follow the S–V and S–V–O patterns. For example, in the *passive* sentence

Mary was followed by Jim

the grammatical subject (Jim) follows the verb, while the grammatical object (Mary) precedes it. For such sentences children must learn special interpretation rules, though they may *sometimes* interpret them correctly without those rules – for example if there are strong semantic or contextual cues to their meanings. A case in which this kind of sophisticated 'guessing' leads to the correct interpretation is:

The flower was watered by the boy

This sentence has only one sensible interpretation – flowers cannot water things, so the flowers cannot be the grammatical subject of *watered*.

Another case in which the S–V/S–V–O rule fails is illustrated by the following pair of sentences:

John is eager to see.
John is easy to see.

These sentences are superficially similar, but only the first conforms to (a slightly modified version of) the S–V pattern. In this sentence John is doing the seeing: John is the grammatical subject of the sentence, and also of the infinitival complement verb *see*. However, in the second sentence, John is not the grammatical subject of the main verb *is*: it is not John who is easy. Neither is John the subject of the complement verb *see*. He is its object.

One of the aspects of syntactic development in children of 5 to 10 years that Chomsky (1969) studied was the understanding of these constructions. She found that the difficult *easy to see* construction posed problems for some children up to 8½. However, there were other children as young as 5 years and 2 months who always interpreted it correctly. It is, therefore, difficult to predict from age alone whether a child will have a problem understanding this construction.

Chomsky argued that the difficulty with *easy to see* arises because children interpret it using a rule that is appropriate for the *eager to see* construction – one that makes the surface subject (John) of the main verb (is) the grammatical subject of the second verb *see*, rather than its grammatical object. However, semantic considerations can override this rule. Most children will interpret a sentence such as *these steps are easy to climb* correctly because it will be obvious to them that *people* climb steps.

A brief description of Chomsky's experimental procedure is in order because subsequent criticisms of her conclusions relate to her task and to children's perception of it. In the experiment, the children were shown a blindfolded doll and asked: 'Is this doll easy to see or hard to see?' and (depending on their answer) 'Will you make her easy/hard to see?' Most 5-year-olds, and some 8-year-olds, answered incorrectly, claiming that the doll was hard to see. Every child who made this error removed the blindfold when asked to make the doll easy to see.

Chomsky's work inspired a large number of follow-up studies. Richard Cromer (1970) extended her findings by testing children on similar sentences with three different types of adjectives: those that follow the *eager* pattern (*happy, glad*), those that follow the *easy* pattern (*tasty, fun*) and those that can follow either interpretation (*bad, nice*). Cromer used a task in which the children were given glove puppets to act out a sentence. He found a closer correlation between mental age, as assessed by the Peabody Picture Vocabulary Test, and performance than between chronological age and performance. Children with a mental age below 5 years 7 months consistently identified the superficial subject of the sentence with the grammatical subject of the second verb. Almost all children with a mental age above 6 years 8 months consistently interpreted the sentences correctly. Children between these ages showed unstable performance, which varied from one day to the next.

Many of the follow-up studies have shown that children can understand *easy to see* sentences earlier than Chomsky claimed, providing that certain misleading features of the task are eliminated. In particular the presence of the blindfold may cause some confusion in children's minds because it draws attention to the doll's difficulty in seeing. As we have already stated, Chomsky found that many children said the blindfolded doll was difficult to see, and she interpreted this response as indicating that the children misunderstood the sentence. Jacqueline Cambon and Hermine Sinclair (1974) point out a further complication: a doll wearing a blindfold is not completely visible. Its face is partially covered and it is not, therefore, easy to see! Some children in their study said that the doll was difficult to see when parts of its body other than its eyes were covered by the scarf used as a blindfold. So children who say a blindfolded doll is difficult to see may not, after all, be misinterpreting the *easy to see* construction. They may be applying a criterion for visibility that the experimenter did not intend. This idea is consistent with the findings of Kessel (1970), who showed, in a study where two dolls were playing hide and seek, that children of 6 to 12 understood 'Lucy is easy to find' comparatively easily. In this situation the problem of blindfolds (for both children and experimenters!) did not arise.

At least some of Chomsky's children did misinterpret *easy to see* in the way she suggests. In a sample interview in her book, one child who was specifically asked who was doing the seeing in *the doll is easy to see* said it was the doll. Nevertheless, these children may have been responding to non-linguistic features, such as the blindfold, rather than systematically misapplying a rule about grammatical subjects.

Cambon and Sinclair also found that a surprisingly large number of 5-year-olds gave correct answers. They suggest these answers might be explained, at least in part, by the fact that 5-year-olds adopt an egocentric viewpoint and interpret *easy to see* as 'I can easily see'. They do not consider other viewpoints. Older children, on the other hand, have to recover the missing grammatical subject of *see* (*anyone* can see the doll easily) if they are to interpret the construction properly. Cambon and Sinclair argue, therefore, that 5-year-olds produce the correct answers in a different way from 8-year-olds.

Cambon and Sinclair further investigated the role of egocentricity by asking children to act out 'the doll is easy to draw'. They argued that, in this situation, it would be more natural for children to draw the doll (egocentric interpretation) than to give the doll the crayon. Surprisingly, out of twenty-four children who gave mixed responses to 'easy to see', nineteen misinterpreted the new sentence and put the crayon in the doll's hand. They did not interpret *draw* egocentrically. This finding shows that, although a blindfold may focus attention on the fact that a doll cannot see, and hence suggest that a sentence of the form '. . .doll . . . difficult . . . see . . .' is about the problem caused by the blindfold, children have genuine difficulties with the '. . . easy to . . .' construction, and these problems cannot be explained away as an artefact of Chomsky's task.

Similarly, Gisela Morsbach and Pamela Steel (1976) showed that, when Chomsky's procedure is altered to eliminate the potentially misleading blindfold cue, by placing the doll behind a semi-transparent screen, only a minority of 5- and 6-year-olds misunderstood the sentences. However, although Chomsky's study underestimates children's ability to understand the *easy to see* construction, some of the 4- to 6-year-olds in Morsbach and Steel's study *did* consistently misinterpret it.

From our present perspective, the important question is whether beginning readers could be expected to have difficulty understanding constructions such as *easy to see*. The evidence suggests that, at least in some circumstances, children over 5 do not understand that the superficial subject of a sentence may be different from its grammatical subject. Although performance on the kind of experimental task Chomsky gave to children depends not just on linguistic abilities but also on more general cognitive abilities – the need to differentiate between one's own perspective and that of others, for example – specific linguistic constructions can cause problems. Furthermore, some studies have found a direct relation between reading skill and the ability to understand such constructions. Brian Byrne (1981) found that poor readers of 7 to 8 years misinterpreted sentences such as *the bird is easy to bite* more often than did good readers of the same age. Goldman (1976) showed that reading skill was significantly correlated with stage of understanding for *promise* (see below) and was a better predictor of performance than was age or IQ.

Understanding of 'promise', 'ask' and 'tell'   Chomsky also investiated how children understand complement constructions with verbs such as *ask, promise and tell*, for example:

John promised Bill to leave.

Again, younger children seem to assume that there is a simple relation between surface features of such sentences and the semantic roles played by the people and things mentioned in the sentences. In this case they assume that all such constructions can be interpreted by the *Minimal Distance Principle* (MDP), which takes the noun phrase that most immediately precedes an infinitival complement (e.g. *to leave*) to be the subject of its verb. This principle works with sentences such as:

John told Bill to leave

in which Bill does the leaving. In this sentence the underlying or grammatical subject of *leave* is *Bill* – the nearest noun. The principle fails, however, for verbs such as promise. In the sentence cited above it is John, not Bill, who does the promising. Chomsky found that children could not interpret such sentences correctly until about 8 years, even though they understood the meaning of *promise*, and could use and interpret it correctly in simpler constructions. Between the ages of 5 and 8 children begin to reject the MDP. They pass through two stages. In the first they recognize exceptions to the principle, but make errors on sentences that follow it as well as on sentences that do not. In the second they revert to error-free performance on sentences that follow the MDP, but only understand *promise* correctly some of the time.

Chomsky found a similar progression in the understanding of sentences with *ask* and *tell*. *Tell* consistently follows the MDP, but *ask* is inconsistent. When it is followed by an infinitival (*to*) complement it obeys the MDP. Thus, in the following sentences:

> John asked Bill to shut the door
> John told Bill to shut the door

Bill is the one who should shut the door in both cases. However, when *ask* is followed by a WH-complement, a question in indirect speech, for example, its interpretation goes against the MDP. When *tell* is followed by a WH-complement it continues to obeys the MDP. Compare:

> John asked Bill what to do.
> John told Bill what to do.

In the first of these sentences, the subject of the complement verb *do* is *not* the NP directly preceding it, *Bill*. In the second it is. Younger children found these sentences highly confusable. They tended to interpret them as synonyms (treating *ask* as though it meant *tell*). However, there was a great deal of variation in the age at which children consistently used *ask* correctly in the questioning sense: responding to 'Ask Kim what to feed the doll' with 'What should *I* feed the doll?'. One child of 5 years 10 months had mastered this use. Another, of 10 years, had not.

Development of the understanding of *ask* with a WH-complement was correlated with that of *promise* and went through similar stages – Chomsky identified five. A full understanding of *promise*, which consistently violates the MDP, was always achieved earlier than for *ask*, which is inconsistent. As Chomsky puts it, in the case of *ask* children must 'learn a rather curious property: keep the MDP, but violate it some of the time' (1969, p. 18). Although Frank Kessel (1970) showed that performance could be improved on a picture selection task (in which children were shown 4 pictures and were required to select the picture that went with the sentence), it was not until 8 years that children could reliably discriminate *ask* from *tell*.

Michael Maratsos (1974) pointed out that even *tell* does not consistently obey the MDP. For example, if the main clause is passivized, as in:

> John was told by Bill to leave

the principle is violated. Even though *Bill* is closer to the complement verb, *leave*, John is its subject – he is the person who is to do the leaving. On the basis of his results, Maratsos suggested that young children are following not the MDP but the *Semantic Role Principle*, which states that the goal (= underlying object) of a verb of instruction should be the actor (= underlying subject) of the action in the complement clause.

Pronouns   Chomsky also investigated how pronouns are understood. She considered two main types of construction with pronouns. In the first type the pronoun may or may not be co-referential with another NP in the sentence but it is usually interpreted as co-referential by adults, for example:

John knew that he was going to win the race.

In the second type the pronoun *cannot* be co-referential with an NP in the sentence, for example:

He knew that John was going to win the race.

Chomsky showed that these constructions are understood quite early. For example, almost all children over 6, though hardly any 5-year-olds, knew the non-identity rule for the second type of sentence. Furthermore, children's errors in understanding pronouns were more highly correlated with chronological age than they were for the other constructions. Chomsky argued that since rules for interpreting pronouns are general and do not depend on the identity of other words in the sentence, they are acquired relatively early. However, other researchers have found that older children still have difficulty in understanding pronouns. This work will be discussed in a later section.

Other complex constructions

Actives and passives   If children interpret sentences by assuming a relatively straightforward correspondence between their surface features and their meanings – if, for example, they think that all sentences follow the S–V and S–V–O patterns – they will have trouble understanding passive sentences such as:

The dog was bitten by the horse

in which the grammatical object comes first, then the verb, then the grammatical subject.

Many investigators have studied how children interpret passives.[2] One of the earliest was Dan Slobin (1966). He gave 6-, 8-, 10- and 12-year-olds and adults a sentence–picture verification task in which they were presented with a picture and a sentence and had to say whether the sentence correctly described the picture. Slobin found that, at all ages, *reversible passives* took longer to verify than *non-reversible passives*. A reversible passive is one in which a reversal of roles produces a sensible sentence. For example:

The boy was followed by the girl

is reversible because a boy can also follow a girl. On the other hand, reversing the roles of girl and flowers in:

The flowers were watered by the girl

is not possible, so the sentence is non-reversible. Adults rarely made mistakes in interpreting reversible passives, but even they found the non-reversible ones easier. Not surprisingly, Slobin reports a decrease in errors with age. However, although the overall error rate was below 20 per cent, even for the 6-year-olds, Slobin provides no further indication as to which sentences produced these errors. Nevertheless, it is likely that the reversible passives proved more difficult than the other types of sentence that Slobin used. Just as with 'easy to see', in the absence of other cues, children may assume that a passive sentence follows the S–V–O pattern and take its first NP to be the underlying subject.

Elizabeth Turner and Ragnar Rommetveit (1967) examined the imitation (i.e. repeating back), comprehension and production of actives and passives in 4- to 9-year-olds. They showed that correct imitation preceded comprehension, which in turn preceded production. It was not until second grade (7 years) that performance in the comprehension test was better than 60 per cent for reversible passives. Nearly all the errors were produced by switching the two noun phrases. However, nearly a third of these errors occurred with non-reversible sentences! In a similar study, Brian Baldie (1976) found that children between 7 years 6 months and 7 years 11 months could imitate and understand reversible, non-reversible and agentless (e.g. 'the dog was bitten') passives, and that it was possible to elicit passive constructions from four out of five children. Nevertheless, non-reversible passives were better understood at all the ages he tested (3 to 8 years), even though they were less often *produced* than reversible passives. In a study of the spontaneous speech of 2- to 14-year-olds, Horgan (1978) found that non-reversible passives with agents (e.g. *The plate was broken by the girl*) do not appear until 9 years.

Margaret Harris (1978) provides evidence for children's awareness of pragmatic constraints in the production of passives. She showed that 5-10 year olds' productions were influenced by noun animacy – most passives were produced when the acted-upon was more animate than the actor, and almost none when the acted-upon was less animate.

To conclude, the large literature on children's comprehension of passives has shown that a number of factors, only some of which we have discussed here, influence the way that such sentences are understood.[3] Children start noticing the difference between actives and passives at about 4 years, but understanding of the relation between them does not begin until about 7 years. One final important observation is that the passive construction is normally used either when the agent of the action is unknown or when the object of the action is the focus of attention, and children find it much easier to act out passive sentences when they are used in this way (see Huttenlocher, Eisenberg and Strauss, 1968).

Relative clauses and embedding   There have been many studies of children's understanding of relative clauses and a number of theories about why children find them difficult. The experimental literature is full of conflicting findings and differing interpretations. De Villiers et al. (1979) review this literature and argue that the conflicts may have arisen, at least in part, because there are two factors that contribute to the structure of relative clauses, and particular researchers have tended to concentrate on one and ignore the other.

These first of these factors is the *embeddedness* of the relative clause, which depends upon its position within the sentence or, more specifically, which part of the main clause it modifies. If the clause modifies the (superficial) subject NP it is *centre embedded* (CE). If it modifies the object NP, it is *right branching* (RB). (These terms are technical terms from syntactic theory and refer to properties of the tree diagrams that describe the structure of the sentences.) In table 3.1, the first two sentences contain embedded, and the second two, right-branching, relative clauses.

The second factor, the *focus* of the relative clause, refers to the function that the head noun phrase – the noun phrase in the main

Table 3.1 Four kinds of relative clause

Embeddedness (role of complex NP in main clause)	Focus (role of head NP in relative clause)	Example sentence
Subject (CE)	Subject	The cat that bit the dog chased the rat
Subject (CE)	Object	The cat that the dog bit chased the rat
Object (RB)	Subject	The cat bit the dog that chased the rat
Object (RB)	Object	The cat bit the dog that the rat chased

CE = Centre embedded.
RB = Right branching.

clause that is modified by the relative clause – plays in the relative clause (subject, object or indirect object). For example, *that the dog bit* is always an object-focus relative clause, because, when it is attached to a head noun, that head noun, whatever role it plays in the main clause, is the underlying object of *bit* in the relative clause. Subject-focus relative clauses are often termed 'subject-relatives' and object-focus, 'object-relatives'.

These two variables in combination result in four main types of relative clause, which are shown in table 3.1. Amy Sheldon (1974) carried out an influential early study of relative clauses. She tested 3- to 5-year-olds and found that neither embeddedness nor focus alone could account for the comparative difficulty of different types of relative clause. She proposed the *parallel function hypothesis* to account for her data. This hypothesis states that sentences in which the head NP has the same function (subject or object) in both clauses will be easier. It predicts, as Sheldon found, that the first (SS) and the last (OO) sentences in table 3.1 should be easier than the middle two, because in the first case *the cat* is subject of both the main and relative clauses and in the last it is the object in both clauses. In the other sentences *the cat* plays both roles, subject and object, once each.

Subsequent studies, for example that of de Villiers et al., have failed to confirm Sheldon's findings. De Villiers et al. set out to resolve some of the conflicting results on the understanding of relative clauses by studying 3- to 7-year-olds' comprehension of nine different types of relative clause in an acting out task. They manipulated embeddedness and focus systematically and included indirect objects in both main and relative clauses, for example:

The kangaroo whispered to the turkey that the zebra shouted to.

They therefore increased the number of types of sentence from four to nine (3 × 3 instead of 2 × 2).

They found that children got better at understanding all types of sentence as they got older. Furthermore, the relative difficulty of the different sentence types was the same at each age. Unfortunately de Villiers et al. do not report how many errors the children made at different ages, but their discussion suggests that 6-year-olds are still having difficulty with relative clauses. Both embeddedness and focus affected ease of comprehension. The SS and OS sentences were the easiest:

The gorilla that bumped the elephant kissed the sheep (SS)
The kangaroo kissed the camel that shoved the elephant (OS)

and the SI (i.e. where the head noun is subject in main clause, indirect object in relative clause) sentences were hardest:

The giraffe that the turkey yelled to pushed the zebra.

Obviously this pattern of results cannot be explained in terms of either embeddedness or focus alone. Neither do the predictions of the parallel function hypothesis fit the data. De Villiers et al. conclude that the children use processing heuristics, and that the NVN strategy (Bever, 1970) can account for most of their errors. The NVN strategy, which we outlined earlier, takes a sequence of noun . . . verb . . . noun to be Actor–Action–Object. To interpret relative clauses using this strategy it is necessary to assume that one noun can be included in two overlapping NVN sequences. As we have seen, such heuristic strategies have wider applications – children also use them to understand passives and other complex constructions. In other words, children pick up on the commonest mappings between surface features and meaning and use them, in the absence of other cues, to interpret all sentences.

The vast majority of studies of relative clauses have used tests of *spoken* comprehension. One exception is a study by Clare Beaumont (1982), who suggested on the basis of previous results that children of 7½ would find at least some types of relative clauses difficult to read. She tested children's ability to understand both embedded subject-relative and object-relative clauses (SS and SO) using a picture selection test and direct questioning. She also varied whether the relative clauses were marked by a relative pronoun (*that*). The sentences she used included:

> The girl that is kicking the boy is short. (subj.-rel.) SS
> The woman following the policeman is tall. (subj.-rel., no pro.)
> The horse that the man is chasing is fat. (object.-rel.) SO
> The lady the man is touching is thin. (object.-rel., no pro.)

Interestingly, and contrary to previous findings, the children found the object-relatives with relative pronouns slightly *easier* than the subject relatives (though Beaumont does not report whether this difference was statistically significant). With the subject-relatives, inclusion or omission of the relative pronoun made no difference. In accordance with the findings of de Villiers et al., subject-relatives, when they were misunderstood, tended to be interpreted as two overlapping NVN constructions. For example, *the woman following the man is carrying a dog* would be interpreted as *the woman is following the man . . . the man is carrying a dog*. With the object-relatives, however, the presence of the relative pronoun was important. Understanding was significantly better when the pronoun was included. The marking function of *that* guided the children's interpretation. Without a relative pronoun, misinterpretations were frequent. The children tended to match up the nouns and verbs according to word order and distance principles. Although the NVN strategy cannot be applied to SO sentences, the misinterpretations are similar to those produced by applying that strategy to SS sentences. Thus, the children interpreted *the boy the girl is pushing is carrying a ball* as meaning *the boy is pushing the girl . . . the girl is carrying a ball*.

In a study of children's spontaneous *production* of relative clauses, Romaine (1984) showed an overwhelming preference for rightbranching (object-relative) clauses in all the ages she tested (6-, 8- and 10-year-olds). This preference reflects the fact that RB structures are syntactically less complex that CE structures.

As with other constructions, there is some evidence that understanding of relative clauses is directly related to reading skill. Byrne (1981) found that although poor readers did not have any *general* problem in understanding relative clauses, they were worse on ones that have an improbable meaning (e.g. *the horse that the girl is kicking is brown*). However, poor readers are, in general, more dependent on extralinguistic knowledge for comprehension (see chapter 5), so the significance of this result for syntactic development is unclear.

It is quite clear from these studies that children have difficulty understanding relative clause constructions, and that they are often unaware of their wrong interpretations. These facts should be taken into account in writing books for beginning readers and in assessing their reading comprehension.

VOCABULARY AND WORD MEANING

Although there is little agreement about how many words children of different ages know, or about how quickly they learn new words, vocabulary clearly develops throughout childhood and into adulthood. However, the fact that a certain word is in a child's vocabulary does not necessarily mean that that child will use it in the same way as an adult would. In the early school years, children's use of a word is often more limited than or different from that of adults. Asch and Nerlove (1970: cited by Cruttenden, 1979) examined children's use of words, such as *bright, hard, sweet*, that can be applied both to physical objects and to people's characters. Such words provide an example of *polysemy* – the possession of two or more related meanings. Asch and Nerlove found that before 7 children only applied the words to physical objects. Between 7 and 8, they started using the psychological meanings but did not consider that the two types of meaning were related. Only the 9- and 10-year-olds showed an understanding of the relation between the physical and psychological meanings. Durkin, Crowther and Shire (1986) have also shown that polysemous words can be misunderstood during the school years and into adolescence, particularly in the fields of music and mathematics education.

Another characteristic of children's vocabulary is that subtle differences between word meanings are often not appreciated. Ervin and Foster (1960) found that for some 6-year-olds *good, pretty* and *happy* are interchangeable synonyms.

Difficult vocabulary directly affects reading comprehension (Anderson and Freebody, 1983; Wittrock, Marks and Doctorow, 1975). However, explicitly teaching children new words does not immediately help them to understand texts containing those words (Jenkins, Pany and Schreck, 1978).

Children also become aware of parts of speech in the early school years. The development of this awareness can be observed in their responses in word association tests. Between 6 and 8 children show a shift from *syntagmatic* responses to *paradigmatic* responses (Entwistle, Forsyth and Muuss, 1964). Syntagmatic responses are words that could occur next to the given word in a phrase or sentence (e.g. *fast* as a response to *car*). Paradigmatic responses are words that could take the place of the given word in a sentence, i.e. they are the same part of speech (e.g. *lorry* as a response to *car*). Some recent (unpublished) work by Annette de Groot and her colleagues at the University of Nijmegen has shown a link between type of response in such word association tests and comprehension skill. Eight-year-old poor comprehenders produced more syntagmatic and fewer paradigmatic associations than did good comprehenders of the same age.

Relational terms

The understanding of relational terms has been studied most intensively in children younger than 5 years. However, Donaldson and Balfour (1968) and Palermo (1973) found that some children up to 7 years take both *less* and *more* to mean *more*. Pike and Olson (1977) found that some 5- and 7-year-olds had more difficulty understanding *less* than *more*. Two out of twenty-one 7-year-olds consistently misinterpreted *less*. However, the majority (fifteen out of nineteen) of the 7-year-olds who showed some understanding of *less* were able to describe relative quantities in terms of both *more* and *less*, and thirteen of them were able to add and subtract in response to both *more* and *less* instructions.

Discourse connectives

Children's understanding of connectives such as *before, after, when, because, then* is reflected in their comprehension and production of sentences with subordinate clauses introduced by those connectives. Such constructions, as we shall see below, may cause problems even for 6- and 7-year-olds. Children younger than about 5 assume that the order of clauses reflects the order of events. They tend, therefore, to misinterpret sentences such as:

John went out to play after he ate his dinner.

They do not understand the meaning of *before* and *after*. However, even when children can understand these words, they may still have problems understanding sentences with them in. Amidon and Carey (1972) showed that 5- and 6-year-olds did not simply assume that events took place in the order in which they were mentioned. However, when they made errors in acting out the sentences, they tended to omit the action in the subordinate clause.

Ino Flores d'Arcais (1978) found a similar focusing of attention on the main clause in Italian children aged 3 years 2 months to 8 years 6 months and Dutch children aged 2 years 10 months to 7 years 4 months. In his experiments with Italian children, Flores d'Arcais explored the comprehension of two types of construction: causal constructions such as

Because the boy has eaten ice cream, the boy is sick.

and final constructions, such as

The girl opens the gate of the garden, so that the dog gets out.

There was a general improvement with age in the children's ability to understand (by acting out) such sentences, but in the oldest group (6 years 7 months to 8 years 6 months), about one-fifth of the responses on both types of sentence were still incorrect. The oldest group of Dutch children (6 years 4 months to 7 years 4 months), who were only tested on causal constructions, were wrong nearly one-third of the time.[4]

Other work by Flores d'Arcais (see, for example, 1981) has shown that when asked which of the connectives 'belong together', second grade children tend to group them by physical or phonemic similarity, whereas older children show an appreciation of their meaning.

Roberta Corrigan (1975) suggests that the understanding of *because* develops in three main stages. In the first stage, children understand only affective links between the clauses ('Peter cried because Jane hurt him'). In the second they also understand physical links ('She stayed at home from school because she was sick'). Finally, they understand 'concrete logical' (or deductive) links as well ('All the blocks were white. John had a white block because there were only white ones'). In Corrigan's experiments, only about half of the 7-year-olds passed two tests of usage of the concrete logical sentences.

Evelyn Katz and Sandor Brent (1968) examined children's comprehension and production of a wider range of connectives and concluded that many connectives are not properly understood until even later. Their findings were based on both a corpus of spontaneous speech and on an experimental task in which first to sixth grade children (and adults) had to select the more appropriate of two sentences. For example, they were asked to say which of the following pair was 'better':

Because it started to rain, we ran into the house.
It started to rain, then we ran into the house.

results showed that children's understanding of *because*, *then* and *efore* changes between grades one and six. The first graders tended to prefer temporal connectives (*then, and then*) to causal connectives (*because, therefore*), whereas the sixth graders showed the reverse pattern. When they were able to give explanations, the first graders almost always gave causal ones, even when they chose temporal connectives, but their explanations rarely focused on the connectives. By contrast, sixth graders gave explanations focusing on *because*, but found it difficult to explain their (comparatively rare) choices of temporal connectives. In addition, Katz and Brent showed that 11- to 12-year-olds had only an incomplete grasp of the meanings of *but* and *although*. Olds (1968: cited by Palermo and Molfese, 1972) found that children up to the age of 9 do not understand *unless*. They take it to mean the same as *if*.

Overall, the studies reviewed in this section show that children beyond the age of 5 have trouble in understanding many conjunctions. Although they may appear to be using a variety of conjunctions correctly in their spontaneous speech, they still have a great deal to learn about their meanings. Robertson (1966: cited by Weintraub, 1968) showed a significant relation between children's understanding of connectives and ability in reading, listening and writing.

Determiners

In narrative discourse, a speaker often wishes to say something about someone or something that has not previously been mentioned. In English, the usual way of introducing such a person or thing is to use an indefinite noun phrase (e.g. *a* man). Subsequently a definite reference may be used (*the* man). Although subtle, the distinction between definite and indefinite noun phrases (NPs) is important for establishing inter-sentential relations in a text. Several studies have explored children's ability to use these linguistic devices to introduce *referents*, and to maintain reference to them. However, there is some controversy about when the ability to use referential expressions correctly is acquired (see e.g. Warden 1976, 1981a; Karmiloff-Smith, 1979, 1980; Hickmann, 1980).

Michael Maratsos (1976) found that even 3- and 4-year-olds could use definite and indefinite articles appropriately and understand the difference between them. This finding suggests that the distinction should not pose any problems for children learning to read. However, in Maratsos's experiment, only isolated forms were tested, in a tightly constrained context. The experimenter told the children a story about, for example, 'A dog and a monkey', or 'Some dogs and some monkeys'. At the end of the story, the children were asked a *who* question about the story. Questions about stories with one animal of each kind should elicit a definite response (e.g. 'the dog'), whereas those about stories with several of each kind would be appropriately answered by an indefinite response (e.g. 'a dog'). Thus, the children were required only to construct simple NPs, and only after the experimenter had set up an appropriate linguistic context.

David Warden (1976) questioned Maratsos's findings. In a story-telling task, he found that although some pre-schoolers sometimes used indefinite expressions to introduce new referents, children up to the age of 7 frequently used the definite article inappropriately to introduce previously unidentified referents. It was not until 9 years that children showed complete mastery of the definite/indefinite forms in discourse. Only the children aged 9 or over (about four-fifths of the time) and adults (all the time) used the indefinite forms significantly more often than definite ones when mentioning a referent for the first time.

Annette Karmiloff-Smith (1979), working with French-speaking children, found similar errors in the comprehension and production of definite and indefinite articles. These articles are multifunctional, and Karmiloff-Smith argues that full control over all their functions is not achieved until about 10 years. In one of her comprehension tasks (experiment 5), where the children had to introduce one of a number of identical objects, the proportion of appropriate referring expressions (for example, the girl pushed *one of the Xs*) increased from below 20 per cent for 4-year-olds to over 80 per cent for 10-year-olds. Adequate reference to one of a set of similar but different coloured objects (the girl pushed *the green X*) was somewhat easier: performance increased from about 60 per cent of appropriate choices at 4 years to near perfect at 10 years. Karmiloff-Smith expresses surprise at the fact that when the children had to refer a second time to the same object in an identical context, even the oldest (11-year-olds) rarely, if ever, used the anaphoric definite article alone – they always modified it in some way, for example, instead of saying *the boy touched the red X, and the girl touched the X*, they responded with . . . *and the girl touched the red X/the same X* (1979, p. 136). However, in our view, the use of *the X* alone is incorrect, at least in English. This result, therefore, has little bearing on when children grasp the *anaphoric* (i.e. referring back) function of simple definite noun phrases.

In another of her studies, Karmiloff-Smith (1979) used a a task similar to Maratsos's. Children had to refer to *one* X. When there is only one X in the story, it should be referred to as *the* X. If there are several (indefinite situation), *an* X is the required form. Karmiloff-Smith found that use of the appropriate article increased only gradually between 3 and 11 years, and only at 9 did children have what could be described as a good grasp of the distinction. Even 7-year-olds used the definite article nearly half the time in the indefinite situation.

Perhaps at least part of the reason for such errors is that even when young children appear to be using the definite article correctly, they do not understand its *anaphoric* function. They may simply be using definite referring expressions to refer to something that is the current focus of attention. In Karmiloff-Smith's experiments, the younger children did try to make their references clear but did not rely on the articles to do so. Karmiloff-Smith argues, therefore, that definite and indefinite articles are not contrastive terms for young children as they are for adults.

David Warden (1976) argued that the discrepancy between his findings and those of Maratsos may have arisen because his story-telling task was more difficult than the simple NP construction tasks used by Maratsos. He suggested that children might be induced to use definite and indefinite articles more appropriately 'by simplifying aspects of the verbal task or communication context' (1981a, p. 94). According to Warden, the communication context is 'simpler' when the referents of referring expressions are not present and 'simpler' when the audience is not present. These claims seem, at first, counter-intuitive, but Warden's idea is that 'simpler' contexts make it more apparent that an egocentric viewpoint is inappropriate. For example, if your audience is at the other end of a telephone, it is obvious that they cannot see the same things as you can.

Warden (1981a) asked children to retell the events in a film, in some cases while the film was running and in some cases after it had finished. The events were told either to another child in the same room, or over the telephone to a child in another room. The results showed that 5- to 8-year-olds do use the indefinite article when introducing a referent for the first time in a discourse, but not consistently. Only eleven of his eighty subjects used them in all their first references. These subjects were evenly distributed across the ages tested. The proportions of correct determiners on first mentions were very similar to those reported by Warden (1976, experiment 3). However, the children were significantly worse than a group of adults who were tested with neither the audience nor the referents present.

Another interesting finding in this study was that the children did not use indefinite articles when a referent was mentioned a second time. The definite article was always used in second mentions, and the indefinite was used only, though inconsistently, when a referent was first introduced. Thus, children younger than 9 understand that *a* should not be used after an initial identification, but they do not realize that it ought to be used for that initial mention. This result conflicts with Maratsos's findings, perhaps, as Warden suggests, because the contextual manipulations failed to simplify the task sufficiently to enable the children to 'surmount their egocentricity'. Describing a series of events may have been too demanding a task to allow the children to monitor whether or not their use of articles was appropriate. Furthermore, when Warden simplified the communication context, he made the children's task cognitively more complex. Most obviously, recounting the events after the film had finished imposed a memory load that was not present in the simultaneous retelling condition. The decrease in the complexity of the communication context may have been offset by an increase in the complexity of the other aspects of the task.

Maya Hickmann (1980) provides further support for Warden's findings. She asked 7- and 10-year-olds and adults to narrate short films, after they had finished, for someone who had not seen them. The 10-year-olds and adults consistently used appropriate forms to introduce referents (85 per cent and 98 per cent of the time, respectively). However, Hickmann argues that the ability to use articles to mark textual cohesion (anaphoric uses) was beginning to emerge in the 7-year-olds. For example, they often produced mixed forms, which included some appropriate and some inappropriate elements (e.g. 'This story was about the elephant and a lion').

One might conclude from this research that beginning readers will have difficulty in understanding the distinction between definite and indefinite articles. If they do not realize that *a* introduces a new referent while *the* refers back to one introduced earlier, they may become confused about how many things have been described in a text and how they are related to one another. However, such confusions seem not to occur. Hickmann and Schneider (forthcoming), in a study of 5-, 7- and 10-year-olds, have shown that even 5-year-olds are good at correcting inappropriate referring expressions, both when asked to retell a story and when repeating back sentences during the telling of a story. When retelling the story, even 5-year-olds used the correct form of referring expression for first mentions in over four-fifths of cases. Thus, in contrast with previous studies of spontaneous story telling, this research shows a relatively early ability to use appropriate referent introductions when reproducing narratives with inappropriate ones. However, only the 10-year-olds in Hickmann and Schneider's study could provide metalinguistic judgements about the anomalous referring expressions. They were far more likely than the younger children to say that there was something wrong with the stories containing infelicitous referring expressions and to explain what was wrong with them.

There are several possible explanations for these different patterns of results. First, the reproduction task used by Hickmann and Schneider may be less demanding than the more complex tasks used by Karmiloff-Smith. The children in Hickmann and Schneider's experiments may have been able to monitor their output carefully and to correct it. Second, Karmiloff-Smith's experiments were testing a different use of definite and indefinite articles. Third, there was never a naïve listener in her experiments. Even if beginning readers can use and understand definite and indefinite noun phrases correctly when given an easy task, such expressions may cause them problems if they are finding other aspects of reading difficult.

REFERENCE AND DEIXIS

We have already seen how definite and indefinite articles can be used to express differences in the 'givenness' of referents. A variety of more subtle differences in meaning can be expressed by appropriate use of referring expressions.[5] In particular, the use of *deictic* referring expressions, such as *this* and *that*, depends on such factors as who is speaking, and how far what is being referred to is from the speaker. *Deixis*, the Greek word for pointing, is used to denote the way that certain linguistic terms (e.g. *this, that, here, there, now, then*) relate to elements of non-linguistic context. Since deixis is more important in spoken language than in written it will not be discussed in detail here, even though the use of deictic terms has not been fully mastered before a child goes to school.[6]

An anaphoric expression is one that takes its meaning from another part of the text in which it occurs. In the discussion that follows, we consider mainly pronouns, but there are many other types of anaphoric expression (see Halliday and Hasan, 1976). Anaphoric definite pronouns (*he, she, it, they,*) typically have the same referent as some other expression. Other types of anaphoric expression, such as the indefinite pronoun *one*, refer to a different thing of the same kind as one that has been mentioned before (e.g. 'Jane has an ice-cream and I want one, too').

Anaphoric expressions are very common in written texts. Figure 3.1 illustrates the large number of anaphoric relations in even a very simple passage. As we saw earlier, Carol Chomsky showed that some constructions containing pronouns are understood by age 6. However, several later studies have shown that older children have problems understanding other kinds of anaphoric expression. Bormuth et al. (1970) found that 9-year-olds failed to understand a variety of anaphoric structures. For example, only about two-thirds of them could successfully answer a simple question following sentences such as:

Joe left the room. He had . . .

Alan Lesgold (1974) also found that children had difficulty understanding anaphoric expressions. The relative difficulty of different constructions was different in Lesgold's study and in Bormuth et al.'s. Lesgold argued that, at this age, understanding of anaphora is not governed by abstract grammatical rules but depends crucially on semantic and other contextual cues. The difference between the two studies probably arises because the semantic cues were different in the two.

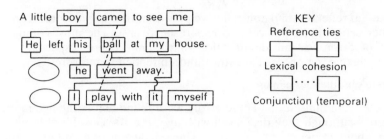

Figure 3.1 Cohesive ties: examples of reference, conjunction and lexical cohesion
Source: Chapman, L.J. (1981). Introduction. In L.J. Chapman (ed.) *The Reader and the Text*. London: Heinemann Educational Books. (p.11)

These quite severe problems that children have in understanding anaphoric expressions suggest either that they need to be trained in the interpretation of anaphora or that children's reading books should be simplified to suit their ability. However, as we shall see below, simplifying sentence structure is not always helpful to children. A similar conclusion follows from Margaret Richek's (1976–77) study of 8-year-olds' understanding of three different forms of anaphoric construction: full noun phrase anaphors (John saw Mary and John said hello to Mary), pronouns (John saw Mary and he said hello to her), and null forms (John saw Mary and said hello to her). She found that the full noun phrase anaphors were easier than pronouns and those, in turn, were easier than null forms. Although such null forms are, Richek claims, widely used in children's readers, and although from one point of view they are simpler than the full versions, only 60 per cent of questions about them were answered correctly.

The studies discussed so far have all investigated *free* anaphors – ones that can have antecedents in other sentences. Other pronouns, in particular reflexive pronouns, are *bound* anaphors, which must have an antecedent in the same sentence. Deutsch, Koster and Koster (1986) investigated the types of error made by 6- to 10-year-olds in interpreting reflexive and non-reflexive pronouns. Following sentences such as:

Pete's brother ties himself up

the children were presented with four pictures (Pete tying himself up, Jan (= Pete's brother) tying himself up, Pete tying Jan up and Jan tying Pete up). They could, therefore make errors on both the pronoun – interpreting *himself* as though it were *him*, or vice versa, and, less interestingly, on the antecedent – mistaking Jan for Pete. Six-year-olds performed equally well on reflexive and non-reflexive pronouns (they were correct just over half the time), but 8- and 10-year-olds scored higher on reflexive than non-reflexive pronouns (the 10-year-olds scored 90 per cent and 81 per cent correct respectively). The most common type of error was misidentification of the antecedent, especially on non-reflexive sentences. Thus, the children tended to interpret:

Pete's brother ties him up

as Pete tying himself up. These errors were found across the age range tested – although they decreased with age, the 10-year-olds still made them about 11 per cent of the time. They made almost no other errors. The results generally support the hypothesis that children find it easier to work out the relation between an antecedent and a reflexive pronoun, because there is only one possible antecedent (see also, Jakubowicz, 1983, who showed that 3-year-olds were able to understand reflexive pronouns). However, even 10-year-olds have not reached the adult level of competence.

The above studies of anaphor resolution all looked at comprehension of isolated sentences or short texts. Annette Karmiloff-Smith (1980) argues that such experiments produce task-specific effects, rather than giving a true idea of children's linguistic competence. Karmiloff-Smith has documented the development of children's use of anaphoric expressions to signal cohesion in text. This work, although interesting, will be summarized only briefly here since it is concerned with the production rather than comprehension of text.[7] Karmiloff-Smith investigated the way that 4- to 9-year-olds refer to things when narrating a story from a picture sequence. The youngest children frequently produced narratives with referentially ambiguous pronouns. She argues that their use of pronouns is deictic – each pronoun refers to an extralinguistic referent, and is not linked with a previous mention of the referent – children do not appreciate that pronouns can be used anaphorically. Later, children learn to produce coherent narratives by using pronouns as intralinguistic referring expressions (anaphors), and they use them appropriately to avoid ambiguity. For example, older children reserve sentence-initial pronouns for reference to the thematic subject (central character) of the story they are retelling. Although Karmiloff-Smith's work is on production, it can nevertheless give us some idea about the expectations that children of different ages have about the appropriate way to refer to something in the course of a narrative.

CHILDREN'S LANGUAGE AND THE LANGUAGE OF BOOKS

For the most part, this chapter has focused on aspects of language comprehension that young school children have not yet mastered. As we have seen, children's language is by no means complete when they enter primary school. In fact, their syntactic sophistication increases up to the age of about 13. Not only do children fail to understand certain syntactic structures that occur commonly in their reading books, but they often do not realize that they are misunderstanding them. The question arises as to whether early reading materials should be simplified to take account of the linguistic structures that children produce and understand. The obvious answer is that they should be, but we shall argue that the issue is more complex than it seems at first.

The first reason to be suspicious of the obvious answer is that, just because children cannot understand sentences in experiments, it does not follow that they will fail to understand the same sentences if they hear them in everyday conversation or encounter them in their reading books. As Karmiloff-Smith (1986, p. 461) points out, most investigators of complex constructions explicitly remove all extralinguistic, paralinguistic and discourse cues to their interpretation. But everyday language understanding does not occur in a vacuum – it depends on interacting cues from syntax, semantics, pragmatics, intonation, context and other factors. Young children are able to use many of these cues if they are available (for example in the interpretation of passives, see pp. 44–6 above).

The converse is also possible: even if psycholinguists can find circumstances in which young children can interpret 'difficult' constructions, those same children may misinterpret them in a text. The research surveyed in this chapter can at best provide only a guide to the sorts of construction that children *may* find problematic if they encounter them in books. As we have seen, the period from ages 5 to 8 is one of rapid change in language development. Children of this age often show inconsistent performance in psycholinguistic experiments, perhaps because the normal cues to understanding are not available. Between these ages children move away from a reliance on semantic, functional and pragmatic cues to comprehension, and towards a more abstract method of interpretation based on linguistic rules (see Karmiloff-Smith, 1986, pp. 460–462). By 8 years plus, therefore, their performance is more consistent.

Learning to read can be regarded as learning to understand language through a new medium. The traditional emphasis on decoding skills has reinforced this view that children have simply to 'break the code'. However, many of the problems that confront beginning readers arise from the fact that it is not *just* the medium that has changed. It cannot be assumed that the child will be able to understand in writing any sentence he can understand when it is spoken. As Romaine (1984, p. 205) points out, proponents of regularized alphabets such as i.t.a. (see chapter 4) seem to have missed this point. In understanding speech, aspects of the non-linguistic context are often very important, but those features are absent from the written text. For example, the physical context and the facial expression of the speaker are absent. So too are the prosodic features of text: stress, intonation, rhythm and pausing. (See Rubin, 1980, for a detailed discussion of the differences between spoken and written language.) Margaret Donaldson and Jessie Reid (1985) make the distinction between spoken language, which is 'embedded' in its context, and print, which is 'disembedded' – children have to learn to rely on the text *alone*.

One result of this disembedding is that there is a relative paucity of cues to syntactic structure in text. In speech, meaningful phrases are often marked by intonation or pausing. The syntactic structure of written text has to be derived by the reader. Apart from punctuation, which in any case is not well understood by young readers, there are no cues to the units of meaning. Katharine Perera (1985) suggests that young and unskilled readers may therefore have difficulty in identifying phrases within sentences – they may not see how sentences break up into optimal chunks. Skilled readers readily divide sentences into such units, as is shown by the fact that if the text is removed suddenly as they are reading, they do not stop immediately but continue reading to the end of a phrase (Levin and Kaplan, 1970; Schlesinger, 1969). The distance they can read after the text is removed is called the 'eye–voice span'. However, beginning readers make many more fixations on each line of print and do not seem to identify phrases in the text (Levin and Kaplan, 1970). They tend to read word by word.

Marilyn Adams (1980) suggests that this failure arises partly because too many of the young reader's resources are devoted to word decoding, and partly because cues to the structure of written prose only become available after considerable reading experience. She also points out that children may fail to recognize grammatical structures either because they do not know how to or because they 'have not figured out that they are supposed to' (p. 23). She emphasizes that structures that exceed the limitations of short-term memory pose special difficulties. When processing text, some words need to be retained verbatim, so that the grammatical relations between them and subsequent parts of the text can be worked out. But memory for exact wording, unlike memory for gist, is very vulnerable (Sachs, 1967). Only a few words can be held in short-term store, and only for a few seconds. Skilled readers (and listeners) can overcome memory limitations by recoding units of meaning, once they have been completed, into a more abstract form and transferring them to a more permanent store. This recoding takes place at the end of each clause. However, on the one hand, a long, complex sentence may impose such a heavy load on a child's short-term memory that its storage capacity is exceeded before the sentence has been recoded. On the other hand, inefficient or inaccurate chunking of information may mean that children try to recode before a meaningful unit has been completed.

Another problem is that sentences in books often have structures that are rare in speech.[8] Donaldson and Reid (1985) suggest that children often experience comprehension failure, and disillusionment, when they meet unfamiliar syntactic structures. Perera, too, argues that many children, although they master decoding skills, never become fluent readers because of the difficulties inherent in written language. Such difficulties, she argues, arise at a number of levels. Not only can the grammatical and discourse structures be unfamiliar, the subject matter and the vocabulary of the text may also be difficult. However, it is particularly in the case of grammatical difficulties that an awareness of the differences between oral and written language and of children's language limitations is necessary if one is to appreciate their problems. Traditional measures of a text's difficulty, such as 'readability', provide only a gross indication of the difficulty of a text since they are based on superficial features such as the lengths of words and sentences. In fact, a readability formula would give the same score to a text with sentences in the correct order and one with all the sentences jumbled up!

There have been several attempts to produce simplified texts for beginning readers. Those based on the phonics approach to reading instruction concentrate on particular spelling patterns. Those based on look-and-say use a restricted vocabulary, with much repetition. But such attempts at simplification have their own problems. Easy words in short sentences often sound stilted and artificial. Take, for example, the much-parodied *Dick and Jane* series, with its inane non-stories:

'Look, look,' said Dick.
'See Sally. See funny Sally and Father.'
'See, see,' said Sally.
'Sally is up, up, up.'
(Gray et al., 1956)

and the like. As Reid (1970) points out, such language takes no account of the way in which the 'words, syntax and sense are bound up with one another' (p. 24). Although these problems with books for beginning readers were pointed out by Huey (1908), they are not always heeded, even in modern reading schemes. David Crystal (1976) has recently found it necessary to renew criticism of the unnatural language found in early readers. Children's motivation is an important factor in learning to read, and they will obviously be better motivated to read books that they find interesting and attractive. This consideration is particularly important at the stage when children have learned some basic reading skills and need practice in independent reading in order to consolidate those skills, and for older children who have reading problems. Eight- or 9-year-olds will find little of interest for them in books intended for beginning readers.

One persisting problem is that attempts to improve early reading books are have not been based on a knowledge of what children's language is like. Strickland (1962) investigated the overlap between the sentence structures in children's speech and those in the books appropriate to their age. She showed that books for first graders varied widely in the patterns they used, and that the overlap between children's oral language and the material in their books was often poor. Strickland did not consider the *frequency* with which various spoken language patterns occurred in the children's books. However, Reid (1970) compared how often the basic speech structures identified by Strickland were used in four British reading schemes. One striking finding was that imperatives (including constructions with *see, look*, etc.) accounted for scarcely more than 1 per cent of the children's constructions, but comprised nearly a quarter of the structures in the four schemes. More generally, the structures in the four schemes differed substantially from those in the sample of speech.

Such mismatches are likely to cause particular problems for young readers, who expect text to make sense, and who use what they know about language to '*predict*' what will come next. This kind of predictive processing, or 'sophisticated guessing', is illustrated by the work of Marie Clay (1969) and Rose-Marie Weber (1970), who showed that when a young child misreads a word, the error is usually a word that is appropriate in the preceding context. Inevitably, beginning readers' expectations come mainly from what they know about spoken language. If the language of their reading books is very different from what they are used to, their 'guesses' are likely to be incorrect. Bullock (DES, 1975, p. 105) stressed the need for 'a close match between the syntactic features of text and the syntactic expectancies of the reader'.

By about 7 years many children have progressed from a basic reading scheme to 'extension readers', which may continue to pose language problems. Research by Ruddell (1965) and Tatham (1970) shows that children of this age have more difficulty reading sentence patterns that do not appear in their speech – even when vocabulary, content and sentence length are controlled. Reid (1972) argues that although the importance of syntactic variables in early reading books has been widely recognized, sentences found in extension readers may not only be difficult to interpret – they may have *predictable* misinterpretations. Reid chose a variety of sentences from extension readers that she judged to be different from the speech forms used and heard by 7- to 8-year-olds. She then created another version of each sentence, in a form which she considered more likely to be found in speech (for example, she removed difficult connectives such as *if, neither, nor, only*). However, the new sentences were generally longer than the originals. For example:

The girl standing beside the lady had a blue dress.

was rewritten as:

The girl had a blue dress and she was standing beside the lady.

In this case, the rewritten version was better understood – 89 per cent of children successfully answered the question '*Who had a blue dress?*'

compared with less than half for the original. In general, the rewritten versions led to significantly better comprehension.

Katharine Perera (1985) argues that grammatical constructions that develop late, or that are found *only* in written language, are likely to be particularly problematic at this intermediate stage in reading, which she terms the 'consolidation' stage. This stage occurs after fluent letter and word identification have been achieved, as children's reading ability catches up with their ability to use the spoken language. Perera (1985, pp. 289-317) lists a number of common written structures that are likely to cause comprehension problems. She suggests how they might be rewritten to ease comprehension. For instance, the following nominalized sentence taken from a junior school textbook:

> The exploration and charting of the coastlines of these new lands was the work of an English seaman.

would be easier to understand if it was rewritten as:

> An English seaman explored and charted the coastlines of these new lands.
> (Perera, 1985, p. 293).

Consolidation should be followed by what Perera terms 'differentiation' – the point at which reading comprehension surpasses auditory comprehension, and processing difficult constructions becomes *easier* in reading than in listening. Oakan, Wiener and Cromer (1971), in a study of children aged 9 years 10 months to 11 years 3 months, showed that good readers were better able to answer questions after reading a text (73 per cent correct) than after listening to it (53 per cent correct). The problem is that some children may never reach this stage.

Perera concludes that the way written language is simplified for beginners is one of the most important factors in early reading. However, the practical question of how to simplify difficult sentences is not as easy to answer as it might at first seem. One approach would be to use the patterns of children's speech but, as we have already seen, that approach has several problems, the most important of which is that structures that are easy in spoken language are not necessarily easy in written language. For example, Reid (1972) suggested that, since children use relatively long sentences in speech, it might be better if they encountered longer sentences in books. However, this suggestion ignores the problems of *decoding* long sentences – the relative slowness of reading, coupled with short-term memory limitations, may mean that readers find long written sentences more difficult than long spoken ones.

A more general problem for all attempts at simplification is that apparent 'simplifications' often make comprehension *harder*. For example, succinct expression often depends on more difficult vocabulary, and short sentences are not always easier, as Pearson (1974–75) showed. He presented 8- and 9-year-olds with four different versions of a sentence and asked them to rank them according to how much help they thought each would provide in answering a question. A sample item was:

> Why did John sleep all day?
> 1. Because John was lazy he slept all day.
> 2. John was lazy. So he slept all day.
> 3. John was lazy, and he slept all day.
> 4. John was lazy. He slept all day.

The children showed a clear preference for the more cohesive, more grammatically complex forms, such as (1). However, Pearson's finding may be specific to the task – the children may have selected the first statement because they expect an answer to a 'why' question to start with the word *because*. They may not prefer more complex sentences in other circumstances.

Nevertheless, as Marion Blank (1985) points out, there is a more general question about simplification of texts to be solved. Short sentences that are easy to understand in isolation may be difficult to link together if cues to the relations between them, usually in the form of connectives such as *because*, are not given. Without such cues, those relations must be inferred, and inference from text is a skill that beginning readers may have yet to develop (see chapter 5). If connectives are omitted to 'simplify' a text, what are classified as the 'simplest' texts may be the least coherent. Blank cites a first-grade passage from Makar (1977):

> Tag is a pup.
> Kit is a cat.
> Kit ran to get Tag.
> Peg has a wig.

She points out that the only method used to link the sentences of this text together – the repetition of words – is not sufficient to produce cohesion. Blank (1985, pp. 32-33) also shows that a short, superficially straightforward extract from a Little Grey Rabbit story leaves many links between the sentences implicit and may therefore pose unsuspected comprehension problems for beginning readers. Indeed, a study by Isabel Beck and her associates (Beck et al., 1984) investigated the effects of revisions that improved the coherence (but did not alter the plot) of stories taken from children's reading books. Although their revisions increased the difficulty of the stories as indexed by readability formulas, they improved the comprehension of both skilled and less-skilled third-grade readers.

Of course, no text makes all cohesive links explicit – a text that did would be very long and boring. However, Blank argues that only if the inferences are kept simple will children be able to cope. Thus, care must be taken when deciding which text connectives to omit, since connectives often provide valuable clues to relations between sentences.

A further problem is that, as we saw above, children have difficulty with some connectives until the late primary years. It is no good including connectives that children are unlikely to understand.

A more general consideration is that difficulties in text should not be entirely avoided or else children will not have the opportunity to learn. However, at any age there are probably only certain things that a child is capable of learning, and it is on those things that instruction should focus. This idea of fostering development within certain limits is related to what the Russian psychologist Lev Vygotsky termed the *zone of proximal development* (Vygotsky, 1978, ch. 6). As Vygotsky points out, although learning should be matched to children's developmental level, they have to be helped to progress beyond that level. In order to provide such help, Vygotsky argued, one must not only know the current intellectual level that a child has attained, but also his or her *potential* level of performance when given some hints or guidance to help with the problem in hand. The zone of proximal development lies between these two levels.

Vygotsky's idea of a zone of proximal development suggests that reading instruction should at every stage be tailored to children's current needs and difficulties. For beginning readers, part of that instruction may be to help them realize that the language of books differs from spoken language, and to understand the nature of the difference. Later, their syntactic knowledge, as well as other reading-related skills, should be taken into account. Even when proficient decoding skills have been attained, there remains a need for structured teaching of reading. An understanding of children's current linguistic abilities and difficulties should suggest how to produce texts that are appropriate to those abilities and that gradually extend them.

Donaldson and Reid (1985) recommend explicit discussion of difficult grammatical structures and suggest that reading *to* children can play an important role in helping them to understand the structures they will encounter in their own reading. By reading aloud texts that are harder than the children's current reading level and explaining any difficult structures if necessary, teachers can help children to progress to reading more complicated texts for themselves. Perhaps, too, children should be prepared for the 'language of books' before reading begins. There is much pre-training in letter and word identification, but little attention is given to familiarizing children with the patterns of written language. Such familiarization could be brought about by reading aloud and discussion of written texts.

The focus of this chapter has been the way in which oral language development limits reading comprehension. However, it is highly likely that, for older children, the acquisition of reading skills influences their syntactic competence in spoken language (see Hall, White and Guthrie, 1986, for a discussion). Children who fall behind in reading may also suffer in their ability to use speech effectively.

Notes

1. For more details of methodology in child language research, see Elliot, 1981. For a discussion of some of the problems associated with an experimental assessment of child language, see Warden, 1981b.
2. A summary of this work can be found in Karmiloff-Smith, 1986, p. 458.
3. For a brief overview of the literature on children's comprehension of passives, see Elliot, 1981.
4. See Flores d'Arcais, 1978, for a discussion of the development of strategies for dealing with causal constructions.
5. See Maratsos, 1979, for a summary.
6. For brief reviews of children's use of deixis, see Elliot, 1981; Wales, 1986.
7. More details can be found in papers by Karmiloff-Smith (e.g. 1980, 1981, 1985).
8. See Perera, 1985, chapter 4 for a thorough discussion of the differences between spoken and written language, and Olson, 1984, for a discussion of the different functions of oral and written language.

Learning to read words

INTRODUCTION

When people talk about learning to read, what they usually have in mind is learning to read *words*. We say that children can read if they can work out what words are on the page and say them out loud. Of course we expect at least reasonable fluency in reading, but we assume that children who can read a passage out loud understand it, at least in outline. We shall argue in the next chapter that a significant proportion of children who can read stories in this sense are still having difficulty understanding them. However, in this chapter we consider how children learn to read words.

Almost all of the vast amount of research on reading has been on reading words in this sense, and in a single chapter we can only outline this work. We have felt it necessary to provide this outline for two reasons. First, the ability to read words is a *prerequisite* for understanding stories. To have a chance of understanding a written story a child must, therefore, have a certain set of skills – skills that we hope to identify in this chapter. Second, this chapter and the following one, taken together, show that the skills required for reading words are different from those required to come to a satisfactory understanding of what a story is about. Once this fact is recognized, it comes as no surprise that there are children who can read words fluently but who have great difficulty in grasping what the stories they are reading are about.

This chapter is in two parts. In the first, we look at some of the skills that young children may need to develop so that they can read words efficiently. We also consider how the development of these skills might be related to reading instruction. The most basic prerequisite for reading is to have the idea that marks on a page correspond, in some way, to spoken language – that there is a code to crack. In general the skills that are necessary or useful for learning to read are language-related skills – the ability to recognize that rhyming words sound the same, for example.

In the second half of the chapter we consider different approaches to teaching children to read words – the whole word (look-and-say) and phonics methods, and the use of special alphabets and other special writing systems. We consider how successful these methods are in practice and attempt to explain their success, or lack of it, in the light of the ideas discussed in the first part of the chapter.

DEVELOPMENT OF READING-RELATED SKILLS

Children who are learning to read already possess a wide variety of skills and are acquiring others. Many of these skills are either prerequisites for reading or are related to it in other, less direct ways. It is on the development of these skills and their relation to reading that we focus in the first part of this chapter. The first set of abilities we shall consider can be grouped under the head of *understanding printed language concepts*.

Before children can start to read, they must realize that the squiggles by the pictures in books are systematically related to what their parents say when they read those books to them. Furthermore, they must realize that only some aspects of those marks are important to what is said – their shape, but not their colour or position on the page, for example. Second, children have to acquire the concept of a word. This concept is such an obvious one to literate adults, and so easily applied to spoken as well as written language, that it is hard to realize that a 3-year-old whose spoken language is fluent and sophisticated may not understand what a word is. Third, despite the (partial) success of whole-word approaches to teaching reading, the ability to subdivide both written and spoken words into recurring units (letters and what linguists call *phonemes*, or sound segments, respectively), is a great help to beginning readers. Furthermore this ability is essential for children who want to recognize for themselves words they have never seen written before.

In particular, children must learn rules that relate written letters or groups of letters to sounds. In English these rules are complex, more so than in languages such as Finnish, Italian and Serbo-Croat. Nevertheless, even in English, the correspondences are often straightforward. The letter b, for example, corresponds to the single sound that linguists represent as /b/. However, some letters, such as c, are sounded differently in different words (*cite* vs. *cute*), and sometimes two or more letters correspond to a single sound (e.g. ch, ough).

The rules for converting letters into sounds are called *grapheme–phoneme correspondence rules* (GPC rules) because they state the relation between small building blocks of written language (graphemes) and small units of spoken language (phonemes). (We will explain the concept of a phoneme in more detail later). To apply grapheme–phoneme correspondence rules, children have to be able to break written words into parts and put the parts back together once the corresponding sounds have been determined (these skills are called *segmentation* and *blending*). All of these aspects of word decoding will be discussed in more detail below.

As has just been mentioned, one of the abilities that children already have to a high degree when they start learning to read is the ability to *use* spoken language. Most children starting school are unlikely to have difficulties with the basic syntax and semantics of language. Although there are some major syntactic developments beyond the age of 5 (see chapter 3), 'almost every kindergartener is capable of understanding utterances far more complex than anything he will be asked to read during the first few years of school' (Rozin and Gleitman, 1977, p. 89). Neither do most children suffer from visual or auditory perceptual problems. However, many children who cannot yet read have vague or even wholly misguided conceptions about it. Even those who do not will find much of the terminology used in reading lessons new. They may not be familiar with the idea of talking *about* language. They may lack the necessary knowledge about words, syllables and phonemes that are prerequisites to the development of an analytic approach to reading. To master the art of reading they will have to learn to pay attention to features of language that they have previously ignored. Although children beginning school have a good command of spoken language, which means they can produce and comprehend speech effectively, they lack the ability to analyse and reflect on the form of language independent of its meaning.

The ability to think and talk about language is sometimes described as a *metalinguistic* skill, one level up from the basic linguistic skills required for using language to talk about the world. However, there is some dispute about where the boundary between linguistic and metalinguistic skills should be drawn (see e.g. Ehri 1979, pp. 81–3). Paul Rozin and Lila Gleitman (1977, p. 93) claim that a major problem in beginning reading is to attain the level of metalinguistic awareness needed to understand the way the alphabet is related to the sound system of the language.

Before discussing in more detail the development of specific reading-related skills, we need to make one methodological point. Many of the findings about how the development of these skills relates to the development of reading are only *correlational* – they show that the age at which a child develops such-and-such a skill reflects the age at which that child develops a particular reading ability, whether before, after or at the same time. However, it is a truism in the social sciences that correlations are not necessarily indicators of causal relations. Furthermore, even when there is a causal relation, a correlation cannot show which direction it runs in. The skills that we shall consider could therefore be related to reading in various ways. Linnea Ehri (1979) identifies four different types of relation. First, skills may be *prerequisites*: skills upon which reading builds, and which must be acquired before reading can be learned. Second, they may have the role of *facilitators*: skills which may speed progress in beginning reading, but which are not essential. Third, they may be *consequences* of learning to read: skills that develop through practice at reading rather than vice versa. Finally, there may be no direct link between a skill and reading ability at all – they may be *incidentally* correlated, perhaps because each is related to some other factor, such as intelligence. Because a variety of explanations are possible for a correlation between a particular skill and reading ability, it is not always clear that training in that skill will improve reading. Training can only be useful if a skill is either a prerequisite for or a facilitator of reading development.

How can causal relations be established? One method, suggested by Peter Bryant (see e.g. Bradley and Bryant, 1983), is by a judicious mixture of longitudinal and training studies. Longitudinal studies establish which of two abilities develops first in the individual child. Since abilities that develop later cannot cause the development of abilities that develop earlier, longitudinal studies rule out whole sets of causal hypotheses. But do abilities that develop earlier cause the development of abilities that develop later in a longitudinal study? Not necessarily, even if the development of the two abilities is strongly correlated (i.e. if children who acquire the first ability at a comparatively early age tend to acquire the second at an early age, too). The development of both may be caused by a third factor – a general facility with language, for example, in the cases we are interested in. However, if training the ability that develops early has a specific effect on the ability that develops later, and if more general types of training do not have the same effect, then a causal relation is indicated, providing that the training programme has been suitably designed. As Wagner and Torgesen (1987) point out, it is important to ensure both that the programme improves the skill it is supposed to and that any other effects it has are controlled for.

Combined longitudinal and training studies are difficult and time-consuming to carry out, and their importance has only recently been recognized. There is, therefore, some uncertainty about which skills are necessary for reading to begin. It follows that the concept of *reading readiness* (e.g. Downing and Thackray, 1975) must be questioned. Readiness tests are supposed to assess whether a child is ready to begin formal reading instruction. They assess the perceptual, cognitive and linguistic skills assumed to be used in reading (for example, visual and auditory matching, letter–sound relations), so that appropriate pre-reading instruction can be given, if necessary.[1] But reading readiness skills (i.e. the skills measured in readiness tests) will only be helpful if the skills taught are important for reading to commence. For example, the ability to name the letters of the alphabet is often assessed in readiness tests but, as we shall see later, it is not needed for reading. In addition, as will become clear from the evidence below, and as Taylor and Taylor point out, 'reading itself may foster some readiness skills rather than the other way round' (1983, p. 358). Another use of reading readiness tests is to predict later reading achievement but, as Weaver and Shonkoff (1978) point out, such measures are no better predictors than teachers' own judgements, or scores on more general tests of intellectual ability.

Understanding of printed-language concepts

Between the ages of 3 and 5 children's ideas about reading change dramatically, as do their ideas about the components of written language. The first of these developments is reflected in children's own assessment of whether they can read. Oliver (1975: cited by Yussen, Mathews and Hiebert, 1982) found that more than half of 3-year-olds thought they could read, although none of them could. When asked to say what reading was, they said things like 'looking at paper' or 'holding a book'. Only about one-third of 4-year-olds thought they could read. Their conception of reading was similar to that of the 3-year-olds, except that they recognized that looking at books had to be accompanied by some 'talking'. By 5, most children who could not read were well aware of the fact. Children of this age thought of reading as 'knowing words' and 'saying words'. However, Oliver's subjects were children from a poor American Indian background, who may not be representative of children of their age.

Young children also have difficulty in understanding other reading-related concepts. Some early studies by John Downing (1970) and Jessie Reid (1966) showed that beginning readers had difficulty answering open-ended questions about reading and reading terminology. For example, they could not give the meanings of terms such as *word*, *letter* and *writing*, or answer questions such as 'what parts of the book do you read?'. Their answers indicated much confusion amongst the terms. However, on simpler tasks such as pointing to letters, words and sentences, children who had just started school performed well above chance level (see e.g. Evans, Taylor and Blum, 1979). Furthermore, Lavine (1977) showed that whereas only some 4-year-olds could distinguish writing from non-writing, most 5-year-olds could. Many could also distinguish between numbers and letters. On the other hand, a study by Clay (1966: cited by Yussen, Mathews and Hiebert, 1982) revealed that two-thirds of 5-year-olds thought that the *pictures* in a book, not the words, told the story, although after 6 months of schooling almost all of the children had reversed their judgement.

In summary, 3-year-olds are more likely than older children to misassess their reading ability, thinking that they can read when they cannot. However, they understand that reading involves interacting with books, and that something has to be in the books. By 5, most children know if they can't read, and know about the importance of *words*. Children's early knowledge of the language and terminology of reading correlates with their later reading skill (see Yussen, Mathews and Hiebert, 1982). However, an explicit understanding of reading-related concepts may not be a prerequisite for reading. Reading instruction may encourage children to develop a more analytic approach and to learn more about the terminology, rather than vice versa.

Word consciousness

Word consciousness or *lexical awareness* is the ability to recognize that both writing and speech are made up of distinct entities called words. Although the concept of a word is one that literate adults take for granted, it is not necessarily obvious to young children. Some 5-year-olds still find it difficult to recognize words as distinct units. An excellent review of research on word consciousness is given by Linnea Ehri (1979), who also addresses some of the broader issues about the relation between word consciousness and reading. Here we simply outline some of the major findings.

A study by Ryan, McNamara and Kenney (1977) showed that performance on some tasks that measure word awareness skills is correlated with early reading ability. For example, in first and second grade readers, reading skill was correlated with ability to judge whether a sound was made up of one word or two words, or whether it was not a word at all. Reading ability was also related to the ability to pick out the word or words that differed between two sentences. The investigators did not find that reading ability correlated with performance on an *oral segmentation task* which required the subjects to tap once for each word in a spoken sentence. However, they acknowledge that the word tapping task has been shown to relate to reading ability in other studies – several studies have shown that pre-school children are generally unable to segment meaningful sentences into words (see e.g. Ehri, 1975; Holden and MacGinitie 1972; Huttenlocher, 1964).

It has not been clearly established whether teaching word consciousness skills enhances reading. Some children are aware of words *before* they begin to read, so word consciousness is not simply a consequence of learning to read. However, there is no evidence that it is essential for reading to begin (see Ehri, 1979).

More surprisingly, first grade children have difficulty detecting word boundaries in printed materials, too, despite the fact that there are clear visual cues to where one word ends and the next begins. The ability to pick out printed words develops with increased reading proficiency. However, Mickish (1974: cited by Ehri, 1979) found that the perception of word boundaries develops only slowly during the first year of instruction. So, again, this skill does not appear to be a prerequisite for learning to read.

Although the relation between word awareness and reading acquisition is not clear, the available evidence suggests that games to facilitate children's understanding of the word concept are likely to accelerate reading. Word awareness might also be fostered by the 'look-and-say' method of instruction, since words are presented in isolation.

Awareness of lower-level features

In order to extend their limited sight vocabulary, children must learn to break both written and spoken words into smaller parts. Teachers call the ability to divide words up in this way *word attack* skills. As we mentioned in the introduction to this chapter, children who recognize that a printed word is made up of a sequence of letters, and that each letter or group of letters corresponds to a sound, can make a good guess at the pronunciation of a word that is new to them, and recognize it from the way it sounds.

In the discussion that follows, the concept of a *phoneme* will be an important one, so we shall say more about it before we continue. Phonemes are the units of speech that correspond roughly, but only roughly, to letters in writing. The sound system of English has about forty-five phonemes (depending on dialect), rather more than the twenty-six letters of our alphabet. Just as written words that differ by only one letter have different meanings, spoken words that differ by only one phoneme have different meanings. Indeed, this feature of phonemes can be used to distinguish one phoneme from another. This task is more difficult than you might at first imagine because different instances of the *same* phoneme can be acoustically more different from one another than instances of different phonemes. For example, the /b/ sound of a deep male bass voice and that of a high female soprano are more different than the /b/ and the /p/ of either.

In a particular language, two sounds are different phonemes if the difference between them *by itself* can signal a change in meaning. For instance, /r/ and /l/ are distinct phonemes in English. We can easily tell the difference between the spoken words *rent* and *lent* and recognize that the different initial sounds signal a difference in meaning. However, in Japanese no two words differ only in that one has a /r/ and one has a /l/. These sounds are perceived as different examples of the same phoneme, and indeed they sound the same to Japanese ears. This feature of Japanese causes characteristic pronunciation problems for Japanese speakers learning English as adults.

To illustrate the fact that it is not only the Japanese who have these problems, consider the /t/ sounds in *top* and *stop*. To English ears they sound the same, though the /t/ in *top* is much more breathy, as you will feel if you say the two words with the back of your hand about an inch from your mouth. This difference is not phonemic in English, although it is in Arabic and other languages.

If children are to increase their sight vocabularies using word attack skills, they must first recognize the letters of which words are made up. Then they can apply the grapheme–phoneme conversion rules that we discussed earlier to get sounds for each letter or group of letters. The use of these rules demands at least an implicit mastery of the phonemic system of the language. The phonemes or sound segments (as they are also known) produced by application of the rules must then be *blended* to produce a pronunciation for the word as a whole. So, in summary, a child who knows the word *cat* but has never encountered it in its written form can use word attack skills to break the word into its component letters, grapheme–phoneme correspondence rules to produce the phonemes /c/, /a/ and /t/, and blending skills to produce a pronunciation for the whole word.

Young children have great difficulty segmenting spoken words into phonemes and written words into letters. The lower-level features such as letters and letter clusters are much more difficult for them to appreciate than the words themselves. Even very obvious features of words, such as their spoken or written length may be difficult for children to perceive. For example, Rozin, Bressman and Taft (1974) showed that kindergarten children were unable to make use of apparently highly salient differences in length to distinguish between two written words. The subjects were shown pairs of written words such as *mow* and *motorcycle* and were asked to say which one was *mow*. Even though the words differed so markedly in length, only a tenth of inner-city kindergarten children could reach the criterion of 7/8 correct, although nearly half of children in a suburban kindergarten could do so.

Orthographic awareness   The orthography, or writing system, of a language such as English comprises more than just an alphabet. There are also rules about which sequences of letters are admissible. For example, the orthographic rules of English would be violated by a word beginning zn . . . Furthermore, some letters appear more often in certain positions in words, and some of the permissible sequences of letters are more common than others. Just as words within sentences are to some degree predictable – for example, we expect articles to be followed by nouns – so are letters within words. To the extent that a letter is highly predictable it is said to be *redundant*, not because it is unnecessary for the correct spelling of the word but because someone who is familiar with the sequential and position-specific constraints on letters within words does not need to pay much attention to the letter. They know it must be there. The ability to use orthographic redundancy to speed word recognition was emphasized by Frank Smith (1971) who argued that more proficient readers are better able to use redundancy at *all* levels of text processing

(We shall return to use of redundancy at the sentence level later.)

Most studies that have explored the development of orthographic awareness have done so with tasks that demand *explicit* judgements. However, children whose reading indicates sensitivity to the orthography of their language cannot necessarily make such judgements. In one type of experiment children are asked to say which of pairs of non-words they think are more 'word-like' (Rosinski and Wheeler, 1972). Their ability to perform this task increases with age and with reading fluency. However, studies that have investigated how orthographic structure affects speed of word identification or naming have found no improvement with age beyond the initial stages of learning to read.

The use of orthographic information to aid word identification is typical of skilled adult reading, as demonstrated in the Reicher–Wheeler task (see chapter 2). Even quite young readers have also been shown to make use of such information. Juola et al. (1978) found that only children in kindergarten did not show a word superiority effect in Reicher–Wheeler experiments. The orthographic structure of the display affected the search times of second and fourth graders as much as it did with adults. Similarly, Krueger, Keen and Rublevich (1974) found that both fourth grade children and adults searched more rapidly for target letters in lists of common words than in lists of non-words. The difference in search time was almost the same for both. Although better readers tended to search faster, there was no consistent relation between reading ability and use of orthographic redundancy.

In a task that more closely approximates reading – lexical decision – younger children are more influenced by the orthographic features of letter strings than older children. In this task, subjects have to decide whether a string of letters is or is not a word. Henderson and Chard (1978: cited by Stanovich, 1980) used non-words that were either similar or dissimilar orthographically to real words. They showed that there was a *larger* effect for second graders than for fourth graders of how word-like the non-words were. The younger children took longer to reject the more word-like non-words as acceptable words. They were distracted by their word-like qualities. So, in this respect at least, Frank Smith's idea that one aspect of skilled reading is increased reliance on orthographic redundancy is wrong – fluent readers are *not* more reliant on this sort of redundancy. In reading tasks, there is either no increase in the use of redundancy with age, or there is a decrease. We shall see later that the evidence about the use of context does not fit Smith's hypotheses either.

Phonemic awareness   Young children experience great difficulty in tasks that require them to be aware of phonemic differences between words. Calfee, Chapman and Venezky (1972) found that kindergarten children could not decide whether two words began with the same sound, or whether two words rhymed, although nearly half of them were able to *produce* four or more appropriate rhymes in eight attempts.

The lack of phonemic awareness in young children is also indicated by the performance of elementary school children on the Auditory Analysis Test. Bruce (1964) asked children aged between 5 years 1 month and 7 years 6 months to say what remained when a particular sound was removed from a word (e.g. /h/ removed from hill). Children with a mental age below 7 were unable to perform the task at all, and for more advanced children middle sounds (e.g. ne-S-t) were harder than first or final ones.

Rosner (1972, 1973: cited by Rozin and Gleitman 1977), also using the Auditory Analysis Test, showed that performance on the phoneme deletion task correlated with reading skill in the first and second grade. Rosner and Simon (1971) used a version of the task requiring syllable deletion (e.g. say 'cowboy' without 'boy') as well as the phoneme deletion version (say 'belt' without /t/). Even kindergarten children in their study correctly deleted final syllables from two-syllable words about 80 per cent of the time, though they performed poorly at phoneme deletion. Rosner (1974) showed that auditory analysis skills could be successfully trained. Pre-schoolers given training over a year performed better than comparable children of the same age, and as well as children one year older who had had an entire year's schooling. However, Rosner does not report the effects of such training on subsequent reading achievement.

Lynette Bradley and Peter Bryant (1978) addressed the question of whether there is a *causal* link between phonemic analysis skills and reading. The innovative aspect of their research was that they compared backward readers (10-year-olds) not only with normal readers of the same age but with normal children (6-year-olds) who had the same *reading age*. They asked children to detect the odd-one-out in sequences of four spoken words (either on the basis of alliteration – *sun, sea, sock, rag* – or of rhyme – *weed, need, peel, deed*), and to produce words that rhymed with other words that they read out. The older normal readers showed the best performance, but the important finding was that the backward readers were poorer on such tasks than the younger normal readers, even though they had presumably had much more experience of written language. Bradley and Bryant argue that phonemic analysis skills do not simply develop through exposure to print, but that they are *causally* related to reading – phonemic awareness helps children learn to read. In a later longitudinal study, Bradley and Bryant (1983, 1985) provided further evidence for this idea. They showed that performance on the odd-one-out task at 4 or 5 was a good predictor of reading achievement, but not of mathematical ability, three years later. In this study Bradley and Bryant tried to eliminate the possibility that the real effective factor was short-term memory span, not phonemic awareness – children who cannot remember the lists of words will not be able to pick the odd-one-out. However, as Wagner and Torgesen (1987) point out, Bryant and Bradley's memory span test – asking children to remember the words used for the odd-one-out task – may not be a good measure of the more complex *working memory* capacity required to hold *and compare* the words to see which was the odd-one-out (see our discussion of the distinction between short-term and working memory in chapter 2).

Another way to determine whether there is a causal link between a particular skill and reading ability is to attempt to train that skill. If improving the skill increases reading ability, the skill probably plays a causal role in reading development (for further discussion of training studies, see chapter 6). Bradley and Bryant (1983, 1985) found that training in categorizing picture names by their sounds did not improve reading and spelling skills in non-readers who were lagging behind in phonemic awareness unless it was supplemented by teaching with plastic letters that demonstrated to the children how words that have sounds in common often have common spelling patterns. For example the teacher would show the children how the word *hand* could be changed to *sand* or *band* by simply changing one letter. The improvement in reading was long-lasting – when the children were re-tested at 13, it was found that those given phonological training were still ahead of the control groups[2] (who were either given no training, or training in an unrelated skill) in reading and spelling, but the children trained in the connection between sounds and letters were still ahead of all other groups (see Bradley, in press). However, Bradley and Bryant did not assess the effects of the training with plastic letters on its own, so the contribution of the sound categorization training to the overall gains cannot be determined. In fact, the later study by Bradley showed that training in sound categorization alone was not as effective as such training together with the training with plastic letters, or even the plastic letters alone.

In this later study, Bradley trained four groups of children, all of whom had normal sound categorization skills. One group was equivalent to the group in the previous study that received training in the two strategies – training in sound categorization and visual orthographic training using plastic letters. A second group received training in the same strategies but in separate sessions. Group three was taught the sound categorization strategy only, and group four the visual orthographic strategy only. The results showed that the reading of the group who were trained in both strategies and were shown the connection between them (Group 1) made most progress, suggesting that teaching the children the connection between the different strategies is more effective than teaching the same strategies independently. However, although they made significantly more progress than Group 2 (strategies taught separately) and Group 3 (sound categorization only), their improvement was not significantly greater than that of the fourth group who *only* received the visual orthographic training (plastic letters). This finding shows that the extensive practice with written words was very important. In this study, as in the previous one, there were no differences between the groups in arithmetic: the training effect was restricted to reading and spelling. Two years after the initial training there were no differences in reading ability between the four groups. This could be because the training was relatively short, or because only children with poor phonological skills benefit in the longer term from training in such skills. Other work by Bradley (mentioned in Bradley, in press) suggests that the latter hypothesis is the more likely. A further study using the same design but with a group of older backward readers showed that only those children who had a specific difficulty in sound categorization benefited from the training.

These studies by Bradley and Bryant have shown that training to rectify a deficiency in the skill of sound categorization can improve reading generally. It is also possible that learning to read improves phonemic awareness. For instance, David Goldstein (1976) gave non-reading 4-year-olds reading instruction and showed that sensitivity to the sound properties of spoken words (phoneme and syllable segmentation and blending) helps children to learn to read, but also that learning to read improves these skills.

Nick Ellis and Barbara Large (in press) have suggested that the causal relation between reading and phonemic skills (they used syllable- and phoneme-segmentation, and rhyming and blending tasks) changes over the first few years of schooling. In a longitudinal study of 5- to 7-year-olds, in which they assessed forty-four different skills, Ellis and Large showed that the phonemic skills of those children who were non-readers at age 5 predicted their reading ability at 6. However, once reading ability begins to develop, it then causes the development of some reading-related skills. For those children who had begun to read, reading skill at 5 and again at 6 predicted phonemic skills one year later. Ellis has suggested that the ability to read 'makes sense of' sound skills and fosters their development. The poor performance of illiterate adults on phonemic awareness tasks (Morais et al., 1979) also suggests that learning to read has a causal role in the development of phonemic awareness.

Phonemic segmentation   Before they can apply an analytic strategy to word decoding, children must become aware of the phonemic segments into which words can be divided. Without such awareness, decoding using grapheme–phoneme correspondence rules and blending are impossible. Experiments with young children have shown that they find segmentation of words into phonemes very difficult. This difficulty is probably related to the fact that there are no *acoustic* boundaries separating phonemes in speech (Liberman et al., 1967). Furthermore, phonemes overlap in speech, largely because of a phenomenon known as *coarticulation*. The way the parts of the mouth move means that, for example, the articulation of /b/ will depend on the following vowel. The first part of *bat* is pronounced differently from that of *but*. The very first bit of the word contains information about the vowel as well as about the /b/.

The difficulty of thinking of spoken language in terms of phonemes is also suggested by the fact that the alphabetic system of writing has been invented only once and only recently (by the Greeks about 3,000 years ago). Syllabic and logographic systems, on the other hand, have existed for thousands of years and have been invented independently several times (Gelb, 1963). Unlike phonemes, syllabic units are clearly marked in speech. Each contains a vocalic nucleus, which functions as a peak of acoustic energy, and these peaks are audible cues signalling (approximately) the centre of syllables. Although they do not signal boundaries, they do signal the number of syllables.

Studies of 4- and 5-year-olds have showed that they find segmentation of words into phonemes almost impossible, although they can of course distinguish between words that differ by only one phoneme (*bet* vs *pet*). Children are much better at dividing words into syllables and putting syllables together to form words (Elkonin, 1973). Rozin and Gleitman cite numerous other sources of evidence that suggest that a syllabic writing system is easier to learn than an alphabetic one. For instance, Liberman et al. (1974) measured segmentation skills in 4- to 6-year-olds by requiring them to tap on the table to indicate the number of syllables or phonemes (one, two or three) in spoken words. The percentage of children who completed six consecutive trials correctly is shown in Table 4.1. These data clearly show that the younger children have great difficulty making explicit the phonemic distinctions needed for many approaches to reading. These children are perfectly able to *perceive* differences at the phonemic level (e.g. they know that two words that differ in one phoneme are not the same). However, segmentation skills may be apparent earlier on some tasks. For instance, Fox and Routh (1975) found that even 3-year-olds could segment some words into their beginning and remaining sounds, if asked to 'say just a little bit' of the word. Overall, Fox and Routh's results concur with those of Liberman et al. (1974). They found that whereas 4-year-olds could identify syllable segments, the ability to extract phonemes did not emerge until 6.

Table 4.1 Percentages of children who achieved a criterion of six consecutive trials correct in phoneme and syllable segmentation tasks

Age group	Phoneme	Syllable
4 years	0	46
5 years	17	48
6 years	70	90

The ability to segment words into phonemes does not necessarily provide the key to reading, as Liberman and Shankweiler (1979, p. 125) point out:

> Because letter-to-sound correspondences have been learned in isolation, the traditional phonics method requires that these be combined or blended to form words. There the methods run afoul of the facts about speech that we have emphasized earlier: The spoken word is not a merging of a string of consecutive sounds. In speech, information about the three segments of the word *cat* is encoded into a single sound, the syllable. Therefore, no matter how fast the consecutive phonemes are spoken, 'kuh-a-tuh' merged together consecutively will produce only the nonsense trisyllable 'kuhatuh' and not the monosyllabic word *cat*.

Pre-reading success on Liberman et al.'s phonemic segmentation task predicts reading success in the second grade (Liberman et al., 1977, p. 214). However, segmentation skills continue to develop after children start to read, although it is not clear whether these skills develop through learning to read or because of more general developmental factors.

Perfetti, Beck and Hughes (1981) examined the relation between phonemic knowledge and reading in a longitudinal study. They concluded that some (less sophisticated) aspects of phonemic knowledge, such as blending, *enable* beginning reading, whereas other (more sophisticated) aspects, such as phoneme deletion, are enabled *by* reading. However, whatever the precise relation between such skills and reading, the results discussed above indicate that young children should find an analytic approach to reading difficult, and that they should find such an approach easier if the units of analysis are syllables rather than phonemes.

Phonological recoding

We have already seen that converting a written word into its spoken form may be a useful way of recognizing the word. In beginning readers the process is typically accompanied by 'sounding out', but skilled readers may convert letters to sounds in fluent reading too (see chapter 2). The ability to carry out this so-called *phonological recoding* may be an important component in the development of reading. Phonological recoding for word recognition requires the use of spelling-to-sound rules, such as the GPC rules discussed earlier. However, a word might be converted to its phonological form *after* it has been recognized, by simply looking up that form in the mental dictionary. Huey (1968/1908) suggested why this kind of recoding might take place: phonological coding provides a more durable medium than visual coding for storing early parts of a sentence so that they can be combined with what comes later. There is, indeed, evidence that the most recently read portion of text is retained in its exact phonological form (Jarvella, 1979). We shall consider evidence for these two types of phonological recoding below.

The sight vocabularies of beginning readers are relatively under-developed in comparison with their aural vocabularies. Phonological recoding is therefore important for these readers in retrieving the meanings of words that have been heard but never before encountered in print. They can identify words that are not in their sight vocabularies by converting the graphemic repesentation into its spoken counterpart. It has been suggested that one use of phonological recoding by skilled readers may be a by-product of this initial learning-to-read process, since it is not essential to convert a printed word to a sound pattern in order to retrieve its meaning (Barron, 1978). Even beginning readers recognize some words directly from their visual appearance. Rod Barron and Jonathan Baron (1977) demonstrated this fact by asking children to make judgements about word meanings (saying whether words 'go together') while repeating the word 'double' over and over again. This repetition was supposed to use up the children's phonological processing capacity and thus prevent phonological recoding of the words whose meanings had to be judged. Barron and Baron found that the interference task did not affect the extraction of the meaning of individual words at any of the ages they tested (6 to 13). Even children who had had less than a year of reading instruction were not affected by having to repeat 'double'. In contrast, the same interference task affected rhyme judgements at all ages. Since rhyme judgements necessarily involve phonological recoding – not all rhyming words have the same spelling patterns – this part of the experiment provides evidence that the interference task does affect performance when the use of phonological information is essential. Barron and Baron concluded that young children are able to go straight from graphemic information to the meanings of printed words.

Pieter Reitsma (1984) argues otherwise. He investigated the effect of a preceding speech sound (usually two phonemes) on 7- to 12-year-olds' ability to access the meaning of a printed word. He showed that phonemic similarity between the sound and the visual word helped the younger but not the older readers. Reitsma argues, therefore, that beginning readers translate print to sound before meaning can be retrieved.

While recoding may not be necessary for retrieving the meaning of words, younger children do seem to make relatively more use of phonological coding than older ones. Estelle Doctor and Max Coltheart (1980) argue that young children encode phonologically when reading for meaning. The youngest children in their study (6-year-olds) found it harder to classify as 'meaningless' sentences that sound correct because they have a (word or non-word) *homophone* substituted (e.g. 'I have know/noe time'). However, this effect may have arisen not because phonological encoding was more prevalent in younger than in older children (they tested 6- to 10-year-olds), but because the younger children were less certain of the spelling of the substituted words. They may, for instance, have been unsure how to spell *no* (while being sure that *blue*, however spelled, was nonsense in the context 'I have . . .time'). There is some support for this conjecture in Doctor and Coltheart's data – the 6-year-olds rejected sentences with non-word homophones (*noe*) nearly half of the time, but those with real word homophones (*know*) less than a third of the time. There was more confusion between the two real words, perhaps because some children could immediately recognize *noe* as a non-word. Doctor and Coltheart did consider an explanation in terms of spelling ability, but claim that the data they present refute it: they asked children to define homophonic words, and found that the wrong meaning was given in only about a quarter of cases by the youngest group. They argued that 'Although substitutions of one homophone for another, its mate, did occur . . . they were much too infrequent to explain the effects . . .'(1980 p. 199). However, performance on this task, where children are being asked to state a word's meaning explicitly, may be very different from meaning extraction when reading a sentence. In a further experiment, Doctor and Coltheart asked the children to spell homophones in context. Although less than a fifth of the youngest children's errors were substitution errors, they made 69 per cent of errors overall, an indication of their very uncertain grasp of the spelling of those words. In any case, Doctor and Coltheart confuse two skills: knowing how to spell a word, and recognizing the correct spelling in context. The former skill might not be a good predictor of the latter.

Some more recent work by Veronika Coltheart and her colleagues (1986) does not support the findings of Doctor and Coltheart (1980). Coltheart et al. suggest that visual (direct) access develops first, and that grapheme–phoneme conversion skills are comparatively late in developing. They found that all 9-year-olds used direct access, and it was only the best readers who had well-developed grapheme–phoneme conversion skills. Other studies (Barron, 1978; Snowling, 1980) have also shown that better readers tend to make greater use of phonological coding to access word meanings. Coltheart et al. suggest that the effects found by Doctor and Coltheart were due to post-lexical phonological recoding, rather than recoding used in access.

Another question is when children learn some of the more difficult GPC rules of English. Richard Venezky (1976) investigated the learning of GPC rules in children from second grade up and compared their performance with college students. This study was based on a detailed set of rules of pronunciation for English described in detail in Venezky (1970). In this earlier work, he listed the possible pronunciations for 60 spelling patterns and showed that in most cases the spelling-to-sound correspondences follow one of 100–200 rules. Sometimes the spelling–to–sound rule is invariant, as it is for the letter r, but in most cases there are alternative pronunciations, and the purpose of Venezky's rules was to specify the environment in which each pronunciation would be appropriate. For example, c is pronounced /s/ if it is followed by i, y or e (as in *circus, cycle, ceiling*) but is pronounced /k/ in most other environments. These two correspondences account for almost all pronunciations of the letter c in English.

Venezky (1976) asked his subjects to pronounce non-words such as *cabe* and *cipe*. The percentage of pronunciations that followed the two main rules can be seen in Table 4.2. Venezky found that the proportion of pronunciations that followed the rules increased with age, but that even the oldest subjects did not always produce the 'correct' pronunciation. He also showed that some rules were learned much earlier than others. He suggested that this finding could be explained by the fact that some correspondences are far more frequent than others – there are more words where c is pronounced /k/ than where it is pronounced /s/.

Table 4.2 Percentages of pronunciations that followed the two main rules for the pronunciation of c in Venezky's study

Rule	Grade 2	Grade 6	College
c before a,o,u →/k/	82	92	88
c before i,e,y →/s/	22	59	70

A more general question that has recently been voiced in the literature on how adults pronounce words and nonsense words is whether GPC rules are needed at all, or whether pronunciation can be effected by analogy with words spelled similarly. Attempts to distinguish these two possibilities have shown that they are not as easy to tell apart as might first be thought, at least for the single-syllable words with four letters on which this work was carried out. However, work with children on multisyllabic words has been used as evidence that analogy plays an increasingly important role in reading as reading skill develops.

In one study, Marsh, Desberg and Cooper (1977) asked children to say nonsense words such as *tepherd*. They claim that GPC rules indicate that the *ph* should be pronounced /f/, but that the analogy with *shepherd* suggests a syllable boundary between the two separate phonemes /p/ and /h/. The results showed that children in the fifth grade use GPC rules half the time and analogies about two-fifths of the time. For college students the respective figures were 30 per cent and 59 per cent. (The other pronunciations were predicted by neither strategy.) Marsh et al. (1981), who found a significant increase in the use of analogies between the second and fifth grades, suggest that analogy is an optional strategy for adults, and that its use depends on the kind of nonsense words in the experiment. Only some of theirs had obvious analogies. However, recent work by Usha Goswami (1986) challenges the idea that use of analogy is a late-developing skill. She has shown that even 6-year-olds can successfully use analogy to decode words. The children in her study were shown 'clue words' such as *beak* and were then asked to read a number of analogous and non-analogous test words, on which they had previously been tested. The provision of clue words improved performance on words that could be read by analogy (e.g. for *beak*, words such as *peak* and *bean*), but not for other words (e.g. *rain*). Even 5-year-old non-readers were able to make some use of analogies to help them decode some of the test words.

We now turn to the use of phonological codes after words have been recognized. It may be that even though children can access word meanings directly, phonological recoding of words plays some part in their reading strategies, as Huey suggested. Indeed, there is evidence that adults use a phonological code to store visually presented letters and words in memory even when it is potentially disadvantageous to do so, as it is when the spoken forms of the letters and words are highly confusable. In a test requiring children to remember a series of pictures, Conrad (1972) found that subjects older than about 6 perform less well if the pictures have confusable names (e.g. *bat, bag, cat*). Younger children make more mistakes overall but are unaffected by confusability. It seems that phonological recoding is preferred by older children and is not suppressed even when it is disadvantageous. Similarly, a study by Erikson, Mattingly and Turvey (1973: cited by Liberman et al., 1977) suggests that Japanese subjects reading Kanji, a logographic script, store the symbols in a phonological rather than in a visual or semantic form. In neither case, pictures or logographs, can the phonological code be produced by grapheme–phoneme correspondence rules. The word must be accessed from the visual pattern – either the picture or the logograph – and its phonological form subsequently retrieved and used as a memory code.

Use of sentence context

The use of sentence context in reading will be discussed in detail for two reasons: it has played an important part in some theories of reading acquisition, and it is relevant to the discussion of good and poor readers in the next chapter. First, a distinction must be made between use of context to correct or prevent errors, and the use of context to speed word recognition. In general, older readers are better at using context to make predictions (e.g. guessing what the next word might be from the context) or to check them, but they do not make so much use of context to identify words that they know.

As we saw earlier, Frank Smith suggested that good readers are better at using contextual information to help them decipher words. However, there is no evidence to support Smith's hypothesis at the level of word recognition (i.e. identificaton of known words). In fact, all the experimental evidence on the effects of context on word recognition points to the opposite conclusion – the use of context *decreases* as reading skill increases.

For example, in a study by Richard West and Keith Stanovich (1978), subjects (fourth and sixth graders and adults) had to name, as quickly as possible, a single word presented to them very briefly. In some cases the target word (e.g. *cat*) was preceded by a congruous context such as:

The dog ran after the . . .

In this case the target word is a sensible continuation and is fairly predictable from the context. In other cases, the target was preceded by an incongruous context, such as:

The girl sat on the . . .

and sometimes the target word was not preceded by any real context at all – just the word *the* (no context condition). This condition served as a baseline against which the effects of context could be assessed. If context is used to speed word recognition, then response times in the congruous context condition should be faster than when there is no context (a *facilitation* effect). Similarly, an incongruous context might slow recognition (an *inhibition* effect). West and Stanovich's data showed that *all* groups of subjects were faster to name words in the congruous context than when there was no context. The size of this facilitation effect was similar for children and adults. However, the *overall* level of sensitivity to context, which was measured by the difference between identification times in the congruous and incongruous contexts, was larger for the younger subjects. The developmental difference occurred because children showed inhibition *and* facilitation, whereas adults showed only facilitation. This trend is precisely the opposite of what would be predicted on Frank Smith's hypothesis – younger readers do *not* make less use of context, as Smith predicted they should. Although there was no developmental difference in the use of context to facilitate recognition, West and Stanovich note that there was a non-significant tendency for the younger subjects to make more use of context.

In a study that used a lexical decision task rather than naming, Schwantes, Boesl and Ritz (1980) varied the amount of context from, for example

The sky was dark and it started to

to 'started to . . .'. They found that relative to a no-context condition, increasing amounts of congruous context facilitated word recognition for the youngest (third grade) subjects, whereas adults were virtually unaffected by the amount of context supplied. Similarly, increasing amounts

ingruous context interfered with word recognition for younger but
der readers. Thus, using a lexical decision paradigm, Schwantes
et al. were able to demonstrate greater facilitation and inhibition from
context in younger readers. Schwantes (1981) extended these findings to
conditions in which extended, meaningful story contexts were used.

In a further study of word-naming, West et al. (1983) showed that
the effects obtained by West and Stanovich generalized to sentences
that were more representative of children's reading materials. They
took the sentences used in their experiment from children's reading
primers. As in the previous experiment, younger children showed
larger context effects.

To explain their results, West and Stanovich invoke Posner and
Snyder's (1975a, 1975b) 'two process' theory, which divides psychological processes into fast-acting automatic processes and slow-acting,
conscious, attention-demanding processes. In word identification West
and Stanovich claim that facilitation, but not inhibition, can be produced
by an automatic process called *spreading activation*. Facilitation can
also be produced by a slower contextual prediction process, which can
also produce inhibition. Roughly speaking, this process corresponds to
thinking what words might come next. The fact that older subjects
show facilitation but not inhibition suggests that contextual effects are
mediated by the automatic mechanism in skilled reading. Because adults'
word recognition is fast and automatic under normal circumstances,
conscious processes do not have time to exert an influence, but spreading activation (the fast, automatic process) can produce facilitation.
Although facilitation can also operate at a conscious level, in adults
it rarely has time to do so (unless the words are difficult to decipher).
Since slower (younger/poorer) readers also show inhibition, it is likely
that they are using the conscious contextual prediction mechanism and
that it produces some of the facilitation as well. West and Stanovich
call their model the *interactive compensatory* model. Contextual and
perceptual information work together in the identification of words –
they interact. However, the primary use of context in poorer readers is
to *compensate* for the fact that they cannot recognize words from their
perceptual properties alone. We shall return to the research on context
effects in the next chapter.

APPROACHES TO TEACHING READING

The contribution of various skills to children's reading development may
depend on their programme of reading instruction. Letter orientation,
order and word detail will be important for programmes that emphasize sight recognition of words, with little attention to letter-to-sound

rules. Differentiation of letters, the association between sounds and letters, and blending of sounds will be more important for phonics programmes. In the second part of this chapter we outline the main approaches to the teaching of reading and discuss in more detail how the various skills described above might be related to teaching procedures. We also outline the relation between the development of memory and reading. We shall not consider the role of social and motivational factors in early reading, although they are undoubtedly of importance.[3]

There are two main approaches to teaching beginning readers to recognize words: the 'phonics' (or 'code-based') approach, which teaches letter-to-sound correspondences and blending skills so that children can decode words on their own, and the 'whole word' (or 'look-and-say') approach which teaches a few words as unanalysed visual patterns, and bases early reading on this 'sight vocabulary' of learned words.

Whole word (look-and-say)

In this approach the overall shape and gross visual features of the word are stressed, not its component letters. Children are taught to recognize a small set of words, each of which is displayed singly on a card called a *flashcard*. Very often, too, pictures and objects around the classroom have written labels attached to them, so that children are constantly confronted by the written names of common objects. By use of the flashcards in conjuction with discussion about the words and labelling games, children are taught a pool of words that occur very frequently in their first reading books. Once children have built up an adequate *sight vocabulary* they progress to the first reading book in the scheme, in which almost all the words are taken from the flashcards.

The assumption behind this method is that children should be taught to read the way skilled readers do, by recognizing words 'directly' without having to analyse them into their component letters. We saw in the first part of this chapter that beginning readers find such analysis very difficult. The method also circumvents the problem that in English there are numerous exceptions to any simple set of grapheme–phoneme correspondence rules. Another advantage claimed for the whole-word approach is that it allows children to read for meaning early, presumably because it does not divert their attention away from meaning towards the structure of words. For this reason, the whole-word approach is sometimes referred to as a 'meaning-based' approach.

The look-and-say method has numerous disadvantages and limitations. The argument that children should be taught to identify words the way that skilled readers do is contentious. Skilled readers may access word meanings directly (without phonological recoding), but beginning readers may, nevertheless, benefit from training in decoding. Indeed, there *are* occasions when skilled readers need to recode phonologically, for example to identify words that are in their spoken vocabulary but which they have not met before in written form. Equipped with only the ability to recognize words as visual patterns, beginning readers will have no tools for deciphering new and untaught words. In addition, memorizing each of the 50,000 or so words in the average adult's reading vocabulary as an independent visual pattern, without the mnemonic link between spelling and speech, would be highly inefficient. So, although a whole-word approach may get the reader off to a good start, there is bound to come a time when a more analytic approach to reading is required.

Phonics

Phonics approaches to the teaching of reading, of which there are many, stress the importance of GPC rules, which is why terms such as decoding, sounding out and breaking the code are frequent in discussion of this method. Children taught this way learn the sounds that the letters of the alphabet usually make, so that they can pronounce unfamiliar printed words. They may have to attain a certain level of proficiency in producing the appropriate letter-to-sound correspondences *before* they are exposed to words. This approach provides children with a much more general reading skill. In principle, they should be able to 'sound out' any new word they come across. In practice, however, things are not so straightforward. Grapheme–phoneme correspondences in English are irregular, and a letter may be associated with several different sounds. Furthermore, the sound that a letter translates to often depends on the surrounding letters.

A more serious problem for phonics methods arises from the difficulty that young readers have in dividing words into their parts. As we saw in the first part of this chapter, most 5-year-olds find it impossible to perform the word segmentation and blending that are fundamental to the phonics approach. The Russian psychologist Elkonin (1973) points out some other difficulties with a phonics method. Because children have learned that every object has a name, they will, he argues, tend to regard printed characters as concrete objects: 'This causes children to distort the true relationship between spoken language and written language. Instead of seeing the truth – that the character is a written symbol for the reality of the sound in the primary spoken form of language – they reverse the facts and consider the sound as only the label or name of the character' (1973, p. 544).

Jeanne Chall (1967) concluded that *systematic* training in phonic rules (where rules are taught early and children have intensive training on the rules, often before any sight words are introduced) was better than *intrinsic* training (where sight recognition is taught first, and phonics is introduced only gradually as one of the cues that can be used to derive the meaning of printed words).

On the question of implicit vs. explicit training, Jeffrey and Samuels (1967) showed that for kindergarten children learning an artificial set of graphemes, systematic training on grapheme sounds was more effective than training on whole 'words' comprised of these letters. The number of unfamiliar words pronounced correctly was considerably higher in the former group. These findings suggest that specific training on GPCs may be the best way to help children to deal with new words.

Given that children have to learn GPC rules at some stage, how do they do it? We have little evidence on whether they do better if taught only regular letter–sound correspondences in the early stages of reading instruction, for example. Neither do we know whether they should be taught rules *explicitly* or be encouraged to figure them out for themselves.

Levin and Watson (1963: cited by Singer and Ruddell, 1976) addressed the first of these questions. They showed that third graders who had been introduced to variable letter–sound mappings from the start were better able to learn new materials that conformed to the variable rules than were the children who saw only one possible mapping.

Special alphabets

Various special alphabets for teaching reading have been developed specifically to overcome the problem of the irregular grapheme–phoneme correspondences in English. Each one reforms the writing system (orthography) in some way, so that the grapheme–phoneme correspondences are completely regular. Since each letter in a special alphabet is associated with only one sound, pronunciation is simplified. One way of regularizing spelling-to-sound rules is by colour-coding the letters of the ordinary alphabet, so that a letter written in a particular colour only ever has one sound. An example of a special alphabet that uses colour coding is the Gattegno system (e.g. Gattegno, 1969). With this approach there is more to learn about the orthography at the outset, but once the mappings have been learned, any word can be decoded successfully. A similar system, the diacritical marking system, adds extra marks to letters to indicate their pronunciation. For instance, a final e is slashed to indicate that it is not pronounced. Figure 4.1 provides an example of a text written in the diacritical marking system.

Onc℮ upon à tīm℮ Little
Red Hen liv℮d in à ba̲r̲n wi̲t̲h̲
h℮r fīv℮ ch̲i℮cks.

Figure 4.1   Text written in the diacritical marking system
Source: Brooks, L. (1977). Visual pattern in fluent word identification. In A.S.
Reber and D.L. Scarborough (eds). *Toward a Psychology of Reading*.
Hillsdale, N.J.: Lawrence Erlbaum Associates. (p.147)

A more radical system, and perhaps the best known, in Britain at least, is the Initial Teaching Alphabet (i.t.a.). The i.t.a. is a modified version of the English alphabet which has extra symbols so that each one maps unambiguously onto a single sound. For instance, the 'th' in *the* and the 'th' in *thin* are represented by two different symbols, as are the 'oo' in *book* and the 'oo' in *spoon*. There are forty-four symbols in the i.t.a. Several of them correspond to more than one letter (e.g. those that correspond to the 'th' and 'oo' sounds described above). Once the symbols and their corresponding sounds have been learned, all words can be 'sounded out' with complete success. However, children who have learned by this method can only read material in the i.t.a. script, and sooner or later the transition to traditional orthography (t.o.) must be made. Figure 4.2 shows a text in the i.t.a. script.

wuns upon a ti℮m
a littl red hen livd in
a barn wi̱th her
fi℮v ℔hicks.

Figure 4.2   Text written in the Initial Teaching Alphabet (i.t.a.)
Source: Brooks, L. (1977). Visual pattern in fluent word identification. In A.S.
Reber and D.L. Scarborough (eds). *Toward a Psychology of Reading*.
Hillsdale, N.J.: Lawrence Erlbaum Associates. (p.146)

John Downing (1967) compared a group of children taught i.t.a. with one taught t.o., both using equivalent materials (the 'Janet and John' books). The i.t.a group were better at word recognition and comprehension after their one-year assessment, and also following transfer to conventional script, even though they suffered an initial setback on transfer. However, other studies have shown that i.t.a. groups are superior only in word-decoding skills and *not* in comprehension (see Taylor and Taylor, 1983, p. 373). Moreover, work on reading ability after the transfer to t.o. has shown that there is no advantage in having been taught initially using i.t.a. (Warburton and Southgate, 1969). Generally, the evidence suggests that problems may arise at the transfer stage, and that the initial advantage of learning i.t.a. is lost on transfer to t.o.

Proponents of revised alphabets such as i.t.a. for the teaching of reading use the fact that some GPC rules are learned very slowly to argue for such teaching schemes. They claim that those schemes are effective because they use invariant GPC rules which are easy to learn. However, if regular GPC rules were the crucial factor in learning to read, completely regular languages such as Finnish should be very easy for beginning readers. However, although reading and ability to pronounce non-words do correlate in Finnish, the latter skill only accounts for about a quarter of the variance in reading scores, so factors other than ability to apply GPC rules must be important (Venezky, 1973).

Richard Venezky (1970) argues against reformed orthographies such as i.t.a. on two counts. First, i.t.a. increases the phonological regularity of English spelling at the expense, in many cases, of other types of regularity, such as morphological regularity. For example, to spell *sane* and *sanity* with different (first) vowels obscures the relation between them. Venezky argues that there is no good reason to prefer phonologically regular spelling to morphologically regular spelling. Second, i.t.a. regularizes the correspondences between single letters and sounds. Venezky argues that many English correspondences are, like those for the letter c, context dependent. Children learning to read in English therefore can, and probably do, make use of the redundancy found in its spelling patterns.

The use of i.t.a. in Britain declined sharply in the late 1970s and early 1980s, and it is now difficult to find. One problem that led to its demise was that it discouraged parental involvement – parents did not understand the system and could therefore not help the child at home. In addition, children learning the i.t.a. script were limited to reading books in that script which were never as widely available outside of school as books in traditional orthography.

Other approaches

There are a number of other approaches to teaching reading. Most are related to the phonics or whole-word methods, or combine aspects of the two. We shall mention some of the better-known ones briefly.

The *alphabetic* method is based on the idea that children should be taught to read by first teaching them the names of letters. The ability to name letters on entering school is a very good predictor of reading ability at the end of first grade (Stevenson et al., 1976). However, it does not follow that teaching children the names of letters will help them learn to read. The relationship may arise because reading and letter-naming skills are each linked to another factor (perhaps general intelligence, or an interest in or facility with verbal materials, or parents who are interested in reading and language development). Indeed, those studies that have investigated the issue have found no evidence that teaching children to name letters will make them better readers (see Onmacht (1969: cited by Crowder, 1982) and Samuels, 1972).

The *linguistic* method attempts to combine the whole-word and phonics approaches by teaching words by the whole-word method, but carefully selecting the words so that children are 'forced' to make generalizations about the correspondence between visual patterns and sound patterns. Beginning readers are exposed to 'stories' such as the following (taken from Crowder, 1982, p. 208), in the hope that they will extract spelling-to-sound rules for themselves:

> Dad had a map
> Pat had a bat
> Tad had a tan cap
> Nan had a tan hat

The *language experience* approach is closely related to the whole-word method, but combines learning to read with learning to write, and relates reading to the child's own experiences and spoken language. The correspondence between spoken and written language is stressed. From the start, children are encouraged to make up written sentences about things that are of interest to them. For instance, they might write their own captions for pictures, and then put together a series of such captioned pictures to make a 'story' booklet, which then becomes a text for learning to read. An example of this approach is *Breakthrough to Literacy* (Mackay, Thompson and Schaub, 1970), a scheme in which children have their own word file or dictionary. The file contains basic words from reading books, each on a small card, together with the child's individual words, which are written on blank cards by the teacher for the child.

The philosophy of this approach is that learning to read should be related to functions of language with which children are already familiar, in particular its communicative function. The first words taught are based on children's own experiences, and their assumed desire to record these experiences. By using these words to compose written sentences about events that are meaningful to them, children learn both about reading and about its connection with writing.

One advantage of the language experience approach is that the real function of written words – that they convey meanings – is emphasized from the outset, and reading is not associated with difficult and perplexing procedures for 'breaking the code'. A second advantage is that a language experience approach can be tailored to individual children's language capabilities and vocabulary, as well as relating reading to topics that are of interest to them. As we saw in chapter 3, the relation between the language of beginning readers and the often very different language of books is an important one, but one which is often overlooked.

A related approach is *invented spelling*, in which children are at first encouraged to make up their own spellings regardless of whether they are correct. This approach is not widely used in schools and has not been systematically assessed. Most of the data has been collected informally (see, for example, Glenda Bissex's fascinating account (1980) of the development of her own son's writing using invented spelling). Proponents of invented spelling argue that in creating their own versions of words and sentences, children will learn reading-related skills, such as phonemic awareness and spelling-to-sound rules, and will develop an interest in learning to read. Charles Read (1971, 1973: cited by Ehri, 1979) and Carol Chomsky (1979) show that children as young as 4 years can use their knowledge of letter names to invent their own words and messages. Chomsky argues that children are ready to write before they are ready to read, and that they should be introduced to the printed word through writing rather than reading. Her suggestions are based on evidence from children of 4 to 6 years who cannot read but who have some knowledge of the letters of the alphabet and their sounds. These children use their knowledge to construct their own messages with invented spelling. Although their invented spellings differ from standard spelling they are systematic, and there are similarities between the inventions of different children. Both Read and Chomsky note that children are not disturbed by the differences between what they write and what they read, and often find it easier to decode standard orthography than their own spellings. Chomsky argues that writing can aid learning to read, not only because it promotes interest in reading but also because it promotes knowledge of how words are made up from letters and of letter–sound correspondences.

An approach that combines the best aspects of the phonics and whole-word approaches is the syllable-based method developed by Paul Rozin and Lila Gleitman (see, e.g. 1977). As we saw earlier, the main difficulty of an alphabetic script is that each letter or letter cluster corresponds to a phoneme, and children have difficulty in dividing words into phonemes. Rozin and Gleitman point out that syllables are the smallest independently pronounceable units of speech, and are much easier to bring into awareness than phonemes (especially for children). They argue that the initial stages of reading should therefore be taught using a syllable-based writing system. With such a system children are taught correspondences between signs standing for syllables and sounds. These signs form a *syllabary*, which corresponds to the alphabet of an alphabetic writing system. Rozin and Gleitman acknowledge that insight into the alphabetic principle of grapheme–phoneme correspondences is crucial for readers of alphabetic scripts. However, they claim that this principle is difficult to teach directly, and that the syllable can act as an intermediate device to aid acquisition of the phonemic principle. In their method, the alphabetic principle is introduced *last*.

At this point we digress slightly in order to clarify the concepts of a *logography* and a *syllabary*. A logography is a writing system in which signs are used to represent the *root forms* of whole words (the 'grammatical' endings are ignored). Thus, *help* and *helped* would be represented by a single logogram, and the words *bow* (to bend over) and *bow* (a weapon) would be represented by different logograms. In such a system, the symbols, or logograms, stand for concepts, and a direct connection can be made between each symbol and its meaning. In a logography words that have a syllable in common, such as *manuscript*, and *emancipate* are represented by completely different logograms. In a syllabary this common syllable *man* is represented by a single sign in whatever word it occurs. So the sign, by itself, stands for the word *man*, it is the first of three signs in the written form of *manuscript* and the second of four in *emancipate*. Just as there is no relation in meaning between all English words with the letter 'a' in them, the use of the 'man' sign does *not* imply that all words with this sign in them have related meanings.

There is some cross-cultural evidence that a syllabary is easier to learn than an alphabetic system. In Japan, for example, there is one logographic writing system (Kanji) and two syllabic systems (Hiragana and Katakana). In the syllabaries the relation between the written symbols and spoken syllables is highly regular – almost every character has a single pronunciation. They are therefore easy to learn. The less complex Hiragana system is used exclusively in the first reading books. Sakamoto and Makita (1973) report that many children learn Hiragana without formal instruction before they enter school, although the acquisition of the logographic writing system (Kanji) goes on into adulthood.

There are five main stages to Rozin and Gleitman's syllabary curriculum.

1. Children are taught that meanings can be represented visually (by pictures).
2. Cards with a written syllable (e.g. wind, hand), and a stylized picture to represent that syllable are introduced. Children are shown how these cards can be used to construct sentences.
3. The principle that speech can be segmented into sounds that can be represented by written symbols is taught. In particular, children are shown that words that have sounds in common are written using the same character. At this stage, too, they learn how to combine pictures that represent one-syllable words to make new words (e.g. wind-ow, hand-y-man, rain-bow).
4. During this stage more syllables are introduced. Most are still accompanied by a picture, though grammatical elements, which cannot be depicted, are also introduced (e.g. *-ing*, *-er*). As this

stage progresses, the pictures are gradually phased out, as are the syllable boundaries.

5. In the final stage, children are taught to apply the word analysis and synthesis skills that they have learned to smaller units – phonemes. They are introduced to phonemes one at a time and shown how to blend them into syllables they already know.

One of the main advantages of this system is that motivation is high. The initial materials are very simple, and children can read with understanding very quickly. Most children from low-achieving populations learned to read the syllabary fluently by the end of the first year at school. Rozin and Gleitman suggest that such children would not have made comparable progress had they been taught the normal alphabetic script. They therefore claim that, for populations who have difficulty with the concept of a phoneme, a syllable-based approach may be beneficial. However, many of these pupils had great difficulty in transferring their knowledge to phonemes. Although upper-middle-class first graders made the jump from syllables to phonemes with little help after only about a month of training with the syllabary, some urban children (i.e. those from lower socio-economic groups) had still not mastered the alphabetic principle by the end of the first grade. In general, the pupils taught the syllabary were no better or worse at the end of the year at understanding the concept of phonemes than pupils who had received traditional phonics instruction. There did not seem to be an automatic transfer of the skills acquired during syllabary training to phonemes.

Other research (Canney and Schreiner, 1977) has failed to show any effect of training in syllabification on word identification or comprehension in second graders. However, they seem to have taught syllabification principles rather than using a special syllabary for teaching *reading*. Indeed, there has been considerable controversy over the efficacy of teaching children to divide words into syllables. Opponents of this method (e.g. Johnson and Pearson, 1978) argue that, in order to find syllable boundaries, one must first be able to pronounce the word – the supposed goal of syllabification. Cunningham, Cunningham and Rystrom (1981) developed a new syllabification strategy which did not require prior pronunciation to divide the words. However, they showed that although third and fourth graders given instruction in this method were better able to divide words into syllables, they were no more proficient than a control group on any other measure of reading achievement.

In summary, the available research shows that teaching the rules of syllabification does not help word recognition because there are so many exceptions to the rules. (see e.g. Zuck, 1974) However, efficient reading does require some strategy for identifying multisyllabic words, and it may be useful to teach spelling patterns that are always pronounced in the same way, such as *ight, ant* and *ish*. Such patterns may be recognized as single units by good readers (see e.g. Laberge, 1979).

Finally, we consider an approach to reading instruction that received much attention in the 1970s – one based on Kenneth Goodman's 'psycholinguistic guessing game' account of reading. (e.g. 1967) This account assumes that readers begin with expectations about the meaning and purpose of the text and use the print only to confirm or disconfirm these predictions. It can be contrasted with an account according to which reading is primarily a process of decoding marks on the page – first, letters are identified, then they are combined into words (possibly using phonological recoding). The words are then used to access meaning representations.

Frank Smith, another proponent of this approach, argues that since adults can access word meanings directly without first deriving a phonological representation, there is no reason to teach children to read by this 'unnatural' method. He further argues that the reading speed of skilled readers proves that they cannot be attending to every letter. Fluent readers make use of all kinds of information – syntactic, semantic and pragmatic – in recognizing words, and Smith's view is that beginners should be taught to read in the same way. He argues that decoding is not only an unnatural and difficult method of learning to read, but that it can be positively harmful. He proposes that in 'making sense' of the text, children will learn whatever rules they need to. In other words, children should learn to read *by reading* – by deriving hypotheses from the context and from prior knowledge of what the text is about (for a summary of these ideas see Smith, 1973).

However, Smith is not explicit about how children should be taught. He simply suggests that children should be immersed in interesting, meaningful materials. Indeed, Smith (1979) admits that his theory is vague and that it cannot specify particular procedures for teaching reading, although he argues that it is useful in alerting teachers to a different view of teaching reading. Ken and Yetta Goodman (1979) proposed a similar approach. They draw a parallel between learning to read and learning to talk, and stress motivation and linguistic environment rather than systematic teaching or rule learning.

One current method of teaching reading that has been motivated by the ideas of Smith and the Goodmans is the *story approach*, in which the similarities between learning to read and learning to speak are stressed, and the emphasis is on books with motivating content and an interesting story line (see e.g. Waterland, 1985). In this approach there is little attempt at formal teaching in the initial stages, which are similar to the sorts of initiation into reading that the child might experience at home. First, children listen to an adult reading to them and follow the story in a book, then they attempt to read along

with the adult until they feel able to 'read' some or a
text themselves.

However, apart from Smith's failure to explain exactly how children
should be taught, there are a number of flaws in his arguments (see
Mitchell, 1982, p. 124). First, his conclusion that guessing from context
is all important in skilled reading is based on experiments with adults in
which the texts were made difficult to read. Under such circumstances,
readers *do* make informed guesses to help them make out the words.
However, there is no good evidence that they do so to help them identify
clearly printed words in normal reading. Such guesswork may sometimes
be useful in identifying a visually unfamiliar word or even for working
out the meaning of a wholly new word. But in general, contextual information is usually available too late to aid word identification in skilled
readers. Such readers have usually identified a word from its appearance
before they have had time to decide what words are likely to appear in
the current context. Smith's theory predicts that skilled readers make
greater use of context in word identification but, as we have already
seen, they do not.

Second, Smith's argument that the subprocesses of reading could
not possibly be carried out rapidly enough to be aided by context is
flawed. He estimates that some people read at a rate of 1,000 words
per minute, four times as fast as they could if they were analysing
every word. However, to arrive at this conclusion, Smith simply divides
one minute by the time it takes to identify a single word. He takes no
account of the fact that, with continuous text, more than one word can
be processed at a time. The final stages of the processing of an earlier
word may overlap with the early stages of identifying a later one. Thus,
although identification time for a single word can be measured fairly
accurately, this measure provides only a poor way of estimating reading
speed for continuous text.

Finally, as we discussed earlier, there is no reason to believe that the
best way to teach reading is to train young children in the skills used
by adults. Reading cannot be simply a guessing game. There must be
some decoding of the printed text so that the guesses can be confirmed
or disconfirmed. Furthermore, decoding must be *taught*. It cannot be
expected to materialize as a by-product of intelligent guesswork, though
some children are undoubtedly able to work out the rules for themselves,
with little formal instruction. Interesting accounts of the characteristics
of children who learn to read before they go to school can be found in
Clark (1976) or Torrey (1979).

We are not arguing that abilities such as prediction from context are
unimportant in reading. Indeed, in the next chapter we suggest that the
teaching of such higher-order skills is a neglected area. However, teaching such skills is not enough. Both decoding and prediction should have
their place in reading instruction, and neither should be stressed at the
expense of the other (Carroll and Walton, 1979).

Which is the best method?

It is extremely difficult to make an objective assessment of methods of teaching reading because there are so many factors that cannot be controlled. Indeed, it has been suggested that children's progress in learning to read is much more closely related to the quality of their teacher than to the programme used (Goodacre, 1971). Some children seem to learn by any method, and some fail by any method. However, presumably some methods produce better results *on average* than others.

Jeanne Chall (1967) surveyed the research then available on the relation between teaching method and reading achievement. Her conclusion was that an early emphasis on phonics led to better reading by the time the children had reached the fourth grade than did a whole-word approach, at least as far as reading new words and reading aloud were concerned. However, teaching method had little effect on comprehension, or on interest and involvement in reading. Chall (1979) reports that, after ten years of further research, no data have come to light to disconfirm her original conclusion, and Williams (1979) in a review of the literature since 1967, concludes that the evidence in favour of a phonics-based approach is, if anything, stronger than it was. However, Elkonin (1973) claims that when the predominant whole-word teaching method was abandoned (in the USSR) because of criticism, the level of literacy among primary school pupils dropped.

A more recent review of this research also confirms that early intensive instruction in phonics produces readers who are more proficient at pronouncing words than are those taught by a whole-word approach (Johnson and Baumann, 1984). Children taught by a phonics method mispronounced fewer words when asked to read either single words or words in context. Although an early phonics emphasis is often criticized as having a detrimental effect on comprehension, there is little evidence to support this claim. Many studies have shown no clear difference in comprehension ability between children taught by whole-word and phonics approaches, but Johnson and Baumann cite some evidence (Norton and Hubert, 1977) that children given meaning-based instruction excel at comprehension. Chall (1967) also found some slight evidence that an early emphasis on meaning led to better comprehension by the end of second grade, although this evidence was not as reliable as that supporting the idea that phonics improved other aspects of reading.

As we saw earlier, within a broad phonics approach, some methods of teaching decoding skills seem to be more efficient than others. For example, the identification of words that have not previously been encountered in written form requires both segmentation and blending skills, and Jeffrey and Samuels (1967) found that specific training on letter–sound correspondences followed by blending instruction enabled more effective transfer to new words than did instruction in blending alone.

Studies of children taught by i.t.a. show that they progress more rapidly than children taught by an identical scheme with traditional orthography. They also do better on word decoding (Schonell) and comprehension (Neale) tests. However, all of this initial advantage is lost once the children transfer to traditional orthography.

WHAT CAN READING ERRORS TELL US?

Beginning readers and older poor readers frequently make mistakes (often called 'miscues') when they are reading aloud. These errors have been studied from two perspectives. First, if children have followed a particular reading scheme closely, the errors that they make can indicate the effects of that method of training. Second, if no scheme has been followed rigidly, or if a mixed scheme has been used, patterns of errors might indicate the stage a child has reached in the normal course of reading development.

The effects of teaching methods

Different teaching methods have also been assessed in relation to *qualitative* differences in word-analysis skills. For example, there is clear evidence from the work of Rebecca Barr (1972, 1974–75) that the type of reading errors that children make is linked to the method by which they have been taught. First graders taught by a phonics method more often fail to produce any response to a word. They are also prone to errors based on orthographic similarity, even though this strategy leads them to produce nonsense words. Barr suggests that some of these children do not understand that written words should correspond to spoken words. When children who have received whole-word instruction make mistakes, they tend to respond with another real word but do not make much use of letter cues. They seem to rely on more global features such as length or overall shape. The errors of children taught by a whole-word approach are more likely to be real words, and more likely to be contextually appropriate. This finding provides some evidence that the whole-word method produces a better understanding of the fact that the purpose of reading is to make sense of the text. However, most teachers now use a mixture of approaches in the initial stages of reading instruction. The question of interest is not so much *which* approach should be adopted, as *when* different approaches should be used – in particular, when phonics should be introduced.

Different errors at different ages

The pattern of reading development provides some evidence about the type of instruction that is appropriate at various stages of the learning process. In particular, children's reading errors may indicate the strategies and the sorts of information they are using. For example, a child who reads 'went' as 'want' is using different information from one who reads 'yesterday' as 'tomorrow'. However, this sort of error data must be interpreted with care, since, as we have seen, certain types of errors are the result of certain teaching methods.

Rose-Marie Weber (1970) showed that 90 per cent of first graders' errors made sense in the context in which they occurred. This high level of attention to meaning was not related to reading skill. Both good and poor readers made use of knowledge of language to help determine their responses. Although children in the early stages of reading tend to use insufficient information – relying on the first letter or overall shape of the word – they are guided by the meaning of the text. They reread the text and corrected themselves three-fifths of the time if an error later resulted in an nonsensical reading.

Three stages in first graders' error responses were identified by Andrew Biemiller (1970). In the first stage, the errors were words that fitted the context but bore little graphemic resemblance to the actual words in the text. In the next stage, children began to 'refuse' words. They often stopped reading when they encountered a word that they did not know. They realized that they needed to take account of what the word looked like as well as whether it made sense in the context, but they did not always know a word that satisfied both these criteria. The word eventually produced, if wrong, was usually visually similar to the actual word. By the end of the first grade children had passed into the third stage. Their errors were both graphemically and contextually constrained more than 70 per cent of the time, and they 'refused' relatively few words. There was also evidence that children who reached the 'no-response' stage early (i.e. those who realized the importance of graphemic information) were better readers at the end of the first grade.

These data suggest some changes in strategy during the first year of learning to read. In the initial stage, children learn some distinctive features, such as the overall shape and length of words, that enable them to distinguish those words from the few others that they know. When they encounter unfamiliar words they guess their identity on the basis of the preceding context. However, such a strategy will obviously lead to many errors when reading books that contain more than a few words. In the next stage, children must learn some rules for deciphering unknown words. It would be extremely difficult to for them to learn to recognize the 50,000 or so words in the average adult vocabulary entirely by a 'look-and-say' approach. To progress beyond a restricted sight vocabulary, children must be able to break words into their component letters and letter groups. They must recognize that specific visual features, such as the orientation of letters, are important. In the final stage, both sources of information – graphemic and contextual – complement each other.

We have outlined the strategies that children use in learning to read words. Implicit in this discussion is the assumption that children progress naturally as the inadequacy of one strategy becomes apparent to them. However, the research of Barr (1972, 1974–5), cited above, suggests that instruction could accelerate the development of more effective strategies.

CONCLUSIONS

When the two halves of this chapter are brought together we find two sets of information that are hard to reconcile. In the first part of the chapter we saw how kindergarten and first graders find difficulty in the task of segmenting words into their constituent phonemes. Yet, in the second part, we saw how reading programmes that require precisely this skill (phonics approaches) are more successful than other approaches, even though the decoding/blending process may be difficult or impossible for beginning readers to perform (though see Elkonin, 1973, who argues that phonics methods do not achieve such rapid or satisfactory results as has been claimed). Certainly, beginning readers should not be started on phonics straight away, as such a difficult approach may well alienate them from reading. Merritt (1970) argues that beginning readers should be encouraged to treat new words as whole units, and 'should not, under any circumstances, be asked to go through the artificial process of sounding out the separate letters to find out what the word "says"'. He further argues that phonics instruction should be introduced at a much later stage, and should 'be handled with great care and sensitivity if the child's interest in reading is to be maintained'.

A general procedure based on what we know about beginning readers' capabilities and limitations would be to start them reading with a limited vocabulary of sight words, and to introduce phonics only gradually, once they are able to read and understand simple stories and have some confidence in their ability to read. Such training could start by pointing out the visual similarities of words that sound the same, to show that parts of words correspond to sounds and that there is some regularity in this correspondence. Phonemic segmentation and blending could then be taught, using first compound words, then syllables and finally phonemes, as suggested by Rozin and Gleitman (1977). However, word recognition in itself is not reading: whatever approach is used, it should be supplemented by instruction to develop comprehension and other language skills. A curriculum rich in language activities seems to foster the development of linguistic awareness skills which, as we saw above, are so important in early reading. Thus, reading to children and giving them opportunities for writing and playing word games etc. can all make an important contribution to the development of early reading.

Regardless of the specific teaching method employed, it is important that early reading materials are related to beginning readers' interests and experiences, even if the difficulty of such materials cannot be precisely controlled. Children will be more likely to make an effort to read a slightly more difficult story that is exciting and interesting than to read a tedious story with a higher proportion of easy words. In this respect, the *Breakthrough* scheme has a lot to offer. In recent years, too, many schools have given children more scope to choose their own reading materials. Rather than using a single reading scheme, many schools now combine books from different schemes with extension readers and other materials to produce a set of books that are coded (usually by a coloured band) to indicate their level of difficulty. The children are assigned to a level in the scheme, according to their reading ability, and can select their own books within that level until they are have achieved sufficient ability to progress to the next level. Most children will thus read only some of the books at a particular level and will be able to choose books that are of interest to them.

The skills we have discussed in this chapter are related mainly to the development of efficient word recognition. However, in order to be able to read for meaning there are a number of comprehension skills that children must develop. These will be the focus of the next chapter.

Notes

1. See Coltheart (1979) for a very full account of the concept of reading readiness.
2. An explanation of the purpose of control groups in psychological experiments is given by Bryant and Bradley (1985, p 61).
3. The interested reader can find reviews in Gibson and Levin (1975, chapter 9) or Layton (1979, chapter 1).

CHAPTER 5

Learning to understand text

In this chapter we examine the skills of text *comprehension* that enable children to progress beyond the initial stages of reading, and to read both for amusement and for instruction. We also consider how deficits in these skills can result in reading problems. In the first part of the chapter we discuss the component skills of text comprehension and their development. In the second part we consider more specifically the differences between good and poor comprehenders.

THE DEVELOPMENT OF COMPREHENSION SKILLS

As we saw in chapter 2, proper understanding of a text results in a mental representation of the state of affairs the text describes, a representation we called a *mental model*. We further saw that, even after individual words have been identified and grouped into phrases, clauses and sentences, a number of other skills are required to construct such models. One is the ability to work out the meaning of *anaphoric expressions*, an ability whose development we discussed in chapter 3. More generally, the meanings of individual sentences and paragraphs must be integrated, and the main ideas of the passage identified. In many cases, inferential skills are needed to go beyond the information explicitly stated, since authors often leave the links between ideas in a text implicit.

In the first half of this chapter we consider how children's ability to make inferences from text develops. We also discuss a number of more specific skills necessary for comprehension. For understanding stories, these skills include: identification of the main characters and their motives, following the plot and deriving the main theme, or the moral, if there is one. In the case of expository texts, they include identifying the topic, deciding which information is important and which peripheral, following the argument, and extracting the gist of the passage.

We also discuss the development of children's ability to *monitor* their comprehension – to be aware of whether or not they are understanding a text. Comprehension monitoring is referred to as a *metacognitive* skill, since it is not one of the basic reading skills but, rather, a 'higher-level' ability to reflect on how such skills are being used. As reading progresses beyond the initial stages, metacognitive skills become increasingly important. The meta-level knowledge needed by young readers who are just beginning to learn to identify words – the technical vocabulary, the need to attend to the written words – is much simpler than the knowledge slightly older children need. Comprehension skills are far more dependent than word recognition and decoding on metacognitive abilities. Once the basics of reading have been mastered, children need to learn how to read for different purposes, how to select the main ideas and important points, how to monitor their comprehension, and how to improve it if it is not adequate.

In our review we consider three main topics. The first two are understanding the organizational structure of the text and deriving the meaning of the text. The third is the development of the metacognitive skills we have just been discussing – the ability to monitor one's understanding and to choose reading strategies appropriate for different purposes. But before we turn to these topics we shall consider briefly the importance of speed of decoding and of accessing the meanings of words in skilled reading.

Speed of decoding

Initially, it might seem odd to suggest that the development of comprehension skills depends on the speed with which words can be recognized. However, rates of lexical and semantic access are closely related to comprehension skill, and as we will see in the second part of this chapter, slow and laboured word recognition can be a major hindrance to comprehension. The reasons why slow word recognition might disrupt comprehension are summarized by Frank Smith (1975), who makes use of the idea, introduced in chapter 2, that short-term memory stores with a strictly limited capacity play a crucial role in reading:

> . . . it is probably impossible to read with comprehension at slower than 200 words a minute – the units we are trying to get into short-term and long-term memory will be too small to be of any use. Similarly it is impossible to read for meaning if we stop to read every individual word; short-term memory will soon overflow with a meaningless clutter of words and bits of words. . . . In fluent reading, individual words come last rather than first. (Smith, 1975, p. 70)

Readers who must constantly switch between the processes of comprehension (working out who or what is being referred to, drawing inferences, building up a mental model) and worrying about the identity and meaning of individual words will, in general, have greater difficulty understanding a text than those who decode swiftly and automatically and can concentrate on the problems of understanding the text as a whole. Beginning readers who are having difficulty with both decoding and comprehension are likely to suffer particular problems. The burden of word recognition may leave little mental energy for comprehension. Furthermore, as Smith points out, the rapid loss of information from short-term memory stores makes it difficult for slow readers to 'hold' information from earlier in the sentence so that they can integrate it with what comes later. If decoding is slow and laboured, much of the prior context may have been forgotten by the time the current word has been recognized.

We saw in the last chapter that decoding skills improve with practice, so presumably as children get older they can devote more attention to comprehension. Indeed, Curtis (1980) has shown that, as children reach the later primary school grades, comprehension skills replace decoding skills as the most important predictors of overall reading skill.

There has been relatively little work on the speed of lexical and semantic access in young children because of the difficulty of obtaining reliable measures. However, Gitomer, Pellegrino and Bisanz (1983) devised a method of measuring semantic processing speed that takes into account the different times it takes children of different ages to make responses in experiments. They found that speed of access increases with age between 8 and 10 years, as does the ability to make use of information about the semantic category (e.g. it's the name of a fruit) of the word. A similar experiment by Chabot, Petros and McCord (1983) also showed differences in semantic processing speed with age and with reading ability. Thus, younger children's comprehension may be limited by the speed with which they can access the meanings of individual words.

Deriving the structure of the text

Once the individual sentences of a text have been decoded and under-stood, their meanings must be combined to provide an interpretation of the text as a whole. This integration of information depends on several skills, in particular the ability to appreciate the main ideas in a text – what it is about – and to understand how it is structured. It is to these abilities that we now turn.

Searching for main ideas   Otto and Barrett (1968: cited by Yussen, Mathews and Hiebert, 1982) found a marked increase from the second to the sixth grade in children's ability to state the main topic of short paragraphs. Fred Danner (1976) showed that most second graders could distinguish between organized and disorganized texts and could, to some extent, abstract the main ideas from a text. However, he found that the ability to group sentences according to topic increased with age. In addition, to provide a more direct index of the awareness of the relation between organization and recall, he asked the children to select review notes for a future recall test. Most sixth graders selected one sentence related to each topic, and explained that the selected sentences would help recall of the rest of the sentences about that topic. Very few second graders did this.

Yussen et al. (1980) showed that there was an increase in ability from second grade to college to pick out the three parts of a story necessary for understanding it (i.e. those that would be needed to communicate the main idea). These three categories were the *initiating event*, the *main action* and its *consequence*. In a second experiment, they replicated these results with second and fifth graders and showed that, at both age levels, children recalled more propositions from the key categories. However, only for the fifth grade children was there a relation between recall of the stories and the ability to select the key categories.

Other work by Yussen and his associates (see Yussen, 1982) has shown that older children (they tested second, fifth and eighth graders) were better than younger children at selecting a statement to convey the main idea of a story sequence. The older children were also better at putting jumbled sequences of pictures into order, although, surprisingly, these two abilities were not related.

As children get older, they not only get better at identifying the most important information in a story, they also change their minds about what that information is. Stein and Glenn (1979) showed that first graders generally rated the consequences of actions as most important, whereas fifth graders picked out the goals of the main characters. Their results, which are broadly consistent with what is known about how children of different ages assess actions, suggest that even first graders may have consistent ideas about what is important in a story, but that their ideas may differ from those of older children.

In summary, even children as young as 5 are more likely to recall main ideas than trivial details, but they have difficulty in stating explicitly what the main ideas are.

Sensitivity to hierarchical structure   Many recent theories of comprehension have drawn attention to the fact that information in a text is hierarchically structured.[1] The hierarchical structure arises because each text is focused round one or more main ideas, with subsidiary ideas and trivial details subordinated to the main ones. Proper understanding of a text depends on sensitivity to the relative importance of the ideas in it see e.g. Eamon, 1978–9; McKoon, 1977; Meyer, 1977).

Ann Brown and Sandra Smiley (1977) showed that children find it difficult to judge the importance of ideas in a (relatively long and complex) text. They tested 8-, 10-, 12-, and 18-year-olds' ability to classify the ideas in folk tales as having one of four levels of importance. Whereas their adult subjects showed high levels of agreement in their classification, 8-year-olds were almost completely unable to perform the task, and even 12-year-olds were only able to distinguish between very important and very unimportant information. However, at all ages, the ideas that the subjects remembered from the stories depended on their importance. Even the youngest subjects remembered more of the more important ideas. Brown and Smiley suggest that this discrepancy between awareness of levels of importance and the effect of levels of importance on recall reflects different levels of *metacognitive* skills at different ages. Younger children have less knowledge about how they understand stories (see below).

In summary, hierarchical structure is a common feature of texts, and sensitivity to that structure is necessary for comprehension. Younger children find it difficult to make explicit judgements about what is important in a story. This lack of insight could result in a failure to direct effort to the more important parts of a text. However, Brown's work suggests that young children do pay more attention to the important ideas in a text, even though they cannot say which those ideas are.

Understanding the logical structure of the text   Another important element in comprehension is understanding how the ideas in a text are related. One way to assess children's knowledge about the logical structure of stories is to ask them to tell stories themselves. Research on children's story production has documented a developing ability to produce coherent narratives (see Baker and Stein, 1981, for a review of children's growing sensitivity to logical structure and knowledge of what makes a good story). For example, Poulsen et al. (1979) showed that even 4-year-olds' narrations of picture sequences, although primarily descriptive in form, were affected by whether the pictures told a story. When the pictures were presented in the correct order, children added details that were derived from their understanding of the story, whereas they often reverted to simply naming the people and objects when the pictures were presented in a random order. However, additions were quite often made in describing the scrambled sequences, particularly by the older children (6-year-olds) – an indication that they were trying to impose a logical structure on the sequence.

Children, like adults, expect certain types of information in stories (see reviews in e.g. Stein, 1979; Baker and Stein, 1981). When those types of information are missing they are often added in retelling, so that the retold story corresponds to what was expected. Similarly, when a story relates events out of order, the normal order is often restored in retelling. As children get older, they are more likely to reproduce an ill-structured story in a well-structured form. For example, Nancy Stein (see Baker and Stein, 1981), using written stories rather than picture sequences, distorted them by moving specific statements from their original position. She tested second and sixth graders' ability to recall the stories and found that although the older children recalled more, the patterns of recall at the two ages were similar: the distorted stories were recalled less well than the well-formed stories, and the distorted stories became more difficult to recall the further the statements were moved from their original position. However, the older children were more likely to move statements back to their logical position, or at least to repeat them in that position. Stein (1979) argues that these findings are evidence for the development of a story grammar but, as should be apparent from the discussion in chapter 2, they may instead reflect increasing knowledge about the world and about typical sequences of events in it.

As they get older, children develop the ability to use connectives, such as *and, then, because* and *although* to mark explicitly relations that are often left implicit in stories. Keith Stenning and Lynn Michell (1985) asked 5- to 10-year-olds to tell stories from picture sequences and found a striking increase in the use of causal connectives after the age of 7. The appropriate use of referring expressions (e.g. *he, the man*) improved at an earlier age, between 5 and 7. Both of these changes reflect an increase in the ability to use linguistic devices to establish *cohesion*. The stories of the younger children also lacked cohesion in a more obvious respect – they tended to describe each picture separately, rather than combining the pictures to form an integrated story.

In summary, even very young children are sensitive to the logical structure of stories – deviations from such a structure make stories difficult for them to understand and remember. The ability to understand how ideas are interconnected in a story probably develops even before children learn to read.

Learning to make inferences from text

In chapter 2 we discussed some of the many roles of inference in comprehension. Inferences are sometimes needed to work out the hierarchical and logical structure of a text, though the ability to make use of those structures is a separate skill. In this section we examine in more detail the development of the ability to make inferences in text comprehension.

To understand a text it is necessary to establish connections between the ideas in the text and to be able to express them in a different form. Since texts leave many things implicit, inferences are crucial to this process of connecting ideas, since they are required to fill in 'missing' information. A detailed account of the functions of inferences in comprehension is given by Warren, Nicholas and Trabasso (1979). As we saw in chapter 2, however, only a tiny proportion of the possible inferences can be made from a text. Those inferences that are made are guided by the emerging model of the text (see Johnston, 1983). The model indicates where the text is incomplete and, therefore, where inferences are needed.

Scott Paris and his colleagues[2] have carried out many studies of children's inferential processing of text, based on the work of John Bransford and his co-workers (see e.g. Bransford, Barclay & Franks, 1972), who stressed that comprehension was a constructive and an integrative process. After discussing the development of inferential processing in general, we shall focus on three specific issues: the use of prior knowledge in inferential processing, the relation between such processing and text memory, and *when* during reading inferences are made.

Scott Paris and Ann Carter (1973) argued that if children construct meaning-based representations of texts, they should 'recognize' sentences that are consistent with the meaning of those texts but do not actually occur in them. The children in their study were read 'stories' such as:

> The bird is inside the cage.
> The cage is under the table.
> The bird is yellow.

They then had to say whether they had seen a series of sentences from the stories, some of which were actually presented and some of which were true inferences (e.g. The bird is under the table). Children aged 7 and 10 consistently accepted true inferences as sentences they had already heard. Indeed, the probability of identifying items from the stories and true inferences as old information did not differ significantly. This finding suggests that children of both ages integrated the information from different sentences of the stories and stored abstract meaning-based representations rather than specific words or sentences. The younger subjects made more errors overall, but the pattern of errors was similar at both ages. Paris and Mahoney (1974) found further evidence for constructive memory in 7- and 9-year-olds for both verbal and pictorial materials.

Robert Kail and his associates (1977) used the same type of materials, but asked their subjects (7- and 12-year-olds) to judge whether the sentences they were asked to recognize were consistent with the stories, rather than whether they had the exact wording of sentences in the stories. They found that under these conditions accuracy did not change with age. Furthermore, both age groups answered questions about sentences in the stories faster than questions about inferences. The discrepancy between these results and those of Paris and his colleagues might be explained by the different methods of presentation: Kail et al.'s subjects read the stories themselves, whereas in the other studies the stories were read to the children. Modality differences in integrative processing have been found for adult subjects, for example by Flagg and Reynolds (1977).

Unfortunately there are problems with Paris and Carter's test items that cast doubt on their conclusions. In the recognition test the original sentences and the true inferences contained only words from the original passages. The other items, to which the children were intended to answer 'no', contained new words. For example, for the passage above, one of these sentences was *The bird is on top of the table.* Unlike the true inference, this 'false' inference contains words (*on top of*) that were not in the original story. As Lynn Liben and Carla Posnansky (1977) have argued, the children may simply have been saying 'yes' to sentences that contained only words from the passage, thus, appearing to confuse original sentences and true inferences. When Liben and Posnansky corrected this defect, they found little evidence of integrative processing in young children: 5- to 6-year-olds' responses were based primarily on the familiarity of words. However, there was some evidence that the 8-year-olds were influenced by semantic content.

Before accepting Liben and Posnansky's results as decisive evidence against Paris and Carter's conclusions, their materials must also be examined more carefully. An example of one of their stories is:

> The surprise was in the box.
> The box was behind the door.
> The surprise was a birthday present.

The proportion of incorrect 'yes' responses to true inferences with no new words, such as:

> The surprise was behind the door

was far greater than to equally valid inferences that had new words in them, such as:

> The door was in front of the surprise.

However, this last sentence is extremely unnatural, and is an unlikely inference from the original information. If we want to investigate children's inference making we ought to look at inferences they are likely to make.

Further evidence against Paris and Carter is provided by Thomas Theiman and Ann Brown (1977). With 8- and 11-year-old children they verified that *false* sentences are more likely to be accepted when they include the same relational term as the original than when both the relational term and the meaning differ. For example, if the original sentences were:

> The telephone is on top of the book
> The book is under the table

then false new items that included one of the original relational terms, such as:

The telephone is on top of the table.

were more readily accepted as 'old' than false new items with novel relational terms such as:

The telephone is over the table.

This pattern of results obtained for both age groups. It seems, therefore, that the interpretation of results from Paris and Carter's 'false recognition' paradigm is complicated by memory for the words in the sentences. However, the examples of new items with novel relational terms again seem less plausible than those with the original relational terms.

Another methodological problem is response bias (Paris and Upton, 1976). The correct response to recognition items in Paris and Carter's study was 'yes' only a quarter of the time, but Paris and Upton found that 5-year-olds made 72 per cent 'yes' responses, compared with 48 per cent made by 10-year-olds. This general tendency to say 'yes' inflates the number of apparent confusions between true inferences and sentences in the original text.

As an alternative to the false recognition paradigm, Paris and Lindauer (1976) developed a cued recall procedure that eliminates some of the problems of the former method. This procedure, in which words are used to prompt recall of previously presented sentences, is not susceptible, in the way that the false recognition paradigm is, to the effects of response bias or the possibility of using lexical overlap rather than semantic matching to produce a response. It therefore provides a more direct test of inferential processing.

Paris and Lindauer (1976) used this procedure to investigate whether 6- to 7-year-olds and 11- to 12-year-olds routinely inferred highly probable instruments (e.g. a knife for cutting steaks) that were not specifically mentioned in sentences they had been read. There were two versions of each sentence, one in which the instrument was explicitly mentioned and one in which it was not, for example:

The workman dug a hole in the ground [with a shovel].

The words in brackets were included only in the explicit version. After the sentences had been presented, the names of the instruments (implied or explicit) were given as cues, and the children were asked to recall each sentence. Fifth graders recalled almost as many sentences when the cue was implicit as when it was explicit. The difference was much larger for third graders and larger still for first graders. The finding that explicit and implicit recall cues were equally effective for older children indicates that those children are better able to make the inferences that enable them to use the implicit retrieval cues. However, even the 6-year-olds could choose the appropriate instrument almost all the time in a subsequent test when they were questioned directly. So first graders *can* make such inferences when it is clear to them that they have to. The disparity between the results of this post-test and those of the cued recall test suggests, therefore, that the younger children did not *spontaneously* infer the instruments, either when they heard the sentences or when they were given the cue words. In a second experiment, Paris and Lindauer asked first graders to act out each sentence as it was presented. In this case, the implicit cues were just as effective as explicit mentions of the instrument. Presumably in this experiment the children had to make the inferences in order to act out the sentences.

In a related study, Paris, Lindauer and Cox (1977) extended the technique to assess children's ability to make inferences about the consequences of events. They compared the performance of 8- and 12-year-olds and college students when given a noun explicit in a sentence or an implicit consequence as a cue. The difference in effectiveness of the two types of cue again decreased with age. However, the older children's superior ability to use implicit cues may have been related to factors other than spontaneous inferential ability, as many of the inferences were rather obscure and by no means *necessary* consequences of the sentences. For example, 'and it itched' was the implicit cue for the sentence, 'He accidentally played in poison ivy'. In a second experiment, they showed that inferential processing and better recall could be induced in 6-year-olds by asking them to make up stories related to the sentences. These results again support the idea that younger children can make the same inferences as older children, although they do not do so spontaneously.

In these experiments on implicit instruments, contextual information (e.g. that a juicy steak was being cut) produces a more specific interpretation of the sentence (e.g. that the cutting was done with a knife). Such inferences have much in common with those that Richard Anderson has termed *instantiations* (see chapter 2). In instantiation a particular *word* takes on a more specific interpretation in context than it would in isolation (e.g. in the context 'The fish attacked the swimmer', the fish is taken to be something like a shark).

The question of whether children select particular referents for words in context was addressed by Anderson et al. (1977). They asked first and fourth grade children to choose which of four pictures best represented the particular meaning of a noun in a sentence. The children selected the picture that was contextually most appropriate more than 90 per cent of the time. However, while this study demonstrates that children *can* instantiate, it does not indicate that they do so spontaneously.

Incorporation of prior knowledge   Another way of thinking about inference is to say that inference making is the incorporation of prior knowledge, memories and personal experience into the mental representation of a text. For example, to infer that a shovel was used to dig a hole is to use the knowledge that holes are typically dug with shovels to go beyond the information explicit in a text about digging holes.

The decision about what prior knowledge is relevant to a particular text is made very quickly during comprehension. To explain this rapid deployment of stored knowledge, an account is needed of how knowledge is represented in long-term memory and accessed during comprehension. Attempts to develop such accounts include *schema* theory, *script* theory and related ideas (see chapter 2). Indeed, some of the most detailed attempts to specify how text representations are constructed have come from researchers in artificial intelligence attempting to program computers to answer questions that demonstrate ability to 'understand' sentences and texts (see e.g. Schank, 1973; Winograd, 1972).

Primary school children are not only developing their reading skills, they are also learning new things about the world. There are many texts they cannot understand simply because they do not have the background information and cannot make the inferences needed to make sense of them. Not surprisingly, there is much evidence that prior knowledge influences memory and comprehension in children (see e.g. Brown et al. 1977; Owings et al. 1980). It can alter the amount recalled, the perception of what information is important, and the types of intrusions that occur.

Inference as an aid to memory   Paris and Upton (1976) showed that making inferences helps children to remember stories. In one experiment, children aged 5 to 11 were read short stories and questioned on each story immediately after having heard it. Half of the questions required verbatim recall and half could only be answered if an inference was made. It was found that memory for the verbatim information and accuracy in answering the inferential questions both increased with age. Even when the improvement in memory for the exact wording of texts was allowed for, there was still a significant increase with age in the ability to make inferences.

Paris and Upton (1976) suggest that making inferences may help in the encoding of text into memory. This suggestion is consistent with Craik and Tulving's claim (1975) that the greater the depth of processing associated with an item, the better it will be recalled (see also Johnson-Laird and Bethell-Fox, 1978).

The connection between inference making and recall has however been questioned by Omanson, Warren and Trabasso (1978). They conducted an experiment in which 8-year-olds had to make inferences about the intentions and actions of the main protagonist in a story. There were three versions of the story. In one the protagonist's motives were not mentioned; in the second they were socially desirable, and in the third undesirable. In all three cases the children listened to the story, were tested on a variety of inferential questions, and asked to recall the story. The inclusion of motive information produced a higher proportion of correct inferences but did not improve recall. Thus, an experimental manipulation that produced more inferences did *not* lead to better recall. In a second experiment, children aged 5 and 8 were matched on their ability to remember the information crucial to the inferences, and the 8-year-olds made more inferences than 5-year-olds. These findings support the idea that the ability to make inferences increases with age, independently of memory. They do not support Paris and Upton's (1976) assertion that making inferences enhances recall.

When are inferences made?   A wealth of studies demonstrate that inferences of various kinds are drawn to understand text. An important question is whether inferences are drawn at the time of reading or only later (see also chapter 2). The literature on this issue has been extensively reviewed by Goetz (1977).

In an attempt to assess when constructive processing takes place, Dooling and Mullet (1973) gave adult subjects a thematic title, which was necessary for the correct interpretation of many expressions in their (admittedly rather obscure) passage, before or after presentation, or not at all. Their results indicate that constructive processing takes place at the time of original presentation. Subjects given the title afterwards did not recall any more than those given no title. Those given the title first recalled more words and sentences and also recalled information related to the theme of the passage (Christopher Columbus discovering America) that did not appear in the passage.

Paul Harris and his colleagues (1980) conducted a similar experiment with children. They tested 8- and 10-year-olds' ability to recall obscurely worded stories with and without information about the setting. For both age groups, setting information aided recall. A follow-up study showed that setting information improved initial comprehension and not later retrieval. When setting information was provided after presentation but prior to recall, no improvement in recall was found. These findings show that children, like adults, can use contextual information to make sense of an enigmatic text but only if they make the required inferences as they process the text.

Til Wykes (1978), studying rather different inferences (mainly elaborative inferences, see chapter 2), suggested that children do not draw those inferences in the normal course of comprehension. She showed that when children were asked to recall a passage *before* being asked questions about it that required an inference, there was no relation between their performance on the two tasks. When the recall test was presented *after* the inferential questions, the amount recalled was positively related to inferential ability. Wykes argued that older children are superior at answering inferential questions because they are able to recall a greater proportion of the explicit information, from which they can make inferences to answer the questions.

Trabasso and Nicholas (1980) have also pointed out the possibility that neither younger nor older children make optional (i.e. elaborative) inferences during comprehension. Furthermore, as we saw in chapter 2, it is no longer clear that even adults make elaborative inferences, in any straightforward sense, while reading. The results of Paris and Lindauer's (1976) study, reported earlier, which showed that fifth graders recall almost as many sentences whether they are given implicit or explicit cues, were interpreted by those authors as evidence that older children more often make inferences during comprehension. However, their results could be explained equally well by assuming that each cue word (e.g. *shovel*) is strongly associated with the corresponding verb (e.g. *dig*), and that the verb acts as a retrieval cue for the sentence. An increasing ability to think of associates to cue words or to use those associates to guide a search in memory could explain the developmental trends reported by Paris and his associates.

Comprehension monitoring

Comprehension monitoring means assessing whether one's understanding is adequate, while reading. Like word consciousness, which we discussed in chapter 4, comprehension monitoring is one of the *metalinguistic* skills that children acquire as their linguistic abilities develop. The primary linguistic skills are those of decoding and comprehension. Metalinguistic skills are skills in the use of those linguistic abilities. They require the ability to reflect on one's use of language. When skilled readers fail to understand part of a text, they take action, such as rereading, asking for assistance, or using a dictionary, to overcome the problem. A reader who takes such action has, in some sense, become aware of a problem. However, Ellen Markman (1981, p. 75) suggests that information about comprehension is often a by-product of an active attempt to understand. In some cases, active comprehension monitoring may not be necessary – all the reader needs to do is to engage actively in comprehension.

All readers monitor their comprehension to some extent but, in general, younger children are less likely to realize that they do not understand, or to know what to do about it if they do realize.[3] They are, for example, less able to detect that crucial information is missing from a text.

Markman (1977) assessed children's ability to detect inadequacies in instructions for how to play a game or to perform a magic trick. In both cases, critical information was left out. The younger children (first graders) generally failed to realize that there was anything missing from the instructions until they tried to carry them out. Older children (third graders) realized more quickly that the instructions were incomplete.

Another study by Markman (1979) used texts that were logically inconsistent. If an adequate model of a text is to be derived, any inconsistencies must be noted and an attempt made to resolve them. Young children are poor at spotting even gross inconsistencies such as those in the following passage:

Ants

Everywhere they go they put out a special chemical from their bodies. They cannot see this chemical, but it has a special odor. An ant must have a nose in order to smell this chemical odor. Another thing about ants is they do not have a nose. Ants cannot smell this odor. Ants can always find their way home by smelling this odor to follow the trail.

Markman asked third, fifth and sixth graders to make suggestions about the changes, if any, that were needed to make the texts easier to understand. A substantial proportion of the passages were judged fully comprehensible, even by the oldest children, although there was some improvement with age. Markman and Gorin (1981) showed that these results could be partially explained by the standards children use to evaluate texts and by their unwillingness to criticize written material. They gave 8- and 10-year-olds different sorts of instructions before they read passages that contained both falsehoods and inconsistencies. Some children were simply told to look for problems, others were specifically told to look either for falsehoods or for inconsistencies. In each case they were given several examples. Both kinds of specific instructions increased the children's ability to identify the kind of problem they mentioned, though the older children's performance improved more.

Children's ideas about reading, which can be elicited in interviews, also provide some indication of their metacognitive awareness. However, there are certain problems with such interviews – in particular young children's responses may be limited by their ability to express what they know about reading. This and other methodological concerns are discussed in detail in Ruth Garner's recent book (1987, chapter 4), and she also suggests some alternative procedures. A typical finding is that younger children tend to think that decoding is the point of reading and do not view comprehension as important (see e.g. Canney and Winograd, 1979; Myers and Paris, 1978). Myers and Paris asked 8- and 12-year-olds about various aspects of reading. Although the younger children knew that familiarity with the content of the text, and strategies such as rereading, would be helpful for learning, they generally had fewer resources to help them to deal with comprehension failures, for example on unknown words or difficult sentences.

Although there is a general tendency for comprehension monitoring to improve with age, this ability can be affected quite dramatically by aspects of the task and by instructions (see Baker, 1984a; Garner, 1987, chapter 5). For example, children are more likely to report problems when they are forewarned of possible difficulties (Markman, 1979). They are also more likely to report failures to understand when the criteria are more explicit, for example when they are assessing instructions (Markman, 1977), than when they have to select their own criteria, for example when they are looking for inconsistencies in text (Markman, 1979). Furthermore, non-verbal measures are better at revealing awareness of comprehension problems than verbal ones (Harris et al., 1981). An example of these 'task' effects is that whereas the third graders in Markman's first study often reported failures to understand instructions even before they tried to carry them out, children of the same age and older in her second study completely missed inconsistencies such as those in the passage about ants. There is even some evidence that pre-school children show some competence in evaluating their own comprehension, if the conditions are right (see Baker, 1984b; Wimmer, 1979).

A further complication, pointed out by Linda Baker (1984a), is that passages can be incomprehensible for several reasons. For instance, the 'ants' passage is *internally inconsistent* – there is a conflict between different pieces of information in the text itself. Other passages, on the other hand, while not inconsistent in themselves, will be incompatible with prior knowledge that children can be expected to have – knowledge that provides an *external* standard against which they can be evaluated. Finally, uncommon words or nonsense words make passages difficult for a different reason – they are not in the child's vocabulary. The abilities to monitor these different sources of difficulty do not necessarily develop in parallel. Ruth Garner (1981) for example, found, that poor readers are less likely to notice problems arising from internal inconsistencies than those arising from difficult vocabulary. Markman and Gorin (1981) found developmental differences when children were specifically informed about the criterion ('does the text contain false information?' or 'does it contain inconsistent information?') by which they should judge whether they had understood a passage, but not when they were left to adopt their own criteria.

Baker (1984a) compared spontaneous and instructed use of the three criteria for detecting comprehension problems outlined above: internal consistency, external consistency, and vocabulary. She tested 9- and 11-year-olds and compared good and poor readers at each age. Half of the children were instructed about the criteria they should apply, and the other half were simply told to look for problems. The younger and poorer readers identified fewer problems than the older and better readers. The older and better readers also used more of the criteria correctly and were quicker to perceive problems they had failed to report spontaneously. Interestingly, when Baker looked at the number of times a criterion was used, regardless of whether it was applied correctly, she found that the younger children complied with the instructions just as much as the older ones. However, they were less likely to use the criteria correctly. These data argue against the idea that younger children are less willing to criticize written material. Baker suggests, rather, that even when the younger children and poorer readers know what problems they may encounter in understanding texts, they may still fail to identify problems because they do not always use the criteria consistently and effectively – perhaps because they cannot cope so efficiently with the competing demands on their cognitive resources.

In summary, children's ability to assess their comprehension increases over the primary school years. Furthermore, the instructions that they are given can sensitize them to incompleteness or inconsistencies in a text.

Markman (1981) suggests that without the ability to reflect on one's own comprehension, comprehension itself will suffer. In the next chapter, we return to the question of whether techniques to improve metalinguistic skills also improve comprehension. Here we simply note that there may be no *causal* relation between metalinguistic awareness and reading skill. Both Vygotsky (1962) and Donaldson (1978) have argued that it is the process of learning to read that is responsible for increasing the child's language awareness, rather than the other way around.

Purpose in reading

If children are to read for instruction and enjoyment, they must progress beyond the idea that reading is primarily a matter of decoding. They have to realize that the main purpose of reading is to extract meaning from the text, and that decoding is just a means to an end. But there is more to skilled reading than reading for meaning. Skilled readers can apply their reading skills for different purposes. Their monitoring skills are also more finely tuned – what counts as adequate comprehension in skimming, for example, will hardly do in a period of concentrated study. Beginning readers have yet to learn that a text can be read for different purposes, and that different strategies might be appropriate for different comprehension goals.

Ernst Rothkopf (1982) showed that the reason for reading a text affects what and how much is recalled from it. Skilled readers are readily able to adjust their reading strategies, for example to skim a newspaper, to read a scientific paper for particular details, or to learn the main points of a book chapter. Young readers find such adjustments more difficult.

Meyer Myers and Scott Paris (1978) questioned children about how they would retell a story to another child. Ninety-five per cent of 12-year-olds indicated that they would try to reproduce the meaning, whereas nearly half of the 8-year-olds thought they should repeat the exact words. These results cannot be explained by assuming that younger children do not understand the difference between verbatim and gist reproduction. A large proportion of both 8- and 12-year-olds knew that word-for-word recall would be harder than remembering the meaning. It is more likely that children understand the difference, but do not know how to adapt their reading strategies. Myers and Paris found that four fifths of 12-year-olds but only a third of 8-year-olds said they read differently if they needed to remember the exact words of the story, as opposed to the gist meaning.

So far we have only considered the role of metacognitive skills in reading for meaning. Such skills also have an important role in reading to memorize. For example, Brown and Smiley (1978) investigated how students of various ages (fifth to eighth, eleventh, and twelfth graders and college students) made use of extra study time. Seventh and eighth graders used the extra study time less efficiently than the older subjects, and fifth graders did not show any improvement of recall after extra study time, even for the important parts of the text.

In summary, younger children do not seem to understand that they might read differently when they have different goals.

THE PROBLEM OF POOR COMPREHENSION

In the second half of this chapter, we discuss the problems of poor comprehenders – children who have adequate word recognition skills but do not understand what they read as well as they might be expected to. As we mentioned in chapter 1, these children are comparatively difficult to identify and have not received as much attention as those with decoding problems, although their difficulties are beginning to be recognized (see Weaver and Shonkoff, 1978).

Before starting our discussion, we should emphasize that we are not talking about the rare group of *hyperlexic* children. Although the problems of hyperlexic children are in some ways similar – their ability to recognize words is well in advance of their comprehension – they have other problems. Their language is often delayed, and they show an intense preoccupation with reading (often reading before they can talk), and preferring books and alphabet blocks to other toys. In addition, such children are often retarded and show autistic tendencies, if they are not actually autistic (Healy, 1982). The children we have in mind make up a sizable proportion of any primary school class. Indeed, in our own studies, up to one in ten 7- to 8-year-olds has shown a significant comprehension deficit.

The research reported in the second half of this chapter overlaps to some extent with the work described in the first half. Indeed, many of those studies included good and poor readers of different ages. Nevertheless, research on comprehension problems has focused on certain topics related to the three main theoretical views on comprehension deficit – our own, those of Charles Perfetti, and those of Ward Cromer. Perfetti and Lesgold (1979) showed that good comprehenders recognize words more rapidly than poor comprehenders. They argue that decoding in less-skilled comprehenders is less automatic, creating a 'bottleneck' in working memory. On this view, poor comprehenders have less working memory 'space' available for comprehension processes than good comprehenders – not because they have *smaller* working memories but because they make inefficient use of them. Cromer argues that the locus of poor comprehenders' problems lies at a higher level. He has shown that poor comprehenders fail to make use of the syntactic constraints in text, tending to read word-by-word and failing to chunk the text into meaningful units. Our own emphasis is on still higher-level processes. We argue that poor comprehenders fail to make necessary inferences from text and do not connect up the ideas, perhaps because of limitations in their working memories. Of course, each of these views may be right in its own way – each may characterize the difficulties of a distinct *group* of poor comprehenders, or each may contribute to the problem without being the whole answer to the problem in itself. We return to these three ideas in the second half of this chapter.

Our discussion will centre around four main areas of research and will attempt to separate possible sources of comprehension problems from the complex network of skills that comprise efficient reading. First, we discuss the decoding of words and the retrieval of their meanings. Although we are primarily interested in comprehension problems, not word-decoding problems, Perfetti has suggested that comprehension failure may arise from difficulties in decoding. In particular, he has shown that the speed and automaticity of word recognition are important factors in skilled reading. Second, we consider how children's knowledge of syntax and semantics, particularly with regard to written language, might affect progress in reading. As we saw in chapter 3, children's command of spoken language may provide only a poor guide to their understanding of written text. Thirdly we assess how reading skills are related to short-term and working memory skills and to the skills of inference and integration required for understanding and remembering discourse. Finally, we discuss the relation between monitoring skills and comprehension.

In the attempt to understand poor comprehension it is usual to contrast the performance of groups of good and poor readers on various tasks believed to reflect components of text understanding. The skills of normal readers must be understood if the problems of the less-skilled are to be described. Many of the studies discussed below have used this method. However, a difference between good and poor comprehenders in, for example, decoding speed is not necessarily *causally* related to differences in their ability to understand text (see chapter 4). It is always possible that a skill that distinguishes between good and poor comprehenders is merely correlated with ability to understand and is not causally linked to it. In order to establish a causal link, it would be necessary to train poor comprehenders in the skills they lack, and show that their reading improves following such training. Some studies of this kind are discussed in chapter 6.

In this chapter, we focus on children who have a *comprehension* problem, rather than a word decoding problem. However, many of the studies have used only a very general measure of reading comprehension skill, often one that depends on both decoding and comprehension. The 'comprehension' problems of the children in these studies may be due to the fact that they cannot decode the words on which the comprehension questions are based. Where subjects' decoding skills have been taken into account, we say so explicitly.

PSYCHOLOGICAL STUDIES OF GOOD AND POOR READERS

Word level influences

There are many ways that the processing of individual words could influence comprehension. However, reading fluency is not necessarily a good guide to comprehension skill. As we have already mentioned, up to 10 per cent of children who can read out loud fluently and who have normal or above normal word recognition skills for their age nevertheless experience considerable problems answering questions about stories they have read. One possible explanation of their problems is that although these children are good decoders, they have no idea of the meanings of the words that they can pronounce. This explanation is not usually the correct one, but it is to the area of vocabulary and word meanings that we turn first.

Vocabulary   As chapter 4 showed, it is possible to pronounce words without accessing, or even knowing, their meanings, for example by using spelling-to-sound rules. This is one way of reading without understanding. However, for most children vocabulary size is a good indicator of reading comprehension skill,[4] perhaps at least in part because both knowledge of word meanings and comprehension depend on general linguistic experience. Difficulty of vocabulary affects text comprehension directly, and Beck, Perfetti and McKeown (1982) have shown that children find texts easier to remember if they know the meanings of the words in them. They also showed that reading comprehension can be improved by vocabulary instruction. However, other research on vocabulary instruction (Pany, Jenkins and Schreck, 1982) has shown it to have only limited effects. Procedures effective in increasing children's vocabularies improved the comprehension of single sentences, but not passage comprehension. Moreover, as Charles Perfetti (1985, p. 97) points out, inadequate knowledge of word meanings is not a complete explanation of comprehension problems since children can fail to understand texts with only very familiar words in them. Furthermore, while we do not deny that vocabulary knowledge is an important factor in reading comprehension, our own studies have shown that children with the same vocabulary knowledge may have very different levels of comprehension skill (see e.g. Oakhill, 1982, 1983, 1984).

Speed and automaticity of decoding   There are other reasons why comprehension problems might arise from problems with single words, apart from an inadequate knowledge of their meanings. In particular, the *ease* with which the meanings of words can be accessed might be an important factor. As we explained in the first part of this chapter, word identification must be not only accurate but fast and automatic if comprehension is to be proficient.

Perfetti's *verbal efficiency theory* or *bottleneck hypothesis* gives speed and automaticity of decoding and semantic access central roles in the explanation of comprehension failure. Perfetti argues that individual differences in comprehension arise because of differences in the efficiency of these 'low-level' processes. LaBerge and Samuels' (1974) shared capacity theory assigns a similarly prominent role to decoding speed and accuracy in comprehension.

These hypotheses assume that the processes of decoding and comprehension compete for a limited amount of space in short-term memory. Processes take up room in short-term memory, so the less efficient a process, the smaller the amount of information it can work on, and the fewer other processes can be going on at the same time. One way in which processes can be more efficient is by being faster. Fast processes need only remain briefly in short-term memory. Slow processes suffer another disadvantage. The contents of short-term memory decay rapidly. The information that a slow process is trying to work on may disappear before the process has the chance to analyse it.

The fact that processing and storage in short-term memory have to be traded-off against each other is a potential source of differences in reading comprehension. The more automatic decoding and semantic access processes of better readers are more efficient in their use of short-term memory and leave more capacity for other processes. If unskilled readers have failed to develop automatic word-decoding skills they will have less short-term memory capacity for other processes in reading, such as making inferences and constructing a model of the text as a whole. When more work is required for decoding, less space is available in the system for other comprehension work. Furthermore, slow decoding may mean that words identified at the beginning of a sentence

have been lost before the sentence is complete and its meaning worked
out. If too much attention has to be focused on the words themselves, it
may be difficult to retain their meanings and to keep track of the overall
meaning of the sentence.

Several kinds of evidence suggest that poor comprehenders are
slow decoders.[5] Charles Perfetti and Thomas Hogaboam (1975a), for
example, found large differences in the time taken to name single words
between skilled and less-skilled comprehenders from the third and fifth
grades. There were differences for both common and uncommon words,
but they were larger for uncommon words. There were also differences
for strings of letters that looked like words but weren't. Although the
groups were not matched for decoding skills, the results could not be
explained simply in terms of word recognition *accuracy* since the skilled
readers had significantly shorter naming times even for very common
words, almost all of which were identified correctly by both the skilled
and less-skilled comprehenders. John Frederiksen (1978) found similar
results with older children.

One possible explanation of these results is that poor comprehenders
take longer not to decode words, but to say them. Other work by Perfetti
(Perfetti, Finger and Hogaboam, 1978) has shown that this explanation is
not correct. Poor comprehenders do not have a general naming problem.
They are just as quick as good comprehenders to name colours, pictures
and numerals. Furthermore, in the case of word naming, differences
between good and poor readers increase as the words get longer. With
colours, pictures and numerals this differential effect is not found. These
results suggest that the poor readers' slow responses can be attributed to
decoding problems rather than problems in saying words.

Perfetti and his associates have further shown that word naming time
is not the only measure of decoding that differentiates between good and
poor comprehenders. Skilled comprehenders are also faster on decoding
tasks that require a manual response (e.g. pressing a button) rather than
a verbal response (see Perfetti, 1985, p. 95).

Although there is a general tendency for fast decoding and good
comprehension to go together, there is no evidence for a direct causal
link between the two. Although children who are good decoders at an
early stage of reading generally turn out to be good comprehenders
at a later stage, at any particular age there are children who are fast
decoders but poor comprehenders, and vice versa (see chapter 1). For
example, Ward Cromer (1970) identified two groups of college students
who differed in comprehension ability, even though they were matched
on IQ, vocabulary and word recognition skills, including speed of
decoding. Furthermore, speeding up decoding does not always reduce
comprehension problems. Perfetti and Hogaboam (1975b) showed that
training can decrease the differences in decoding speed between skilled
and less-skilled readers. Such training, however, has little effect on
comprehension ability.

Lisa Fleischer, Joseph Jenkins and Darlene Pany (1979) tested the strong form of Perfetti's 'bottleneck' hypothesis (i.e. that fast decoding automatically results in good comprehension). They trained poor readers from the fourth and fifth grades to recognize words as rapidly as the good readers. Both this single-word training and subsequent training in rapid phrase decoding increased decoding speed for single words but did not improve comprehension, even though the passages to be understood were made up entirely of the trained words. Similarly, a new training study (Yuill and Oakhill, in press), which will be discussed in more detail in the next chapter, shows that training in rapid decoding has a negligible effect on comprehension skill in poor comprehenders, compared with training in inferential skills and question generation. These results show that the ability to decode rapidly is necessary but not sufficient for understanding written texts. Perfetti and Lesgold (1979) acknowledge this fact and argue that fast decoding may result from extensive reading practice, which good comprehenders are more likely to have. However, a study by Lesgold, Resnick and Hammond (1985) argues against this idea. They showed that, whereas there was a clear relation between early word recognition efficiency and later comprehension skill, early comprehension skill was *not* associated with later word recognition efficiency. Their data suggest that word recognition skills facilitate the acquisition of comprehension skills, but not vice versa. It might however be the case that fast and automatic decoding has only an indirect influence on comprehension skill – allowing it to develop, rather than influencing it directly. It seems that, at the very least, children need instruction in comprehension as well as training to increase their decoding fluency. We return to the question of training in rapid decoding in the next chapter, under the head of remediation.

Some of our own work (Oakhill, 1981) has shown that skilled and less-skilled comprehenders with the same decoding accuracy do *not* differ in decoding speed. In one study, the children had to sort pairs of words into two piles depending on whether they rhymed. Visually similar rhymes (e.g. ride–hide) and visually dissimilar rhymes (e.g. side–cried) were used. In the latter case, a phonological code must be used to decide whether or not the two words rhyme. There was no difference between the skilled and less-skilled comprehenders in the speed or the accuracy with which they sorted either type of word pair. However, the words in this experiment were all very common, so the task may not have been sensitive to differences between good and poor comprehenders. This possibility was examined in a further experiment in which reading times and errors for both common and uncommon words, and also pronounceable nonsense words, were measured. Again, there were no differences between the groups for any of the materials used.

In summary, poor comprehenders tend to have inadequate decoding skills, both for single words and for words in context. However, training that improves decoding does not improve comprehension, so there is probably no direct link between fast decoding and good comprehension. It may be precisely *because* decoding is such a basic part of reading that children who read more decode faster. Furthermore, speed and automaticity of decoding often go hand in hand with a large vocabulary and *accurate* decoding. When these two factors are taken into account, fast decoding is not such a reliable indicator of good comprehension.

Another difference between good and poor comprehenders is the kinds of decoding error that they make. Rose-Marie Weber (1970) found that poor comprehenders not only made more errors than good comprehenders, but also that more of their errors resulted in words that were inappropriate at that point in the text. Furthermore, poor comprehenders were less likely to correct such errors. This finding is hardly surprising. By definition, poor comprehenders do not understand sentences very well. They are therefore less likely to notice that what they say does not make sense.

Weber's data suggest that good comprehenders make greater use of context in reading. They are less likely to make inappropriate errors, and more likely to correct errors they do make. However, as we pointed out in chapter 4, a distinction must be made between use of context to correct or prevent errors, and the use of context to speed word recognition. In general, good comprehenders are better at using context to make predictions (e.g. guessing what the next word might be) or to check them (Perfetti, Goldman and Hogaboom, 1979), but they do not make so much use of context as poor comprehenders do to speed word recognition. Keith Stanovich (1982) reviews twenty-two studies, which used a number of different paradigms. All failed to show that good readers use context to aid word recognition more than poor readers. If anything, poor comprehenders make *more* use of context in such tasks.

Perfetti and Roth (1981) argue that good readers may not show context effects in word-naming time because their fast decoding ensures that the word has been recognized before context has time to exert any effect. To equate decoding time for good and poor comprehenders, they degraded the words for the good readers so that their recognition times were similar to those of the poor comprehenders. However, even with decoding time equated, good comprehenders made no more use of context than poor comprehenders. Thus, skilled comprehenders can be characterized as more *sensitive* to context, but less (or, at least, no more) *dependent* on it.

Richard West and Keith Stanovich (1978), whose work we discussed in more detail in the previous chapter in relation to developmental differences in the use of context, also found that the less skilled readers in their study relied more on context than the more skilled readers. They argue that this is because these children use context to supplement their poor decoding skills. This conclusion is supported by the work of Simpson, Lorsbach and Whitehouse (1983). They showed that poor readers make even greater use of context with degraded stimuli – as decoding becomes harder, they become increasingly reliant on context. The data are consistent with Stanovich's (1980) *interactive compensatory* model of word recognition – if word analysis is deficient, other sources of information will be used to compensate (see chapter 4). However, less-skilled readers show reliable context effects on word recognition only when they can *understand* the context, and this factor, Stanovich (1986) suggests, may underlie the apparent conflict between the findings of experimental studies and case reports of poor readers. You will recall from our discussion in the last chapter that top-down models of reading, such as Frank Smith's, would predict that good readers would be more reliant on context in on-going word recognition. If anything, the reverse pattern has been shown to hold in experimental studies. However, in the very earliest stages of learning to read, the slow and inaccurate decoding processes of poor readers may prevent them from understanding enough of the context for it to be useful. Under such conditions, poor readers cannot make use of context, simply because their decoding is so poor. For instance, a recent longitudinal study by Stanovich, Cunningham and Feeman (1984) found that a group of first grade good readers showed larger context effects than poor readers, simply because their decoding was sufficiently good to enable them to make use of context. Later in the year, when the poor readers could decode as quickly and accurately as the good readers could originally, they showed a similar level of facilitation to that originally shown by the good ones.

One factor that may influence the speed with which words are decoded is the ability to use orthographic information (see chapter 4). If good readers know more about constraints on the way letters can combine to make words, they should be able to recognize words faster. The experimental evidence on this topic is, however, equivocal and varies with the particular task that the subjects are set. One task makes use of the 'word superiority effect' (see chapter 2). Adults are better able to identify individual letters when they are presented in words than in non-words, presumably because their knowledge of permissible letter patterns helps them. Mildred Mason (1975, Experiment 1) investigated whether good and poor comprehenders can make use of orthographic constraints. The two groups had to search through sets of words or nonsense words for particular letters. The good comprehenders were better, but only on the constrained (word) displays.

A further experiment (Mason and Katz, 1976) showed that good comprehenders can very quickly *learn* sets of constraints, even if those constraints are novel. They presented their subjects with strings of (non-alphanumeric) symbols and varied the redundancy of the strings – some symbols appeared in particular positions more often than others. Adults quickly learned to use this redundancy, and so did good, but not poor, readers from the sixth grade (11-year-olds). Good and poor readers did not differ, however, in their ability to search non-redundant strings.

This finding is important because it indicates that good readers' use of redundancy is a general ability and not something that develops simply because they have had more exposure to print than poor readers.

However, as with context, there is no direct evidence that older or better readers make more use of their superior orthographic knowledge in word *identification*. In fact, in a task that more closely resembles reading, Stanovich and West (1979) showed that poor third grade readers (8-year-olds) made more errors than good readers in a word search task. The task was to look for a target word in different types of list – the other stimuli were either real words, pseudo-words (such as *fornt*) or non-words (such as *rtlno*). There were no differences in search *times* between the groups as a function of orthographic structure (both groups searched faster through the non-word than through the pseudo-word lists, and faster through the pseudo-word lists than through the word lists), and the better readers did not show a bigger effect of orthographic structure. However, the poor readers made more detection errors, and their errors were *more* affected by the other stimuli than were those of the good readers – they made most errors when the other stimuli were other words. Their errors tended to arise because they selected words that were similar in shape or contained some of the same letters as the target word. Thus, poor readers were identifying words on the basis of *less* information and making *greater* use of orthographic redundancy.

Semantic access This section looks at the ease with which good and poor readers access the *meanings* of words. The role of word meaning in comprehension is obvious but, as with decoding, semantic access may be more or less efficient. Readers who can recover the meanings of words quickly are likely to understand text more easily. Inefficient semantic access might be a result of decoding problems and, since the meaning of sentences are put together in short-term memory, should have consequences similar to those of slow decoding.

An experiment by Perfetti, Hogaboam and Bell (cited by Perfetti and Lesgold, 1979, p. 66) examined the relation between comprehension ability and skill at retrieving word meanings. They found that good and poor comprehenders did not differ on tasks that required matching spoken words with printed words or pictures – tasks which they argue require only low-level semantic information. However, they did find that good comprehenders were better at a categorization task, in which they had to *make use of* the information accessed to decide whether a word presented belonged to a given category (e.g. apple is a kind of fruit).

Similar tasks – picture-word matching and categorization – were used in one of our own studies (Oakhill, 1981) to compare semantic access in skilled and less-skilled comprehenders who were *matched* for word recognition ability. If the groups differ in the speed with which they can retrieve the meaning of single words, they will differ on both tasks. If, however, the less-skilled comprehenders are slower only when they are have to process meaning, they will be slower than skilled comprehenders at categorization but not at matching. In fact, there were no differences between the groups in speed or errors on either task. The less-skilled comprehenders were, if anything, slightly faster. These findings contrast with those of Perfetti, Hogaboam and Bell. The less-skilled comprehenders did not seem to be slower at accessing the meanings of single printed words, even when the task required the use of word meanings. However, the words in the categorization task were all obvious exemplars of their category. A task using less-salient examples of category members, or a more subtle distinction between category and non-category members, might differentiate between the groups.

The automaticity as well as the speed of semantic access may be important in comprehension. Roberta Golinkoff and Richard Rosinski (1976) examined the relation between decoding, processing the meaning of single words and reading comprehension. Single-word processing was measured in a picture–word interference task. The children had to name twenty pictures aloud as quickly as they could, and to ignore words (or nonsense words) superimposed on the pictures. Sometimes the superimposed word conflicted with the picture (e.g. *pig* printed on the picture of a cat). If the meaning of the printed word is automatically accessed, it should interfere with naming a picture with a different name and, if this interference effect is semantic, it should be larger when conflicting words are superimposed on the pictures than when nonsense words are superimposed. The good comprehenders completed the interference task more quickly, but they did not show a larger semantic interference effect than the poor group. These findings imply that decoding and semantic access are independent processes, and that the ability to retrieve word meanings becomes an almost automatic process as soon as minimal decoding skills are attained. However, in this study, the measure of reading comprehension depends on both word recognition and comprehension abilities, so the implications of the results for skilled comprehension are unclear.

Oakhill (1981) replicated Golinkoff and Rosinski's experiment with skilled and less-skilled comprehenders who were *matched* for decoding ability. The less-skilled comprehenders took slightly longer to name the nonsense words, but not the words. However, as in Golinkoff and Rosinski's experiment, the interference effect was similar for skilled and less-skilled comprehenders. In addition, this experiment also replicated Golinkoff and Rosinski's finding that less-skilled comprehenders are slower to name pictures. This result may reflect differences between the groups in more subtle aspects of their semantic knowledge (see also the experiment on instantiation discussed below).

In summary, poor comprehenders readily obtain the meaning of common printed words, although they may not be able to access detailed semantic descriptions as readily as good comprehenders.

Syntactic and semantic knowledge

Once the words in a text have been identified, readers have to use knowledge of semantic and syntactic categories and of the rules of syntax to derive the message that the text conveys. Skilled and less-skilled comprehenders may differ in their ability on one or more components of this task.

As we saw in chapter 3, knowledge of sentence structure is still developing beyond the age at which children learn to read, so an inadequate grasp of syntax may adversely affect the comprehension ability of some children. Obviously, knowledge of syntax is not specific to reading, and one might assume that as long as decoding skills are adequate, readers should understand any written sentence that they could understand if it were spoken. However, since there are prosodic cues to guide syntactic processing in listening but not in reading, the identification of syntactic constituents might be difficult for young readers. Both comprehension and memory for text will then suffer. Although texts contain punctuation, its efficient use is a skill that develops relatively late.

The idea that poor comprehenders fail to make use of syntactic constraints in text, has been explored extensively by Ward Cromer and his colleagues.[6] Cromer (1970) identified two main groups of poor comprehenders: a 'deficit' group and a 'difference' group. The deficit group had poor vocabulary and decoding skills as well as poor comprehension skills. They seemed to have a general reading problem. The difference group, meanwhile, had vocabulary and decoding skills similar to those of good comprehenders of the same age. Cromer showed that the comprehension skills of the two groups were different. His study will be described in detail since it is germane to our argument that many experiments on comprehension do not take decoding ability into account.

Cromer presented texts in four different ways: as whole sentences, in meaningful phrases (e.g. the cow jumped / over the moon), in fragmented phrases (e.g., the cow / jumped over the / moon) and as single words. Comprehension questions followed each text. Overall, the poor comprehenders answered fewer questions correctly. However, the 'difference' group performed as well in the meaningful phrase condition as did good comprehenders. Furthermore, this group's scores were the same for the normal sentence, single-word and fragmented phrase conditions, whereas good comprehenders did worse in the single-word and fragmented phrase presentations. These results suggest that the 'difference' group ordinarily reads word-by-word, so they are not affected by the disruptive conditions. Nevertheless, dividing the sentences in a sensible way improves their comprehension. They can make use of structure if it is given to them. The 'deficit' group was not helped by dividing the sentences into meaningful phrases. Their problem is not simply the result of inefficient text organization. The fact that good comprehenders were not helped by division into meaningful phrases but were disrupted by fragmented phrases and single-word presentation, suggests that they normally organize text into phrase-like units. Unlike poor comprehenders, they use sentence structure as well as word identification to aid their comprehension.

This conclusion was confirmed by Steiner, Wiener and Cromer (1971), who argued that an advance summary might help poor comprehenders to read for meaning instead of word-by-word and would, therefore, lower their error rate. Good and poor comprehenders were asked to read stories out loud with or without summaries. The stories were sometimes presented one word at a time and sometimes as paragraphs. The results were the opposite of those predicted: the advance summary led good comprehenders to pay less attention to word detail. They made *more* reading errors when given such information. The poor comprehenders' error rate remained unchanged; they continued to read word-by-word even when given the summary. This reading style is similar to the list-like style that Clay and Imlach (1971) describe poor comprehenders as using.

Eye–voice span measures, cloze procedures and geometrical transformation of text (see Gibson and Levin, 1975; Willows and Ryan, 1981) have also shown that unskilled readers are less sensitive to syntactic cues than skilled readers, and that these differences persist even when IQ and decoding skills are taken into account.

A few studies have investigated more directly whether good and poor readers differ in their sensitivity to syntactic structure. Rhona Weinstein and Sam Rabinovitch (1971) studied memory for spoken 'sentences' such as:

All the rak ibnu lurmed and wabed elirly. (structured)
And all rak elirly, wabed ibnu the lurmed. (unstructured)

The two groups performed equally poorly with unstructured 'sentences'. However, good readers, but not poor readers, found structured strings easier to memorize than unstructured strings. These results held even when IQ differences between the groups had been taken into account. Although decoding skill was not controlled, decoding differences could not account for the results since the sentences were spoken.

In contrast, Mann, Liberman and Shankweiler (1980) found that syntactic structure did not differentially affect good and poor readers' (= decoders) ability to repeat spoken sentences. This discrepancy might have arisen because Weinstein and Rabinovitch required their subjects to learn sentences, whereas Mann and her associates asked for immediate repetition.

Richard Isakson and John Miller (1976) showed that poor comprehenders who have adequate word recognition skills, are less sensitive to both syntactic and semantic cues in text. Their subjects had to read aloud sentences that were either meaningful:

The old farmer planted the bean seeds in the rich, brown soil

or semantically anomalous:

The old farmer paid the bean seeds in the rich, brown soil

or both semantically and syntactically anomalous:

The old farmer went the bean seeds in the rich, brown soil.

Isakson and Miller argued that children who extract the meaning of a sentence as they read should experience difficulty when they encounter the anomalous verbs, and might actually misread the text to impose some sense on it. By contrast, children who read word-by-word should be no more likely to make errors on anomalous words than elsewhere. They found that the good comprehenders' errors increased from normal sentences to those with anomalies, whereas the poor comprehenders' errors were similar (and fairly high) for all types of sentence. Isakson and Miller conclude that instead of using syntactic and semantic cues in the text to integrate the meanings of the individual words, poor comprehenders seem to treat each word separately.

As we saw in chapter ·3, comprehension skill is related to the understanding of difficult syntactic constructions. We mentioned the work of Goldman (1976), who showed that skilled comprehenders were more likely to understand correctly sentences containing *promise* and *tell*:

Bill promised John to leave.
Bill told John to leave.

However, this difference was apparent only when the children *read* the sentences, and not when they listened to them. Indeed, reading comprehension skill was a better predictor of the ability to understand such sentences than age or IQ.

Memory

Most recent accounts of reading emphasize the importance of various types of memory. Short-term memory is needed for temporary storage and integration of information, long-term memory for more permanent storage and as a source of relevant knowledge, for example for inference making. Both therefore play an important role in comprehension. Two sorts of short-term memory deficit are particularly likely to affect comprehension: below average capacity, and failure to make efficient use of available capacity. Problems can also arise if children cannot or do not use information in long-term memory to help them understand text. We shall discuss this kind of problem below under the heads of inference and integration.

Short-term memory   Short-term retention of information in an immediately (though not necessarily consciously) available form is important in *parsing* and in integrating information from neighbouring sentences in a text. The comprehension of a complex syntactic structure depends not only on understanding that structure *per se* but also on remembering the bits of a sentence while the overall structure is being worked out. We saw in chapter 3, for example, that embedded relative clauses are more difficult to understand than right-branching ones. One standard explanation of this finding appeals to the different demands that the two structures impose on short-term memory. A limitation on the size of this store could be a source of comprehension problems for the more difficult sentences. More generally, if it is hard to recall the immediately preceding text, it might be difficult to link the current word or sentence with previous, related, information.

In general, children with reading problems are found to have less short-term memory capacity than normal readers, as measured by the standard digit span technique, which requires the immediate repetition of a sequence of spoken or written numerals (see Torgeson 1978–9). However, Perfetti has failed to find such differences on similar tasks (see Perfetti and Lesgold, 1979; Perfetti and Goldman, 1976). One reason for the diversity of these findings may be that children in the different studies had different reading problems. Few studies have addressed the question of whether children with a specific comprehension problem (as opposed to a more global reading problem) have deficient short-term memory. Some of our own work that relates to this question is discussed below.

More general psychometric studies show that digit span is not strongly related to verbal comprehension in the population at large (Hunt, Lunneborg and Lewis, 1975). Furthermore, the increase in memory span with age reflects children's developing ability to encode information in a useful way, rather than changes in the capacity of short-term memory itself (Chi, 1976; Huttenlocher and Burke, 1976).

Growth in memory span could occur through a decrease in the proportion of the space that must be devoted to basic operations, so that the *available* resources increase even if the total capacity remains constant. Both speed and automaticity of basic processes could contribute to such an increase in resources (see also Case, Kurland and Goldberg, 1982).

It may be that good and poor readers differ in their information-encoding strategies rather than in their memory capacity. For example, Mann, Liberman and Shankweiler (1980) showed that, although good readers' recall of word lists and sentences was superior overall to that of poor readers, they were more disrupted if the words had similar sounds. Mann et al. suggest that the poor readers fail to make use of phonetic coding in short-term memory. However, this explanation is unlikely since the materials were presented aurally, and it is unclear how else they could have been encoded. A more plausible explanation is that good readers rehearse (i.e. say the words to themselves) more than poor readers, and that the confusions arise during rehearsal. The investigators do not rule out this possibility but they note that both groups of readers *appear* to rehearse. Perhaps the good group were rehearsing more efficiently.

Results on the relation between short-term memory and comprehension skill are equivocal. However, there is stronger evidence that good and poor readers differ in their ability to remember recent parts of continuous discourse. Goldman et al. (1980) used a probe task to examine short-term retention of prose. In this task, reading is occasionally interrupted and a word is presented that occurred fairly recently in the text. The subject's task is to produce the word that followed the probe word. The number of words between the target (i.e. the word sought) and the re-presentation of the probe, and the structure of the intervening text, were both varied. Although both groups tended to remember more from the sentence they were reading than from the preceding sentence, skilled readers were better at remembering the previous sentence than less-skilled readers. These differences are not specific to reading – Perfetti and Goldman (1976) found comparable differences in a listening task. They also found that the differences between skilled and less-skilled comprehenders (from the third and fifth grades) were large for two-clause sentences but small for one-clause sentences, especially when the probe was very recent. These data suggest that the processes that integrate information from two clauses may be an important source of comprehension differences, and that the ease with which children can integrate information from discourse may be a source of comprehension differences even when short-term memory size, as measured by a digit-span task, is not.

These results suggest that a language-specific memory store, which can hold information for rather longer than the short-term memory measured by digit-span, is an important component of comprehension skill. Perfetti and Lesgold (1977) propose that this memory might be more enduring because words and phrases are subjected to several types of processing during comprehension. Digits, on the other hand, are simply named, using labels from a small, well-defined set. More varied processing produces a better 'memory trace'.

Another possibility, already mentioned above, is that differences between good and poor comprehenders are attributable to differences in *working* memory capacity. The idea of working memory provides a more active conception of how information is retained for short periods than the passive idea of a short-term store. Robert Kail et al. (1977) suggest that the capacity of working memory differentiates skilled and less-skilled readers. They used Paris and Carter's (1973) 'false recognition' task (see the first part of this chapter), but asked the children whether the inference sentences were true rather than whether they had previously been presented. Better comprehenders made their judgements more quickly. Kail et al. argue that these results cannot be explained in terms of the capacity to retain information, but reflect the facility with which good comprehenders are able to manipulate and integrate information in working memory. This conclusion is consistent with recent research showing that good comprehension depends on an efficient working memory.[7] These experiments, discussed in chapter 2, show that adults' working memory capacity correlates with measures of reading comprehension, with how readily facts can be accessed from long-term memory and with facility in resolving pronominal references.

The articulatory loop, which is a component of working memory, may play a particularly important role in reading. To enter the articulatory loop or its associated phonological store (Salame and Baddeley, 1982), printed words must be recoded into a phonological form. Phonological recoding is important in comprehension because phonological codes are more durable than visual codes for storing early parts of a sentence to combine them with what comes later (see chapter 4). Several studies have shown that good and poor readers differ on memory span tasks, due primarily to differences in the efficiency of phonetic recoding in working memory, independent of general intellectual ability (see Stanovich, 1986; Wagner and Torgesen, 1987). To see whether skilled and less-skilled comprehenders who do not differ in decoding skills use phonological recoding to different extents, we ran an experiment (Oakhill, Yuill and Parkin, 1986) using a technique developed by Hitch and Halliday (1983). Children were asked to remember short lists of one-, two- or three-syllable spoken words. Both skilled and less-skilled comprehenders recalled more short than long words, but there were no differences between the groups. The children were also presented with series of pictures corresponding to the words in the lists. Sensitivity to word length would indicate that the children were recoding the pictures to a phonological form. Again, we found a main effect of length of the picture names, but no difference between the skilled and less-skilled comprehenders. Both showed evidence of verbal recoding of picture names. These results provide additional support for the idea that there is no general difference in memory capacity between the skilled and less-skilled comprehenders.

The tasks described above are primarily tests of storage capacity. Oakhill, Yuill and Parkin (1988) suggested that good and poor comprehenders might differ on a task that makes heavier demands on working memory – one that requires simultaneous storage and processing. As we wished to discover whether the groups differed in working memory independently of their comprehension skill, we used numerical rather than verbal materials. The subjects had to read out groups of three different digits, one group at a time (processing requirement), and after reading two, three or four such groups, they had to recall the final digit in each group (storage requirement). The results showed that whereas both skilled and less-skilled comprehenders did equally well on the easiest task – recalling the final items from two groups of three digits – the skilled comprehenders were significantly better than the less-skilled comprehenders at recalling the final items from three or four groups of digits. Thus, although the skilled and less-skilled groups do not differ in short-term recall of word and picture lists, they do differ on a task that requires concurrent processing and storage, which is probably closer to the requirements of comprehending written material.

Taken together, these studies suggest that poor readers who are not severely retarded do not have a general deficit in short-term memory capacity. However, they do not necessarily have adequate *functional* capacity, especially the kind of functional capacity needed for understanding text. Good readers are better able to use the linguistic properties of sentences, such as their structure, to increase their memory span. The difficulties of poor comprehenders may, at least in part, be related to their poorer use of working memory. In the next section we argue that working memory may also explain differences in text comprehension at the level of integration and inference.

Higher-order processes: text integration and inference

In chapter two, and in the first part of this chapter, we discussed the very important role of integration and inference in text comprehension. In this section we examine differences between good and poor comprehenders in the ease with which they combine information from different parts of a text and in inferential ability.

Integration   As we saw earlier, Smiley et al. (1977) demonstrated that sensitivity to the relative importance of different parts of a text is quite poor in beginning readers and develops with reading experience. They found the same sort of insensitivity in older children who were poor readers. Their results cannot be attributed to differences in other reading skills since they were similar for both reading and listening. However, several studies have failed to find that skilled and less-skilled comprehenders differ in their sensitivity to the thematic structure of a passage (see Perfetti and Lesgold, 1977).

Many studies indicate that skilled and less-skilled comprehenders differ in the extent to which they integrate the information in a text, and in their use of inferences. For example, some of our own work (Garnham, Oakhill and Johnson-Laird, 1982) has shown that less-skilled comprehenders who have adequate word recognition skills have difficulty taking advantage of cohesive links in text. We gave skilled and less-skilled comprehenders short stories that varied in cohesiveness. The normal stories described a readily understood sequence of events. Two other types of story were constructed by scrambling the sentences, thereby destroying the plausible sequence. In the ordinary *random* versions, the sentences were simply moved around. These stories had neither a plausible sequence of events nor cohesive links between the sentences. In the *revised random* stories the cohesive links were restored, for example by replacing uninterpretable pronouns with full noun phrases, but without restoring the original sequence of events. Both skilled and less-skilled comprehenders found the scrambled stories difficult to remember. However, only the skilled comprehenders were helped by the restoration of 'referential continuity'. They remembered more of the revised than of the random stories whereas the less-skilled comprehenders were equally poor at remembering both types. Furthermore, several of the skilled comprehenders tried to impose a structure on the scrambled stories (albeit different from the original structure), adding information and rearranging the sentences to try to impose some sense on the texts. The less-skilled comprehenders showed no such tendency. Their recall of the scrambled stories was usually very sparse.

One way of exploring children's ability to link up the ideas in text is to assess how easily they can interpret pronouns. We found (Oakhill and Yuill, 1986) that less-skilled comprehenders had difficulty in supplying an appropriate pronoun (*he* or *she*) in simple sentences, such as:

Sally gave her shoes to Ben because . . . needed them.

When the link between the first and second clauses was slightly less straightforward, as in:

Steven gave his umbrella to Penny because . . . wanted to keep dry

the poor comprehenders had even more difficulty, making almost twice as many mistakes as the skilled comprehenders.

In a further study (Yuill and Oakhill, in press) we investigated skilled and less-skilled comprehenders' understanding of pronouns in text more directly. We asked the children what pronouns and other anaphoric links (see chapter 2) in the text 'pointed back to', and also asked them very specific questions such as 'who is *he* in this sentence'. Less-skilled comprehenders were considerably poorer at both these tasks than skilled comprehenders.

Inference Many results, including some of our own, show that skilled comprehenders make more inferences from text, which helps them not only to understand the text but also to remember it. However, inference not only aids memory, it relies on it. If poor comprehenders make fewer inferences than good comprehenders, one must always ask:

is it because they have poorer inferential abilities, or is it because they cannot remember the information on which the inference is based? This question is pertinent because many measures of text comprehension impose demands on memory, so 'poor comprehenders', as identified by such tests, are likely to have relatively poor memory for text.

We investigated skilled and less-skilled comprehenders' ability to answer questions both from memory and when they were allowed to refer back to the text (Oakhill, 1984). Some of the questions had answers that were explicitly stated in the text, others required inferences. The skilled comprehenders were better able to answer both literal and inferential questions when they could not see the passages. When the text was made available, the less-skilled group remained poor at answering questions that required an inference, but their performance on literal questions improved to the level of the skilled group. Thus, the poorer question-answering ability of the less-skilled group cannot be explained in terms of poor verbatim memory, at least for the inferential questions.

Further support for the idea that less-skilled comprehenders fail to make inferences from texts comes from another of our experiments (Oakhill, 1982; see also Oakhill, Yuill and Parkin, 1986). In this experiment, groups of skilled and less-skilled comprehenders listened to short stories, which they were told to try and remember. Following the stories, they were asked whether a series of sentences had appeared in the stories. As well as sentences from the texts there were some stating valid inferences and some stating invalid inferences. The number of errors on the original sentences was similar for the two groups, and both groups wrongly identified more valid than invalid inferences. However, among the inferences, the bias towards valid ones was more pronounced among the skilled comprehenders, who tended to respond 'yes' only to original sentences and valid inferences from the story. This pattern of results suggests that skilled comprehenders devote more effort to the active construction of meaning than the less-skilled group.

In chapter 2 and in the first half of this chapter we discussed *instantiation*, a type of inference in which the interpretation of a word is made more specific by context in which it appears. Some of our own work (Oakhill, 1983) has shown that skilled and less-skilled comprehenders who are matched for word recognition skills differ in the extent to which they instantiate. We investigated the relation between comprehension skill and instantiation in 7- to 8-year-olds. Children were read a series of sentences, such as:

The people built their houses out of ice.

Later, either the general noun that appeared in the sentence (*people*) or a particular noun suggested by the context (*eskimos*) was given as a cue for its recall. Both skilled and less-skilled comprehenders recalled the sentences equally well given the original nouns as prompts. However, the skilled group recalled the sentences better than the less-skilled group when they were given the particular word cues. Furthermore, the skilled comprehenders were as quick to respond to original as to instantiated cues, whereas the less-skilled comprehenders took longer to respond to instantiated cues. These data show that the skilled and less-skilled comprehenders differ in the extent to which they spontaneously infer particular interpretations for words. The less-skilled comprehenders do not simply have difficulty in recalling the sentences – they remember them when they are given the general cues. Rather, the groups appear to differ in the extent to which they make use of context and knowledge, for example about the kind of people who build houses from ice, to interpret the sentences. However, a further test showed that the differences could not be explained by differences in general knowledge, only by the extent to which knowledge is used in comprehension. Finally, the response times suggest that the skilled comprehenders were instantiating at the time of initial reading.

Work by Merrill, Sperber and McCauley (1981) also supports the idea that less-able readers do not select the contextually most appropriate interpretation of a word. They asked fifth graders to read a series of sentences in which certain attributes of a key word were emphasized. For example, in *The boy sat near the fire*, some attributes of *fire*, such as *warmth*, are more immediately brought to mind than others (e.g. *smoke*). Immediately after reading each sentence, the children had to name the colour of the ink in which a word (e.g. *smoke* or *warmth*) was printed. It is well known that the meaning of a word, and how salient that meaning is, can increase the time taken to name the colour of its ink. The tendency is to say the word, not the colour. In addition to sentence contexts, the investigators also used word contexts. With these contexts, all subjects showed equal increases in interference when the word whose colour was to be named followed a semantically related word (e.g. *cat–fur* or *cat–claw*) compared with the condition where it followed an unrelated word (e.g. *man–fur*). For the sentence contexts, good comprehenders showed interference for words that were related to the attribute emphasized by the context (*warm*), but not for words related to unemphasized attributes (*smoke*). Poor comprehenders showed interference for both types of words. The investigators argue that these findings point to differences in the way good and poor comprehenders encode sentences. Good comprehenders derive a contextually appropriate encoding almost immediately, whereas poor comprehenders have a more general but presumably less useful encoding, so that more of the target word's attributes are available to them.

Inference can be thought of as a type of reasoning or problem-solving. Indeed, it has sometimes been suggested that reading itself is a form of reasoning.[8] R. Thorndike (1973–74) found that performance on a number of reading tasks depended on a common ability that had much in common with verbal reasoning. Kavale and Schreiner (1979) required subjects to describe aloud their reasoning for accepting or rejecting answers to questions that followed a passage. They found that both average and above-average readers made use of reasoning strategies in comprehension, but, although both groups used similar strategies, average readers applied them less frequently and less successfully. If reasoning ability is a fundamental factor in reading comprehension, then a lack of such ability may be a major source of comprehension difficulty.

Taken together, investigations of less-skilled comprehenders who do not have word decoding or vocabulary problems, particularly our own studies, show that their problem cannot be attributed to a straight-forward memory deficit. It seems, rather, that skilled comprehenders more readily integrate the ideas in a text, making inferences where necessary, to derive its overall meaning. One of our early studies (Oakhill, 1981, experiment 6) provides additional evidence for this idea. Skilled and less-skilled comprehenders' memory for sentences was similar when a verbatim criterion was used to assess recall. However, when scoring was relaxed to include gist recall, the skilled comprehenders' performance was significantly better than that of the less-skilled group. The better gist recall by the skilled group suggests that they made a more active attempt to understand the sentences, rather than simply retaining their wording. These findings are consistent with the idea that less-skilled comprehenders have poorer working memory capacities than their skilled counterparts. Since working memory is important in making inferences and in the construction of a meaning representation of the text, it is not surprising that less-skilled comprehenders are deficient in these text comprehension skills.

Metacognition and comprehension skill

We saw in the first part of this chapter that the ability to moni-tor comprehension during reading is important, and that studies of young children have shown that they often fail to realize that they have not understood a text. Good comprehenders seem to have a better awareness of what comprehension is and when it has occurred (Golinkoff, 1975–76) and there is evidence that poor comprehenders' problems arise partly because they fail to monitor their comprehension, or at least because they make less use of monitoring strategies. For example, Olshavsky (1976–77) found that good and poor tenth grade readers described themselves as using the same sorts of comprehension strategies, but that good readers reported using them more often.

Ruth Garner (1980) has shown that poor comprehenders tend to be less aware of their lack of understanding. She asked good and poor comprehenders from the seventh and eighth grades to read passages that contained obvious inconsistencies. The children were asked to say how easy each section of the passage was to understand. They also had to explain why the difficult sections were difficult. Garner found that good comprehenders classified the inconsistent sections as harder to understand than the consistent ones, and their comments revealed that they were aware of the source of their problems. Poor comprehenders, by contrast, did not discriminate between the consistent and inconsistent sections and, even when they reported a lack of understanding, they did not pick out the inconsistencies. Instead, they explained their difficulty with comments such as: 'The words were longer' or 'I didn't like that part as well'. Garner points out that poor monitoring ability could be either a cause or a result of poor comprehension: 'lack of attention to glaring gaps or blatant inconsistencies might occur because of a history of print's making only minimal sense to a reader' (1980, p. 61). In other words, poor comprehenders might *expect* most texts to make little sense, because they always find understanding difficult!

Another study by Garner (1981) investigated the monitoring skills of fifth and sixth grade poor comprehenders, all of whom had adequate or above-average word recognition skills. She found that they rated a passage containing inconsistencies as easy to understand as one that was consistent, but that they rated a passage containing polysyllabic modifiers that they did not know the meanings of (e.g. *expeditiously, multifarious*) as being less comprehensible because it contained 'tough words' or 'long words'. Garner characterizes the poor comprehenders as being more concerned with individual words than with the text as a whole.

Further work by Garner (Garner and Kraus, 1981–82) showed that almost all of a group of seventh grade good comprehenders detected inconsistencies in a text, but none of the poor comprehenders reported them. Garner and Kraus's study provides further evidence that poor comprehenders do not integrate the information in different parts of a text (and therefore do not detect inconsistencies) because their attention is directed to other parts of the text. They also gave the children a questionnaire about reading. Their responses were revealing: although none of the poor comprehenders had decoding problems, most of them mentioned the importance of word decoding in reading (a response *never* made by the good comprehenders), and few mentioned understanding or extracting meaning. For instance, when asked what makes a person a good reader, the good comprehenders gave responses that stressed comprehension, whereas the poor comprehenders stressed 'knowing all the words' and 'pronouncing the words right'. Similarly, when asked what makes something difficult to read, typical replies from good comprehenders were 'not being familiar with the main ideas', 'badly written stuff where the ideas are hard to get', whereas the poor comprehenders again emphasized problems at the word level: 'small print', 'long words'. These responses certainly reinforce the idea that poor comprehenders, even when they are not poor decoders, put the emphasis on accurate decoding rather than attending to the meaning of the text.

Work by Scott Paris and Meyer Myers (1981) has come to similar conclusions. They gave fourth graders passages to read that contained difficult or anomalous information, and used three indices of comprehension monitoring: spontaneous self-corrections during oral reading, underlining of incomprehensible words and phrases, and study behaviour (asking questions and using a dictionary). Poor readers showed less evidence of comprehension monitoring on all three measures. An additional measure to assess the children's perception of the effectiveness of a number of reading strategies revealed that the poor readers were less aware than good readers of which strategies could be detrimental to understanding. The poor readers seemed to focus on word decoding, rather than comprehension goals. For instance, they rated the strategy 'saying every word over and over' as very helpful.

Linda Baker (1984a) has extended this research on comprehension monitoring. A detailed account of this work was given in the first part of this chapter. She found that poorer readers, like younger children, identified fewer problems with texts than better readers did, and also used fewer criteria for deciding texts were incomprehensible. Baker suggested that the poorer readers may have the same criteria available to them as better readers but be unable to use them consistently. As she says, this ineffective use of the criteria may be the result of a more general cognitive deficit.

We have already discussed the role of working memory in comprehension, and the evidence that less-skilled comprehenders may have working memories with a reduced capacity. Here we add that readers with poor working memories will have little scope for the sorts of processing required to monitor comprehension. Indeed, our own work on anomaly detection suggests that less-skilled comprehenders' inability to detect inconsistencies increases with memory load. Using a technique borrowed from Ackerman (1984), we read children stories describing an adult's apparently inconsistent response to a child's action (Oakhill, Yuill and Parkin, 1988). For example, in one story, a mother is pleased with her son when he refuses to share his sweets with his sister. The inconsistencies were either preceded or followed by information that resolved them – in this case, that the sister was on a diet. We expected that resolving information would be more difficult to use when it followed the anomaly than when it preceded the anomaly, since, in the latter case, resolution could only be retrospective. The difficulty of resolving the anomaly was further manipulated by varying the distance between the anomalous and the resolving information. After each story, the children were asked whether the adult should have responded as he or she did, and why. Only by using the resolving information could the children respond appropriately. Other questions were included to ensure that both sets of children remembered the stories properly and that they knew whether the action in question (in this case, refusing to share sweets) was usually blameworthy. As expected, both groups found it harder to use resolution information when it followed rather than preceded the anomaly. In this more difficult condition, the skilled and less-skilled comprehenders performed similarly when there were no sentences between the anomalous and the resolving information, but the less-skilled comprehenders were worse than the skilled comprehenders when there was an additional memory load created by the intervening sentences.

Text reinspection would be an obvious strategy to help overcome the memory load in comprehension. A study by Ruth Garner and Ron Reis (1981) examined the use of this strategy in good and poor sixth, seventh and eighth graders. They asked them to read passages with interspersed questions about difficult-to-recall details on a preceding page of text. The better, but not the poorer comprehenders, recognised the problem, but only the oldest (grade 8) good comprehenders frequently and spontaneously looked back to the text to answer such questions. Garner and Reis (1981) concluded that only the oldest successful readers recognized their comprehension difficulties (a finding that is consistent with the other studies discussed above), and only they did anything to try to remedy the failure.

Are poor comprehenders poor listeners?

In general, children who are poor at understanding text are also poor at understanding spoken language (see Rubin, 1980). Listening comprehension ability is related to that part of reading comprehension skill that cannot be explained by poor decoding. For example, Berger (1978) found that poor fifth grade readers were deficient in listening as well as reading comprehension. Smiley et al. (1977) found a large listening comprehension deficit for seventh grade poor readers and a high correlation between reading and listening comprehension.

In addition, many of the studies discussed above have found differences in ability between good and poor comprehenders even in listening tasks (e.g. Oakhill, 1982; Oakhill, Yuill and Parkin, 1986). These findings again support the idea that decoding speed and accuracy can only be a part of the poor comprehenders' problem. The sorts of skills on which good and poor comprehenders differ also suggest that they will experience difficulty listening too. Problems with syntax, memory and metacognitive monitoring would certainly be expected to be general comprehension problems and not restricted to reading. We do not, of course, wish to argue that reading is no more than decoding plus oral comprehension skills. As we argued in chapter 3, there are many important differences between oral and written language that the child has to learn to deal with. The point we wish to make here is that children who have trouble understanding written language quite often have trouble understanding spoken language too. So although slow decoding may contribute to reading comprehension problems, at least in the initial stages of beginning to read, it is unlikely to be their only cause.

SUMMARY

In the first half of this chapter we showed that a number of important comprehension skills develop only gradually over the primary-school years. The absence of no single one of these skills can by itself account for comprehension failure, but younger readers and those who have a specific comprehension problem have particular difficulties in making inferences from and integrating the ideas in text. In addition, several sources of evidence suggest that younger children and poorer readers have metacognitive deficits. Younger and poorer readers have inadequate conceptions of reading. They do not realize that the primary purpose is to make sense of the text, and focus on reading as a decoding process, rather than as a meaning-getting process.

Fortunately, as we will see in the next chapter, procedures to help such children have proved quite successful.

Notes

1. See, for example, Meyer (1975), Kintsch (1977), Bower, Black and Turner (1979); see also ch. 2.
2. See, for example, Paris (1975), Paris and Carter (1973), Paris, Lindauer and Cox (1977), for accounts of the original work. For extensive reviews see Paris (1975, 1978), Paris and Lindauer (1978), Trabasso and Nicholas (1980).
3. See Baker and Brown (1984), Markman (1981). For a review of the whole area of comprehension monitoring and reading, see Ruth Garner (1987).
4. See Rosenshine (1980) for a review; also Perfetti (1985, p. 83).
5. See, for example, J. Frederiksen (1978), Golinkoff and Rosinski (1976), Mark, Shankweiler, Liberman, and Fowler (1977), Perfetti and Hogaboam (1975a), Perfetti and Lesgold (1977, 1979).
6. See W. Cromer (1970), Steiner, Wiener and Cromer (1971), Oakan, Wiener and Cromer (1971). But see Calfee et al. (1976) for a criticism of these studies.
7. The work of Daneman and Carpenter (1980, 1983), and Baddeley, Logie, Nimmo-Smith and Brereton (1985), mentioned in chapter 2.
8. See, for example, E. Thorndike (1917), Davis (1972), R. Thorndike (1973–74), Kavale and Schreiner (1979).

CHAPTER 6

Educational implications

Chapter 2 described in detail the processes that underlie reading comprehension in skilled adult readers. Chapter 5 discussed how those processes fail in poor comprehenders. In this chapter we consider the practical implications of the theoretical perspectives and research findings of those two chapters. In the first part of the chapter we discuss the diagnosis of reading problems, particularly the comprehension problems we identified in chapter 5. In the past, these problems have gone largely unnoticed in educational settings. In the rest of the chapter we describe three methods for improving reading comprehension skills: adding items, such as illustrations and questions, to the text; encouraging the use of traditional study aids, such as underlining, note-taking and summary writing; and instigating training procedures based on the deficits of less-skilled comprehenders identified in chapter 5.

IDENTIFYING POOR COMPREHENDERS

Comprehension tests: their scope and limitations

Our aim in this section is to discuss, in general terms, methods of measuring reading ability, in particular the ability to comprehend text, and their shortcomings. We are not concerned with such technical questions as whether norm- or criterion-referenced tests should be used, or how items and tasks should be selected.[1] Neither do we explicitly discuss the notions of test validity and reliability, though we do address the more general question of *what* reading tests measure. Our focus will be on the philosophy behind the tests and on why it might be inappropriate.

Children's reading ability is commonly assessed using tests in which printed words of increasing length and difficulty have to be read out loud. These tests do not distinguish between children who recognize the words directly, from their visual appearance, and children who recognize

144

them via their sound pattern, by 'decoding'. Indeed, it is not necessary to recognize words with a regular spelling-to-sound correspondence at all to say them aloud. Children who are skilled at using grapheme–phoneme correspondence rules can pronounce many words that are not even in their listening vocabulary (see chapter 4). The ability to recognize words directly, the ability to decode them, and the ability to relate spellings to sounds all undoubtedly play an important part in learning to read. Furthermore, these abilities are probably highly correlated with comprehension measures, at least beyond the early stages of reading. However, as we saw in chapter 5, not all comprehension problems can be attributed to inadequate word identification. The ability to recognize individual words is necessary but not sufficient for comprehension, so standard reading tests may give a very inaccurate picture of some children's ability to understand texts. As we saw in chapter 1 and again in chapter 5, there are children who can 'read' a story, and who know the meaning of each word in it, yet who have no understanding of the text as a whole.

The assessment of reading comprehension, as distinct from word identification skills, poses numerous problems. As we saw in chapter 2, psycholinguists find it difficult to provide a criterion for saying when someone has understood a text. People read for different purposes, and there are as many kinds of understanding as there are ways of assessing understanding. Certainly, no two people will extract exactly the same meaning from a text – what they get out of it will depend on their individual characteristics, especially what they know about the subject matter of the text. Although it would be impossible for a commercially produced test of comprehension to take such factors into account, an attempt could be made to reduce the effects of factors such as general reasoning ability in test performance by using assessment techniques that are relatively insensitive to differences in reasoning skills (see Royer and Cunningham, 1978, for a further discussion of this point).

There are tests specifically intended to measure reading comprehension. One kind requires children to read a short text and to answer either open-ended or multiple-choice questions. Another kind uses a completion task called the cloze task, which was initially devised to assess 'readability' (see chapter 3), but which is also used to test and even to train reading comprehension. For instance, Kennedy and Weener (1973) showed that visual training with the cloze procedure improved both listening and reading comprehension in below-average readers. In cloze tests, children read texts with every nth word deleted and are asked to fill the gaps. Their completions show how well they understand the text, assuming that they can accurately decode the words that have not been deleted. Indeed, poor performance on both types of comprehension test might be attributable to lack of decoding and vocabulary skills. It might also be caused by lack of the ability, the knowledge or even the motivation necessary to integrate and interpret the text. Hence, much of the research that purports to distinguish between good and poor comprehenders is not able to differentiate between these reasons for comprehension failure. Obviously, a child who performs well on a question-answering or cloze test has adequate decoding skills, but a child who performs poorly does not necessarily have a problem specific to comprehension. One way that decoding and comprehension skills might be successfully disentangled would be to give children a *listening* comprehension test, so that their understanding can be assessed when they are unhampered by decoding problems.

A further problem with question-answering comprehension tests is that the questions are sometimes based solely on the explicit content of the passage and sometimes they require inferences from that information, usually in conjunction with general knowledge about the world. Indeed, as chapters 2 and 5 suggest, the second type of question is more important for assessing comprehension skills. Correct answers to questions that require no more than verbatim memory for the text are a poor indication of how well it has been understood.

The only British test known to us that enables an independent assessment of decoding and comprehension skills is the *Neale analysis of reading ability* (Neale, 1966). In this test, children read through a series of passages graded in difficulty and answer questions about each one. Once it becomes clear that a child cannot identify a word, the person administering the test says it, so that failure to identify some of the written words does not necessarily result in comprehension failure. Both the number of words incorrectly read or omitted, and the number of questions correctly answered are recorded. So age-related scores for both decoding accuracy and comprehension are obtained, and any mismatch between the two skills can be diagnosed. The test, however, has several shortcomings. First, it is old, and some of the stories are dated: for instance, one of the early stories, in one version of the test, features a horse-drawn milk cart! Second, the test is time consuming to administer. Each child has to be tested separately, and it may take 20 minutes to test a reasonably fluent 8-year-old. The test is thus impractical for the average classroom teacher. Third, the comprehension questions are mixed. They include literal questions and ones that require inferences based on general knowledge. No attempt to distinguish between these types of question is made, although, as we have seen, good and poor comprehenders differ primarily in their ability to answer inferential questions (Oakhill, 1984).

Although a new version of the Neale test has recently been published (Vincent and de la Mare, 1985), which is an improvement on the old version in terms of presentation, content and accompanying illustrations, this test retains some of the problems of the old Neale test and has several additional shortcomings. Each raw score corresponds to a wide range of reading ages – twelve to fourteen months for the reading accuracy scores, and seventeen to twenty-one months for the comprehension scores. Thus, the test provides only very imprecise measures of reading ability, and will be of little help to teachers who want to relate that ability to chronological age. For example, it is of little use to know that a child has a comprehension age within the range 8 years 1 month to 9 years 10 months. More worryingly, the standardization of the test was carried out on only 600 children, from two London boroughs, so that the age-related norms may not generalize to children from other social, geographical and cultural backgrounds.

Most tests of reading – those that use recall or question-answering measures – assess comprehension *after* it has happened. It has recently been suggested that *process* measures, such as reading errors (or 'mis-cues'), eye-movements and reading times are more direct and hence potentially more useful in assessing comprehension (see e.g. Pearson and Johnson, 1978; Johnston, 1983). However, even process measures are indirect indices of comprehension. They do not show exactly what the reader has understood. They just indicate certain things that happen in the process of trying to understand a text. Johnston (1984) further suggests that a useful addition to oral reading tests might be the 'think aloud' approach developed by Olshavsky (1976–77) and Kavale and Schreiner (1979). In a 'think aloud' test, readers are asked to say what they are thinking while they are reading, in the hope that what they say will indicate, either directly or indirectly, any difficulties that they are having. Hare and Smith (1982) used the think-aloud procedure with seventh grade children and concluded that it could provide important diagnostic information about the strategies of individual readers. In addition, as a study by Alvermann (1984) has shown, this method can be used successfully with children as young as second grade, although they need fairly extensive individual practice sessions and do not make explicit their cognitive processing activities in the way that older children are able to. However, as part of a standardized test, this technique would be very time consuming to use, and the interpretation of the 'think aloud' protocols would probably require extensive training.

Can comprehension be divided into subprocesses?

In research on reading development it has often been assumed that comprehension comprises a number of independent subskills (see also chapter 1). This assumption, if true, has important consequences for teaching and for helping children with comprehension problems. If specific skills can be identified and assessed, then appropriate remediation can be given.

A number of taxonomies of subskills exist (see e.g. Barrett, 1976; Pearson and Johnson, 1978). Barrett, for example, suggests a five-fold division of reading skills into those of literal comprehension, reorganization, inferential comprehension, evaluation and appreciation.

Attempts have been made, particularly in the USA, to devise comprehension tests and training programs to diagnose and improve ability in the separate skills. However, although many different sets of subskills have been identified by factor analysis (see chapter 1), there is considerable lack of agreement as to their number and nature (see Drahozal and Hanna, 1978; Rosenshine, 1980). Peter Johnston (1983) argues that a major influence on the subskills identified by factor analytic techniques is the choice of texts for the tests. Furthermore, unlike the components of reading, such as word recognition, parsing and inference, identified in chapter 2, these skills are not derived from an explicit model of text comprehension – they are generally based on a researcher's intuitions about what might be important. More worryingly from a practical point of view, since the taxonomies have no theoretical grounding, it is by no means clear how performance on different comprehension tests can be translated into a useful diagnosis of a particular reader's problems, or into guidelines for instruction.

An alternative view, advocated by Edward Drahozal and Gerald Hanna among others, is that comprehension is a holistic process which cannot be divided into distinct subskills. One version of this view, suggested by E.L. Thorndike as early as 1917, is that reading comprehension is a form of reasoning. More specifically, Thorndike compared comprehension with problem-solving. Although Thorndike's research is now recognized as having many flaws, his conclusions have been endorsed by R.L. Thorndike (1973–74), who also found that performance on a number of reading tasks depended on a common ability that was hard to distinguish from verbal reasoning. Indeed, Frederick Davis (1972), using factor analytic techniques, found that knowledge of word meanings together with an ability that he termed 'reasoning in reading' accounted for 89 per cent of variability in reading comprehension skill (p. 673). So, although test publishers often provide subscores in comprehension tests, and although these subscores may *appear* useful to teachers, they are often alternative measures of the same thing. As Drahozal and Hanna (1978) point out, subscores would be useful if they allowed the identification of children's relative strengths and weaknesses in reading comprehension, but 'providing several scores for the same attribute and giving these scores different labels would serve no legitimate purpose; it would serve only to confuse' (1978, p. 419). Furthermore, although a particular child on a particular occasion of testing will score better on some subtests than on others, the reason is likely to be that the subscores are unreliable. Each subscore is based on only a small number of items, and statistical theory shows that such scores are inherently unstable.

In summary, factor analytic studies have had little success in identifying distinct subareas of comprehension skill (see Simons, 1971). The only thing the studies agree on is that knowledge of word meanings is a separate and necessary factor for skilled comprehension, and one that accounts, not surprisingly, for a great deal of the variability in children's ability to understand text – children with poor vocabularies tend to be poor comprehenders. The remaining subskills of reading are generally thought to be so overlapping and interrelated that they cannot be separated. However, calling reading comprehension a unitary skill makes it difficult to pinpoint and remedy the difficulties that some children experience.

Fortunately, this conflict between the conclusion suggested by research findings and the need for specific help for specific comprehension problems is more apparent than real. It has arisen because the research has focused on the *products* rather than the *processes* of comprehension (i.e. on comprehension test scores – see our earlier discussion). Factor analysis of test results is too crude a tool to elucidate the mental *processes* underlying the responses in the tests (see also Pearson and Johnson, 1978). Furthermore, the fact that results of different tests, for example tests of decoding and tests of comprehension, are closely interrelated for the population *as a whole* does not rule out the existence of relatively large groups of readers for whom that relation breaks down. Hence, factor analysis not only tells us little about the processes of comprehension, it provides no indication of how to improve understanding in cases where it is lacking.

How, then, can comprehension skill be measured so that intelligent decisions about educational practice can be based on the results of comprehension tests? As we mentioned above, part of the problem with most attempts to identify subskills of reading is that they are not based on any theory of what it means to comprehend. In recent years, as we showed in chapter 2, considerable progress has been made in understanding the nature of comprehension in skilled readers, and it is to current theoretical ideas that we should turn for guidance in the search for subskills of comprehension. At a very general level, comprehension can be thought of as the building of a mental model of the meaning of the text. A more detailed analysis suggests that the ability to utilize appropriate prior knowledge and to identify the central ideas of a text are subskills that almost certainly contribute crucially to such model building.

The relation between text memory and comprehension

Many tests of text comprehension also require texts to be remembered for some time. For example, in the Neale test, the children are prevented from looking back to the text when they are given the questions. The assumption behind this method of testing is that poorly understood material will not be well remembered, and there is certainly evidence that understanding and memory are highly correlated (see e.g. Bransford and Johnson, 1972; Dooling and Lachman, 1971). Gordon

Bower (1978, p. 212) even claims that 'superior memory seems to be an incidental by-product of fully understanding a text'. However, it does not follow that something was poorly understood just because it has been forgotten. Moreover, as Johnston (1983, p. 3) points out, perhaps text comprehension and text memory appear to be inextricably linked simply because psychologists have usually tested them together.

WAYS OF IMPROVING TEXT COMPREHENSION AND LEARNING FROM TEXT

In this section we consider a wide range of methods for improving comprehension of and learning from text. In many cases normal readers can also benefit from the aids and strategies we discuss, but our focus is on how to improve the comprehension of poor readers. Studies comparing good and poor comprehenders and studies of normal readers alone will be discussed throughout the section. Any method for improving comprehension is likely to help poor comprehenders, though specific proof that a particular method helps these children may not be available.

Since the process of remediation always takes time, some measure should ideally be obtained of how children given no specific remediation progress over the same period – if improvements are to be attributed to the remediation instruction, it must be shown that these improvements occur *over and above* any improvement that would occur anyway. The groups who do not receive remediation, or receive some form of instruction that is not expected to improve their comprehension are termed *control* groups. Their scores can be used as a baseline against which the effectiveness of the remediation treatment can be measured, though not all of the studies we discuss have used adequate control groups.[2]

We shall consider three main ways of improving comprehension and learning. First, there are various additions or changes that can be made to texts to enhance their comprehensibility and memorability. Such additions and changes are provided *for* readers and require no active effort on their part. Additions to the text include pictures, titles and summary statements; other changes are usually aimed at improving the global organization of the text. These additions and changes are generally intended to make texts easier to understand rather than to facilitate learning. Second, we shall consider *activities*, such as note-taking, underlining and writing summaries, that readers can engage in during or after reading the text, and that have traditionally been referred to as 'study aids'. Study aids are generally thought of as means by which students *learn* from text but, as we show, they can also be used to improve comprehension. The third set of aids to comprehension are processing strategies that children can be taught to apply as they are reading – ways to think about the text, about how it relates to what they know and about whether they understand it. These strategies are designed primarily to improve comprehension rather than to aid learning. They differ from the first two types of aid in that they rely entirely on what goes on in the reader's head, rather than on 'external' aids to understanding and learning. Most remediation studies have trained children in the use of strategies of this kind because poor comprehenders can most usefully be helped by giving them procedures that they can apply to any text. Children cannot easily provide their own illustrations or text organization and, particularly in the case of younger readers, they are often unable to make good use of traditional study aids. Training in processing strategies aims to give younger/poorer comprehenders the skills that better readers naturally use. We believe that skills training is the most important way of improving comprehension, since skills can be applied to any text once they have been learned, and they can be taught to primary school children. Most of the remainder of this chapter will therefore be devoted to the discussion of such aids.

Comprehension aids in the text

Anything that is not in the main body of a text is potentially an aid to comprehension. Such aids are not procedures or strategies that can be taught but adjuncts supplied by authors or editors to help comprehension – for example titles and subtitles, questions, supplementary explanations, pictures and diagrams. They have two main purposes: they can provide additional relevant information, and they can guide and foster the learning process, for example by drawing attention to important aspects of the text. Comprehension aids in the text fall into two main categories: those that provide orienting information for readers before they look at the text (for example, titles or summaries), and those that are interspersed in the text (for example, questions at the end of subsections). There is a vast literature on the efficacy of such aids (see e.g. the review by Tierney and Cunningham, 1984), so our discussion will be brief.

Pictures and titles Language is usually meant to be understood in a particular context. Titles and accompanying pictures form part of the context for interpreting written texts. Failure to provide these cues can considerably disrupt comprehension, particularly if the text contains vague words, such as *thing* or *part* that only have a specific interpretation in context (see e.g. Dooling and Lachman, 1971; Bransford and Johnson, 1972).

A number of studies have demonstrated the beneficial effects of providing titles and other 'verbal organizers' for young readers of normal ability. For example, Arnold and Brooks (1976) gave second and fifth graders verbal descriptions of unusual situations (such as three children flying through the air on a giant swan). Each description was preceded by a summary statement. The statement either related the characters in the text ('two boys and a girl riding a swan') or simply listed them ('two boys and a girl and a swan'). Although the integrated titles did not facilitate verbatim recall of the text, they enabled subjects to make more correct inferences than did the non-integrated titles. Similarly, Paul Harris et al. (1980) showed that titles that provided setting information resulted in better gist recall in 8- and 10-year-olds than titles simply listing the characters in the story. Furthermore, the children reported that the stories with setting information made more sense to them than those with character information only.

Doctorow, Wittrock and Marks (1978) showed that the comprehension of 10- to 12-year-olds was substantially improved by giving them headings for paragraphs in a text. They suggest that headings (theirs were words central to each paragraph's topic) help readers to locate relevant background information in memory which they use to make sense of the passage.

Accompanying pictures can also help normal readers to understand text. Joel Levin and Alan Lesgold (1978: cited by Levin, 1981) reviewed nearly twenty studies that showed improved learning when texts included pictures. Children provided with illustrations that are relevant to the story can be expected to recall 40 per cent more than those given no illustrations. Other studies have shown that pictures can help children learn from factual texts as well as from stories.[3] However, pictures are not always helpful.[4] Schallert (1980) suggests that pictures do not aid comprehension when they are inconsistently or vaguely related to the text, and that to be useful they must illustrate information that is central to the text or new content that develops the overall meaning.

William Rohwer and Wendy Harris (1975) showed that mere repetition of information in a text does not necessarily aid comprehension. They presented information to fourth graders in seven different conditions: print only, picture only, spoken only, print and picture, print and spoken, spoken and picture, and print, picture and spoken. They found that subjects in the picture-only condition performed less well than any of those in the print conditions. Not surprisingly, the picture by itself did not convey the information in the text very well. More interestingly, the children in the spoken-with-picture condition performed better than those in the spoken-with-print condition. This comparison shows that having information repeated in a different modality, for example by hearing and reading the same story, does not improve understanding. Pictures aid comprehension not simply by restating what is in the text, but by providing a different perspective on the same information.

Ruch and Levin (1977) also showed that pictures can improve comprehension more than rote repetition. In particular, partial pictures, in which crucial information is strongly suggested but not actually present, because it is either outside the picture or behind something in it, improved the performance of third graders on both verbatim and paraphrase questions. Repetition improved performance only on verbatim questions.

Peeck (1974) presented 9- and 10-year olds with stories both with and without accompanying cartoon strip pictures and investigated the effect of the pictures on longer-term memory for information in the text. The pictures provided some information in addition to what was in the text. Sometimes that information conflicted with the text. There were therefore four categories of information: that provided exclusively by pictures, that provided exclusively by the text, text information correctly depicted in the pictures, and information inconsistently presented in text and pictures. When the memory test was immediate, the presence of pictures had no effect on memory for the information that was presented consistently in the pictures and text. But when the test was delayed for either a day or a week, memory for information that was represented both in the pictures and in the text was improved for the children who had originally seen the pictures. Furthermore, where pictures and text provided inconsistent information, children who had seen the pictures often responded on the basis of pictorial rather than textual information, although they were instructed to answer on the basis of the written material. Memory for information presented only in the text was never improved by the pictures. So, in the longer-term, pictures help children to remember textual information that they specifically complement, but not other information. Furthermore, where pictorial information conflicts with what is in the text, it may be favoured.

The question of whether 6-year-olds understand stories better if they provide their own illustrations was investigated by Alan Lesgold et al. (1975). In a series of studies, they found that children's recall and ability to answer questions about stories was improved by illustrations, but that it did not make any difference whether the experimenter provided the illustrations, or the children made their own using cutout figures. However, the illustrations had to represent the information accurately if they were to be effective – they only had an effect when children were given the correct pieces for the illustration, or had the illustration constructed for them. As in Peeck's study, the effect of pictures on comprehension was found to be highly specific. In a later study, Lesgold, DeGood and Levin (1977) found further evidence that pictures have to provide accurate and specific representations of the information in the text in order to facilitate retention.

Another study suggesting that pictures have very specific effects in aiding comprehension is that of John Bransford and Marcia Johnson (1972). They asked adults to recall a passage that appeared meaningless because it described an unlikely situation in an obscure way (a man serenading a woman in her fifth-floor room by playing an electric guitar with its speaker floating near the woman's window, held up by gas-filled balloons). Subjects who were given a picture that showed the people and objects in the story in the correct spatial relations recalled the passage better than subjects given no picture. Furthermore, subjects given a picture showing the same people and things but not in the correct relation to one another recalled no more than subjects who saw no picture. These results suggest that pictures are only helpful if they provide a detailed framework for the interpretation of a text.

Drew Arnold and Penelope Brooks (1976), whose experiment on titles we described above, also investigated how different types of pictures help children to understand texts. They found that both second and fifth graders made more correct inferences about short texts with integrated pictures (e.g. the children shown riding the swan) than with non-integrated pictures (the swan and the children shown in different parts of the picture). However, as Nicola Yuill and Trish Joscelyne (in press) point out, in both Arnold and Brooks's and Bransford and Johnson's experiments, the texts were unintelligible without the pictures, and the unhelpful pictures were misleading. Since children's reading books do not contain passages and pictures of this sort, a more pertinent question is whether some types of picture that are true to the text are better than others.

Yuill and Joscelyne (in press, experiment 1) investigated the effects of different types of picture and title on the comprehension of and memory for short stories in skilled and less-skilled comprehenders. This study, like some of those described in the last chapter, used less-skilled readers whose problem lay in comprehension but not decoding. Although the stories were not obscure, some information was not explicitly stated, though it could readily be inferred by skilled adult readers. Yuill and Joscelyne suggest that if less-skilled comprehenders are unable to integrate information from different parts of a text, they, but not skilled comprehenders, should be helped by pictures and titles that indicate how the different pieces of information fit together. They investigated the effects of pictures and titles of two types. The pictures were similar to those normally found in children's story books: either large ones that summarized the whole story, or small ones that illustrated separate events. Yuill and Joscelyne argued that the first sort of picture would be more helpful than the second, relatively disjointed type, since it would provide a better organizing framework for the events in the story. In contrast to earlier studies, both types of picture were plausible representations of the story content. Similarly, they used two types of title: integrative titles, which made the main consequence of the story explicit, and non-integrative titles, which described the main protagonists. The results of the experiment supported Yuill and Joscelyne's conjectures. Both integrative pictures and titles improved the comprehension of the less-skilled but not the skilled comprehenders, though the effect was more striking for the titles.

In sum, appropriate pictures presented with a text improve understanding, though their effects are specific to the part of the text they illustrate. Inappropriate pictures can disrupt understanding.

There are a number of reasons why pictures might help people to understand and remember text. Jennifer Rusted (1984) suggests that their main function is to provide a conceptual framework within which the text can be understood. In addition, they may help the reader to elaborate on the text, for example by suggesting images of the action it describes. Diane Schallert (1980) suggests that pictures are particularly useful when the text conveys spatial or structural information. However, whatever the precise mechanism of their effects, there is no doubt that pictures can be a useful aid to comprehension.

Background knowledge   As we pointed out in chapter 2, it is easier to understand a text if one can bring an appropriate packet of background knowledge, what Bartlett (1932) called a *schema*, to bear on it. For example, a reader with a rich background knowledge of the rules of football and of the teams involved will find a report of a football match easier to interpret and will give it a fuller interpretation than one who lacks that knowledge. The effects of such knowledge on comprehension and memory are illustrated by the work of James Voss and his associates.[5] They presented groups of adults who had either high or low knowledge of baseball with a passage about a baseball match and asked them to recall it. Not only did the high-knowledge group recall more, but they tended to recall more significant information. They remembered the order of events better, and integrated the events in the passage more successfully. The low-knowledge subjects tended to recall peripheral information, such as what the weather was like.

In a study of the relation between comprehension ability and prior knowledge in fourth graders, Mary Marr and Kathleen Gormley (1982) found that prior knowledge about the topics of passages was a better predictor than comprehension ability of the children's ability to draw inferences from and elaborate on the passages.

Further support for the importance of prior knowledge in comprehension comes from a study by Pearson, Hansen and Gordon (1979). Two groups of children from the second grade, who were matched for IQ but who differed in their knowledge of spiders, read a passage about spiders and answered explicit and implicit questions about it. The explicit questions could be answered from the text, but the implicit ones required the integration of text information and background knowledge. The high-knowledge group performed better overall, mainly because of their superior ability to answer the implicit questions. In this study, as in Voss's, all of the subjects had *some* relevant background knowledge, but the extent and quality of that knowledge determined how well the texts were understood. Thus, if a text is about an unfamiliar topic, it may be helpful to provide as much background *as is necessary to facilitate comprehension*. Isabel Beck and Margaret McKeown (1986) argue that insufficient background knowledge may be a major factor in reading failure, and that 'teachers need to be on the alert for knowledge problems masquerading as reading problems' (p. 133).

Can provision of relevant background knowledge immediately prior to reading facilitate comprehension? A series of studies by Michael Graves and his colleagues suggests that it can (see e.g. Graves and Palmer, 1981; Graves, Cooke and LaBerge, 1983). They found that short previews that provided relevant background knowledge, introduced key story elements and attempted to engage the children's interest improved performance on a number of comprehension measures. These results held for both high- and low-skill fifth and sixth grade readers (Graves and Palmer, 1981) and for low-ability seventh and eighth grade children (Graves, Cooke and LaBerge, 1983). The results of questionnaires showed that the children generally liked being given the previews and reported that they found them helpful.

Such procedures can also be effective for younger children. A study of third graders by Beck, Omanson and McKeown (1982) compared standard reading lessons with revised lessons in which relevant prior knowledge was introduced and concepts important to the text were highlighted to help the children to identify and interrelate the main story ideas. The children who received the revised lessons recalled more of a story and answered more questions correctly than did the control group.

It appears, therefore, that the provision of background knowledge does improve comprehension, although the difference between the experimental and control groups in these studies was never simply the provision of knowledge. However, there are obvious problems in trying to provide background knowledge in an educational setting. How much knowledge should be given, for example, and precisely what knowledge can a child or a group of children be expected to have?

A slightly different approach, used by Judith Langer (1984), overcomes some of these problems. She used a pre-reading discussion of the key concepts of the text in an attempt to help the children (sixth graders) become aware of *what they already knew* about a topic. This activity increased available knowledge and improved performance on comprehension questions, but only for average and above-average readers – those of lower ability were not affected.

Summaries and 'advance organizers'   A summary of a text can be helpful in providing an overview of the material to be covered and some pointers to its structure and its main arguments. A summary can also be helpful *after* the text has been read. 'Advance organizers' (Ausubel, 1963) are more abstract and general than summaries – they are intended to provide a cognitive framework within which the reader will be able to understand the text. Numerous studies of the effectiveness of advance organizers have produced inconsistent results (see Jenkins and Pany, 1981). A major problem has been the lack of specific guidelines about what advance organizers are and how they should be produced, so that their quality may have varied considerably from study to study.

Questions   Questions within or immediately after a text have usually been found to make it easier to understand and remember (for a review see Anderson and Biddle, 1975), though results inconsistent with this general conclusion have sometimes been reported (see Jenkins and Pany, 1981). Questions in the passage direct readers' attention to more material. Attending to more material usually means that more is remembered. Questions after a passage not only improve performance on later questions about the same information but also enhance memory for information that was not previously questioned. However, presenting questions before a text tends to make readers focus on the answers to those questions. Such questions improve performance on later questions about the same information but tend to have a negative effect on the retention of other information. They cannot therefore be relied on to improve general understanding of and memory for a passage.

This section has outlined several ways in which additions or adjuncts to a text can make it easier to understand and remember. However, as we indicated at the beginning of the section, we have only touched on this vast area of research.[6]

Study aids

Since, as we have stressed before, there is no average reader or text and no standard goal of reading, there can be no best way of studying a text. What readers do while reading will depend on a number of factors, such as whether they want to understand the text or to learn it, and whether they are more interested in the main themes and ideas or the detailed facts. The same reader may read the same text in different ways on different occasions. For example, we were familiar with the theoretical ideas and main findings of many of the articles cited in this book, but it was not until we came to write about them that we consulted the articles at a different level, to extract details of the experimental procedures and findings. Recipes provide another example of this phenomenon – you might skim through the ingredients and method to see whether a recipe appeals to you and how long it would take to make, but you would have to read it more carefully to check which ingredients you needed to buy and to cook the dish. To adopt appropriate study strategies, readers must take into account what they want to get out of the text and why.

Any study strategy will be more effective if the reason for studying the text (sometimes called the *criterion task*) is known. Skilled readers usually know why they are reading a text, but beginning readers and poor comprehenders may not.

Most people have their own preferred aids to learning, such as highlighting, note-taking and writing summaries. They use these procedures because they *feel* they will help. Research findings suggest that no one strategy is best, and that almost any strategy will be effective if it is used properly and if it focuses the reader's attention in a way that is appropriate to the learning task. Children might be taught to use these study strategies as *comprehension* aids, though, as we shall see they seem unable to benefit from them before the later years of primary school.

We shall briefly outline the main findings on three commonly-used study strategies: underlining (or highlighting), note-taking and summarizing. (Again, there are extensive reviews of this literature, to which the interested reader is referred – for example, T.H. Anderson, 1980; Anderson and Armbruster, 1984).

Underlining   Underlining provided *for* readers and underlining generated *by* readers both improve immediate memory for text. Underlining produced by readers themselves is best, perhaps because the effort expended in deciding which parts to underline improves memory. However, underlining only helps readers to answer questions about material they have underlined, not ones about other parts of the text.

Note-taking   The effectiveness of note-taking obviously depends on the quality of the notes. For example, students who simply copy out parts of the text are unlikely to benefit as much as those who rewrite the material in their own words. In principle, note-taking is an extremely effective study aid, because it allows students to restructure information in a way that is meaningful to them. However, note-taking has not in general been found to be more effective than other study aids, such as underlining (see T.H. Anderson, 1980), perhaps because students do not usually take the opportunity to restructure the information. When notes that reflect the organization of a text are compared with ones that change that organization, the latter are found to be more effective, presumably because restructuring requires thought and effort. Shimmerlik and Nolan (1976) demonstrated this fact both when memory for the material was tested immediately and when the test was delayed.

Note-taking may have qualitative as well as quantitative effects on memory. For example, Einstein, Morris and Smith (1985) showed that note-takers concentrate on the main ideas in the text at the expense of other ideas. The students in their experiment either took notes on or simply listened to a lecture. There was no overall difference in the amount remembered, but the note-takers recalled more of the important information.

Ann Brown and Sandra Smiley (1978, Experiment 2) investigated the use of underlining and note-taking in fifth to eighth grade children. They found that the children who were best at learning from text were those who spontaneously took notes or underlined while they were reading. Children who did not usually use these study aids did not benefit from a suggestion that they should. This finding is not surprising since the children were not shown *how* to use the aids effectively. They tended to produce notes and underlinings of inferior quality.

Summarizing   As with other study aids, the usefulness of summarization depends on the criterion task. A summary is of little use to someone who needs to remember the details of the text, but will be effective for someone who wants to remember the main points. Teaching children to summarize might help to improve their reading comprehension. Brown, Day and Jones (1983) studied summarization in children from the fifth, seventh and tenth grades and college students. The youngest children could produce summaries but mainly did so by deleting irrelevant or redundant material. The older children and college students used a wider variety of rules for summarization. Children younger than fifth grade would probably be poor even at using such simple deletion rules, because they would have difficulty in explicitly identifying the main points and important ideas in a text (see chapter 5). Learning to summarize might help them to focus on the more important aspects of the text, though perhaps only after their ability to say what is important has begun to develop.

A study by Thomas Bean and Fern Steenwyk (1984) showed that sixth graders could be successfully trained in summarization skills. Compared with a control group who were simply advised to write summaries by finding the main idea, the children given explicit instruction were superior both at summary writing and comprehension. In addition, some limited positive effects of training in summarization skills have been found for fifth graders. Barbara Taylor (1982) found that instruction in summarization that focused on the structure of the ideas in the text improved both recall scores and the organization of recall protocols, compared with simply answering questions about texts. The results were very similar for above- and below-average readers. However, considerable practice in generating summaries was needed before it had any effect. Furthermore, children who generated better summaries tended to recall more than those who produced poorer summaries. Younger children, who cannot identify the important points of a text, are unlikely to benefit from such training.

Training in isolating important aspects of a text might also be important in improving comprehension, but again Brown and Smiley (1977) have shown that young readers find this task very difficult.

Doctorow, Wittrock and Marks (1978) showed that writing a summary sentence after reading each paragraph of a text increased the performance of sixth graders by about 50 per cent on both immediate and delayed memory tests when compared with a group who only read the text. Children of the age tested (about 11) were able to cope with the task. Their summary statements were appropriate about four-fifths of the time. Low ability students showed a greater improvement in performance than normal readers.

To summarize, almost any strategy for studying is effective if it focuses the reader's attention in a way that is appropriate to the task. However, the study aids discussed in this section are most suited to skilled older readers. Even the oldest primary school children probably cannot make effective use of the aids we have been discussing. If younger and poorer readers are encouraged to use them, they may do so in such an inefficient way as to render them practically useless. Part of the reason is that the ability to use study aids is closely linked to ability to monitor comprehension – a skill which, as we saw in the last chapter, primary school children are remarkably bad at.

Training procedures and remediation

As we have seen above, there are a number of general methods for improving comprehension and learning that could be used to advantage with any student. We now look at the possibility of improving comprehension by teaching younger and poorer readers to use the types of processing that are normally used by highly skilled readers, for example, making inferences and integrating the information in the text with relevant prior knowledge. We have also included mental imagery training in this section, though it might also be regarded as a study skill.

Children not only need to acquire skills that will help them understand better, they also need to be alerted to the necessity of employing them. These skills and strategies, as opposed to study aids, are particularly important in remediation, for two reasons. First, study aids are primarily designed to promote learning rather than comprehension, though, as we have emphasized, they might also help children to understand text. Second, as we stressed above, study aids are only effective for children who can use them properly, and younger and poorer readers are often unable to do so.

Until fairly recently, most research on reading addressed questions about decoding. Teachers have therefore been given a great deal of advice on how to teach word recognition and decoding skills, but little on how to help children to progress from efficient decoding to skilled comprehension. Most children make the transition satisfactorily, but teachers do not have the same degree of control over this phase of learning to read. In teaching the skills necessary for comprehension they must rely more on intuition than on recommendations from research.

Kenneth and Yetta Goodman (1979) and Carl Frederiksen (1979) suggest that many comprehension problems have their origin in early reading programmes. Instruction that emphasizes decoding skills may encourage children to regard reading as a process of identifying words and may interfere with the development of reading comprehension skills. Even the practice of reading aloud may make children think of reading as essentially different from understanding spoken language. The Goodmans and Frederiksen suggest that a better approach would be to teach children the techniques of skilled reading from the start. However, it may be unhelpful or even harmful to deny beginning readers the opportunity to focus on decoding, to which they may need to devote most of their attention for a while. Moreover, several studies carried out in the USA have failed to support the idea that too much emphasis on decoding in the initial stages of reading is detrimental to the development of comprehension skills (see Resnick, 1979). On the other hand, there is no support for the claim that if decoding skills are well learned other reading problems will not arise – programs that emphasize decoding do not solve all reading problems. What appears to be needed is instruction in decoding, together with some attention to comprehension, probably increasing as time goes on, so that children do not get overly rigid ideas about the purpose of reading. Early reading instruction should concentrate on decoding but there should also be some mention of comprehension. Attention to comprehension from the start could be achieved by asking children questions about texts that they have read, giving them plenty of opportunity to read meaningful and enjoyable books of an appropriate level of difficulty, and telling children that the real purpose of recognizing words is to help them to understand whole texts.

Once difficulties with comprehension have arisen, however, one must consider how they can be overcome. If a skill that poor comprehenders lack is *causally* related to their comprehension problems, training in that skill may improve their comprehension (see chapter 5). Joseph Campione and Bonnie Armbruster (1984) describe several possible outcomes of studies that compare trained and untrained groups of good and poor comprehenders. The outcome that suggests a causal role for the trained skill most strongly is when training brings poor comprehenders up to the level of good comprehenders, who remain at the same high level of ability. The good comprehenders presumably do not benefit from training because they already have the skill being trained.

Training in speeded decoding In the last chapter we saw that many people regard decoding speed as a crucial factor in reading comprehension. However, we also saw that attempts to improve comprehension by training in rapid decoding have generally failed (Fleisher, Jenkins and Pany, 1979; Spring, Blunden and Gatheral, 1981; Yuill and Oakhill, in press). Such results suggest that rapid decoding, though necessary for efficient comprehension, may be only one of a number of skills required, and that training in rapid decoding may have no *direct* effect on comprehension – it may need to be trained together with other reading skills. Alternatively, since training in speeded decoding has little effect on comprehension, rapid decoding may be a by-product of practice and skill at reading, rather than vice versa.

Organizational strategies   As we saw in chapter 5, poor comprehenders have trouble 'chunking' text into meaningful units. However, there is very little research on whether training this skill can aid comprehension. Phyllis Weaver (1979) showed that, after only 3½ hours of instruction in unscrambling sentence anagrams (and hence grouping the words in a meaningful way), third graders were not only better than controls on the anagram task but also on cloze tests and on a test of sentence recall. They were not however better on a comprehension test that required them to answer questions about a passage. White, Pascarella and Pflaum (1981) conducted a similar experiment with groups of learning-disabled children (of 10 and 11 years) who were also substantially backward in comprehension. One group of children was given a sentence anagram task, together with training in word grouping – identifying main verbs and other word groups in sentences. The other group engaged in such tasks as identifying sentences as statements, questions or commands, and replacing nouns with pronouns. The group given the anagram/word grouping training showed better performance on a cloze test than did the sentence study group.

Other studies have attempted to teach children sentence combining and sentence reduction – techniques that help them see how several simple ideas can be expressed in a complex sentence, without explicitly teaching them grammatical rules. Such training is intended to improve children's understanding of how the ideas in a text are expressed and related. However, these studies have produced disappointing results, perhaps because training in such skills is only helpful to the comparatively small number of children who have a specific problem with syntax (see Tierney and Cunningham, 1984).

Background knowledge, inferences and question-generation   Less-skilled comprehenders *can* make inferences and use their background knowledge to interpret text (Oakhill, 1982, 1983). They might make more use of these skills if they were more aware of the value of doing so. These children may not understand that they ought to bring their knowledge and experience to bear on the text. One way of encouraging poorer readers to make information explicit that is only implicit in a text would be to train them in the selection of pictures or summary statements that integrate the information in the text. Another way would be for teachers to read and discuss stories with children, with the teacher encouraging the children to make predictions and asking them questions to guide their inference making. Such strategies would also impress upon children the legitimacy of going beyond what is explicit in the text.

Such methods do meet with success. Au (1977: cited by Wittrock, 1981) reports that the reading comprehension of Hawiian children was improved considerably by a one-year training programme that emphasized the construction of meaning from text. The children verbalized their experiences as they read stories and were encouraged to relate what happened in the stories to their background knowledge and to make inferences from the text. Similar methods have helped 11- to 15-year old English children to learn factual materials (Lunzer and Gardner, 1979).

Jane Hansen (1981) tried to train children to be more aware of how their prior knowledge could be used in story comprehension. The subjects were second graders whose reading ability was at or above the level expected for their age. There were three groups: the first (control) group read a series of texts that was followed by a mixture of approximately one inferential to five literal questions; the second group received only questions requiring an inference; the third, 'strategy', group was encouraged, prior to reading, to integrate text and prior knowledge. A weaving metaphor was used to suggest how prior knowledge and information from the text should be put together, and the children were induced to predict what might happen next in the text, using relevant experience of their own. Both the strategy group and the inferential question group showed better performance than the control group, with strategy training tending to be more effective. However, these results held only for the passages used in training and did not transfer to new stories, though there was some improvement on a standardized reading test. These results emphasize the need for children to be taught when to apply newly acquired skills.

Such training procedures may be particularly helpful for children with comprehension problems. Hansen and Pearson (1983) used a training programme, with 9-year-old good and poor comprehenders, that combined Hansen's strategy training with inferential question techniques. Another feature of this study was that training was given by the classroom teachers rather than the experimenter. The training helped the poor readers both in understanding the original passages and in understanding new ones, but there was no training effect, and hence no transfer effect, for good readers. These findings suggest that encouraging children to make inferences can be effective if they are young or if they are poor readers. Older and better readers make inferences spontaneously.

Nicola Yuill and Trish Joscelyne (in press, experiment 2) provide further support for this conclusion. They instructed 7- to 8-year-old skilled and less-skilled comprehenders in how to make inferences from specific words in texts. In their stories, the locations and main consequences were not explicit and had to be inferred. For example, one story was about a boy reading a schoolbook in the bath. He gets soap in his eye and drops the book. The main consequence, that the book fell in the water and got wet, was not explicitly stated, but could be inferred from particular words in the text. Likewise, the setting could be worked out from the use of certain words: the room was 'steamy', the boy was 'lying down', there was 'soap' and a 'towel'. Once it has been inferred that the boy is reading in the bath, the clues to the main consequence, the splash and the boy's exclamation of horror, suggest that he dropped the book in the water. This inference is supported by the further information that the boy was worried about what to tell his teacher, and that he planned to buy a new book. The children were trained to use 'cue words' in the story to infer the missing information. Trained less-skilled comprehenders, but not skilled comprehenders, were significantly better at answering comprehension questions than corresponding control subjects who were given no training.

In a further study of good and poor comprehenders, Yuill and Oakhill (in press) combined training in asking questions about texts with the inference instruction used by Yuill and Joscelyne (in press). Control groups spent the same time either working on standard comprehension exercises or having practice in the rapid decoding of words. The biggest improvement was for less-skilled comprehenders given inference and question-generation training. Their comprehension ages increased by 17 months, on average, over a period of 2 months. This improvement was significantly higher than that of the decoding group (6 months), and slightly, but not significantly, more than that of the comprehension exercise group (13 months). None of the three groups of skilled comprehenders showed much improvement. The improvement of the less-skilled comprehenders is particularly striking since it was measured by a standardized test. Many training studies produce improvements only on the particular skills being trained. For example, we saw in the last chapter that less-skilled comprehenders are poor at understanding anaphoric expressions. However, training them to understand such expressions better has had only very circumscribed effects. For example, Dommes, Gersten and Carnine (1984) gave children explicit training in working out who or what a pronoun referred to. These children learned to perform the task better than children given no training or practice in retelling the main points of the same passages. However, this improvement did not enhance their recall of facts from texts, even though establishing what those facts are often requires that pronouns be understood.

Other studies on self-generated questions have failed to show effects (see Tierney and Cunningham, 1984 for a review). However, as Tierney and Cunningham point out, very few studies have trained students or given them practice in question generation, and in other cases the training procedures have often severely limited the types of question that can be asked. They suggest that further research is needed before any firm conclusions about the usefulness of self-generated questions can be drawn. As Weaver and Shonkoff (1978) argue, only generating factual questions might mean that children need to think very little about what they are reading and are often missing the major points of a text. What is needed, they suggest, is a mixture of questions that require responses at various levels – literal, inferential, interpretive, evaluative, etc.

One of the few studies that has included training in question generation is that by Marli Andre and Thomas Anderson (1978–9). They studied the effects of teaching high-school children to ask questions as they read texts. Some children were simply told to make up and answer questions as they read, while others were instructed in how to formulate the questions and use them in their learning. Both groups did better than a group who just reread the texts, and the group given training in question formulation did best of all. They generated a higher proportion of good comprehension questions, and their comprehension scores on a subsequent test were slightly higher than those of the untrained question group, though not significantly so. In addition, lower ability subjects benefited most from the training. Training in question generation has also been shown to be effective with much younger children. Ruth Cohen (1983) showed that training in question generation, together with instruction in how to apply such skills to reading short stories, improved comprehension of third graders.

Although many of the studies of question generation were of children older than those we are primarily concerned with, the work of Ross and Killey (1977) shows that younger children (9- to 10-year-olds) can also benefit from generating questions. They showed that asking questions about pictures taken from children's books, and being provided with answers to them, improves memory. Furthermore, retention of information was better when that information was acquired through the child's own questions rather than through those asked by another child. Ross and Killey suggest that this effect occurs because children's attention will be more strongly focused on the answers to questions generated by their own curiosity. However, because this study was of memory for information related to pictures (which were accompanied by only a brief descriptive written statement), it may have limited applicability to learning from text.

Michele Linden and Merlin Wittrock (1981), like Yuill and Oakhill, combined different types of comprehension training in an attempt to get children to generate associations from the text and to relate different parts of the text to one another and to background knowledge. They taught 10-year-olds to generate summaries, images, analogies and inferences as they read stories. Such training increased the number of images, analogies, inferences and summary statements that children produced and also improved their comprehension.

We argued in chapter 2 that comprehension is a constructive process, and in chapter 5 that good readers engage in constructive processing more often than poor ones. The results of the studies reviewed above show that relatively simple procedures can increase constructive processing and enhance reading comprehension. A prerequisite for such processing is that children have the relevant prior knowledge to draw inferences and to elaborate on what is explicit in a text. Either texts should relate to the child's existing knowledge, or the necessary background should be provided. However, readers may possess the relevant prior knowledge, but still fail to access and use it in comprehension (see also Oakhill, 1983). Strategies for organizing and retrieving information might also have to be taught.

Training in metacognitive skills   The results of the studies discussed above suggest that children who have a specific comprehension problem may benefit from inference training. However, in those studies the children were usually given guidance about the sorts of questions they were likely to be asked. They were therefore prompted to check whether they understood the central parts of the texts, such as characters' main goals. However, our interviews with poor comprehenders suggest that, when they are not specifically instructed about what they should get out of a text, they are not generally aware of their comprehension problems. For example, they are less likely than skilled comprehenders to notice anomalies in text.[7]

The ability to decide when a text has been understood is a crucial step towards becoming an independent reader. As we saw in the last chapter, poor comprehenders and younger children have inferior metacognitive skills. Young children are often not aware that their understanding is inadequate and that they are poor at detecting omissions or inconsistencies (Markman, 1977). However, work by Heinz Wimmer (1979) has shown that even 4-year-olds are capable of recognizing problems with text under favourable circumstances, and, encouragingly, it appears that training in such skills can be effective. In this section, we discuss some of the studies that have shown how training in metacognitive skills can aid comprehension.

In the last section, we saw that question generation can be used to improve comprehension. Although the ability to generate and answer questions is not itself a metacognitive skill, question generation can be used as part of a metacognitive training program if children are taught to make up questions so that they can find out if they have understood the text. Summarization can also be used in this way, again on the assumption that children learn that trying to identify and recall the important points of a passage provides a check on whether the passage has been adequately understood.

Ron Reis and Nancy Spekman (1983) showed that poor comprehenders from the sixth and seventh grades were considerably better at detecting 'reader-based' inconsistencies (i.e. those that violate what the reader knows about the world) than they were at detecting 'text-based' inconsistencies (conflicting information in the text). In addition, even those children who were very poor at detecting inconsistencies could be trained to do so, but such training only improved their ability to detect reader-based, and not text-based, inconsistencies. Reis and Spekman suggest that poor comprehenders can evaluate their comprehension to some extent, but tend to use different standards to those employed by better readers – they are able to monitor how a text relates to their knowledge about the world, but not whether the text is internally consistent.

Brown, Palincsar and Armbruster (1984) combined training in question generation, summarization, clarification and prediction in a program specifically designed to enhance the metacognitive skills of 12-year-olds with specific comprehension problems. The children were also informed about how and why the activities were important. Their ability to ask effective questions and to produce good summaries improved dramatically during the training period, but again it emerged that fairly extensive training may be necessary before children can incorporate such skills into their repertoire and can use them effectively. The children also showed reliable, lasting improvements on various measures of comprehension, including standardized reading tests, and they generalized their new abilities to classroom tasks. Similar studies by Scott Paris and his associates have also shown that training in meta-cognitive awareness can improve both reading strategies and comprehension. Paris and Jacobs (1984) showed that fifth graders benefited from 4 months' training in 'how, when and why' they should use reading strategies to improve comprehension. In a more extensive study Paris, Cross and Lipson (1984) gave third and fifth graders training in a rich variety of comprehension strategies, including understanding the purpose of the text, attending to main ideas, monitoring comprehension and drawing inferences. They found that the children given such training performed better on cloze comprehension and error-detection tasks, though not on standardized comprehension tests.

Another comprehension aid that could be used to encourage comprehension monitoring is mental imagery. For instance, Bales (1984) showed that below-average fourth and fifth grade readers could benefit from mental imagery instructions. The children given the imagery instructions were told to 'make pictures in your head to help you determine if there is anything not clear or not easy to understand'. Compared with a control group who were told to 'do whatever you can to help you determine if there is anything not clear or not easy to understand', the imagery group were able to detect more of the inconsistencies in a text. These findings suggest that imagery can act as a monitoring strategy, and that poor readers can use it.

Allan Collins and Edward Smith (1982) argue more generally that in teaching children to read, too little emphasis is placed on the *process* of deriving an interpretation of a text. They suggest a three-stage programme of training in comprehension monitoring and predictive skills. In the first, 'modelling', stage the teacher takes the lead, reading stories and commenting on various aspects of what is entailed in understanding them. For example, the teacher generates hypotheses about the text, points out sources of difficulty and how to overcome them, and comments on ways of gaining insight into the text. During this stage, the teacher gradually encourages the children to take part in these activities, in preparation for the next, 'student participation', stage. In this stage, the teacher shifts the responsibility for generating hypotheses and for spotting and remedying comprehension failures to the children. In the final, 'read silently', stage, the children are expected to use the skills they have learned when reading to themselves. Collins and Smith suggest that children can be encouraged to use these skills by giving them texts with problems to spot, or texts with questions that encourage them to predict what will happen next.

Ellen Markman (1981) points out several ways in which children's comprehension monitoring might be fostered. First, she suggests that children should be given practice in formulating expectations: predicting words and consequences of causal sequences, and otherwise generating hypotheses about the text. Second, children should be given practice at making and evaluating possible inferences from the text – explaining why some follow and others do not. Lastly, children could be trained to examine texts for inconsistencies and errors. Their own writing could provide material for such analysis. It may also provide clues about their conception of reading: as children become less egocentric they should become increasingly aware of their readers' needs and expectations, and should adjust their writing accordingly.

Imagery   In the preceding section we discussed the use of imagery to improve comprehension monitoring, but suggesting that subjects form mental images of the events in the text can also improve comprehension itself. Forming images has certain similarities to looking at pictures (see Schallert, 1980), but the effect of imagery is typically smaller than that of illustrations (Levin, 1981). Imagery may help comprehension by maintaining attention, or it may promote deeper semantic processing of the text.

Sandra Steingart and Marvin Glock (1979) showed that imagery instructions increased the number of inferences made by adults and improved their recall of texts. Imagery instruction has also proved successful with children. For instance, Michael Pressley (1976) taught 8-year-olds to generate images for sections of stories as they read. Compared to children who only read the story, those who produced images were better able to answer questions about the story, even though both groups spent a similar amount of time studying it.

The ability to use imagery instructions improves with age. Only when children reach about 8 can they learn to use self-generated images to improve their comprehension of stories (see Wittrock, 1981 for a review). For example, Guttman, Levin and Pressley (1977) found that the reading comprehension of third graders, but not kindergarteners, could be improved by imagery instructions or by the kind of 'partial picture' used by Ruch and Levin (1977). The children who saw the partial pictures were told to use them to help to construct an image of what they could not see. In contrast, the same study showed that children from kindergarten, first and third grades all recalled more information when complete pictures illustrated the stories, and that the amount of improvement was similar at all three ages.

By age 10 children benefit from simply being told to use mental images, but between 8 and 10 they need to be *taught* an imagery strategy. However, as with many of the other comprehension aids, imagery instructions do not always enhance comprehension, even for children older than 9 (see Levin, 1981, for a review). Levin argues that part of the reason for these discrepancies is that not all types of image are equally helpful, and that different types of passage and different subject matter may call for different types of image. Peters et al. (1985) discuss forms of imagery instructions that might be suitable for different passages.

Some children seem to derive special benefit from visual imagery instructions – in particular, those children with adequate word recognition skills who nevertheless have comprehension problems. Levin (1973) tested two groups of fourth grade poor comprehenders – those with decoding and vocabulary problems (the 'deficit' group of W. Cromer 1970) and those with adequate vocabulary skills (Cromer's 'difference' group). Both groups were given a text and were told to try to think of a picture in their mind for each sentence as they read it. The difference group improved substantially with the imagery instructions, but the deficit group did not.

Reading and listening   As we discussed in the last chapter, the ability to understand spoken language is closely related to reading comprehension skill, once decoding skills have been acquired. It is not surprising, therefore, that training in listening comprehension also helps with reading. Sticht et al. (1974, cited by Jenkins and Pany, 1981) reviewed twelve studies of training in listening comprehension. In ten of them there were improvements in reading ability of a similar magnitude to those found in listening. These studies provided instruction in vocabulary along with such skills as recalling events, extracting main ideas, predicting outcomes, drawing conclusions and making inferences. Thus, training that expands children's general facility with language is likely to have beneficial effects on reading comprehension as well.

Reading and reasoning   Another way of improving comprehension might be to give instruction in reasoning tasks that are not normally associated with reading. Learning to think and learning to read are inextricably related (see E. Thorndike, 1917; R.L. Thorndike 1973–74), so an increase in general thinking skills might be accompanied by a corresponding increase in comprehension ability. A number of programmes in the USA (e.g. Whimbey and Lochhead, 1980) are designed to teach logical reasoning together with awareness of reasoning processes, but the extent to which such skills are applied in situations such as reading where *spontaneous* reasoning is required has not been assessed. Moreover, there may be restrictions on the extent to which the ability to make inferences can be trained, since that ability depends on the relatively unalterable capacity of working memory. So, at any particular age, there may be a limit to how much less-skilled comprehenders' performance can be improved. More research is needed on the extent to which inferences necessary for text comprehension are restricted by limitations on working memory, on how such limitations change with age, and on which reasoning strategies, if any, are effective in improving children's comprehension.

FINAL REMARKS

We have not provided an exhaustive survey of the many different learning aids and strategies, but we hope we have given some idea of how comprehension might be improved, and which aids and training procedures are likely to be successful with children of different ages. There is obviously no 'best' aid or strategy that can be recommended, and, as we have seen, effects are often crucially dependent on the type and length of training given. An important consideration in educational settings is that some of the methods are more practicable than others. Furthermore, in many ways it is better to spend time teaching children general comprehension strategies than to focus on adjuncts such as pictures and subtitles that many texts do not have.

We end this chapter with three notes of caution. First, most methods for improving comprehension are based on the assumption that less-skilled readers will benefit from being taught to use strategies that skilled readers use naturally. However, the fact that poor comprehenders have not acquired these strategies might indicate, at least in some cases, that they are unable to acquire them. For example, asking questions about causes and effects ought to promote comprehension because it encourages or forces readers to find connections between events. But if some children are not capable of identifying those connections (or not capable of identifying them when they hold between events described in a text), they may not benefit from training designed to make them more like good comprehenders. In such cases, training programmes are doomed to failure. The study by Brown and Smiley (1978) provides a further illustration of this 'chicken-and-egg' problem. The children who learned best were those who spontaneously took notes or underlined, but less proficient learners did not benefit from the suggestion that they should use these strategies. We are not wanting to sound a note of despair; indeed, since Brown and Smiley did not use extensive training, it is possible that poor comprehenders can learn how to make good notes. We are simply pointing out that the efficacy of training programmes must be proved. It cannot be assumed that poor comprehenders will become good ones if they are 'taught' the skills that good comprehenders possess.

Second, as Yussen (1982) points out, instruction in skills such as comprehension monitoring should be restricted to children who have reached the stage where they are reading to learn. Introducing such training when children have not yet mastered decoding may be counterproductive because they may not have enough processing capacity to learn both aspects of reading together. It is therefore sensible to wait until decoding skills are reasonably proficient before introducing training in comprehension strategies. This view is not in conflict with the idea put forward in earlier in this chapter that children should learn from the outset that comprehension is the *purpose* of reading. The claim is only that *training in conscious comprehension strategies* should not be introduced too early.

Third, we pointed out earlier that the training programmes discussed in the latter part of this chapter have the advantage that they are not restricted to specific texts. Once learned they can, in principle, be applied to any text. However, Tierney and Cunningham (1984) caution against training that puts into practice a theorist's prescriptive beliefs about the 'right' way to read, particularly beliefs about strategies that readers 'should' adopt. We do not yet know enough about reading strategies to make such prescriptions. However, what we can do is to try to induce children to develop strategies for themselves that lead to the required end product – comprehension.

Notes

1. Readers interested in the more technical aspects of test construction are referred to Vincent and Cresswell's (1976) book or to Johnston's (1983, 1984) more recent work.
2. See Jorm (1983, p. 114–117) for a fuller discussion of the evaluation of remediation studies.
3. For a review see Schallert (1980).
4. See Levin (1981), Rusted (1984), Schallert (1980).
5. See, for example, Chiesi, Spilich and Voss (1979), Spilich, Vesonder, Chiesi and Voss (1979).
6. A more extensive discussion of the text-based aids we have discussed and a variety of others can be found in Tierney and Cunningham (1984).
7. See, for example, Oakhill, Yuill and Parkin (1987), see also chapter 5.
8. See Wittrock (1981), for a review.

Afterword

Literacy opens doors, and minds. But becoming a skilled reader is a far more difficult task than becoming a fluent user of spoken language. Far too many of our children are still failing to acquire a satisfactory degree of literacy.

It is our belief that a better understanding of the mental processes that underlie the ability to read can provide the foundation for better educational practices. We are not, of course, under the delusion that they automatically will. The gap between theory and practice is a large one, and one that must be bridged by people with practical experience. What we *are* convinced of is that, given good-will on both sides, practitioners of reading education have better long-term prospects of instilling literacy if they have a sound understanding of the psychology of reading, in the broadest sense of that term.

In this book we have tried, among other things, to provide that. We have described, in chapter 2, the abilities of the skilled adult reader, and discussed, in chapter 3, those linguistic abilities of beginning readers that might affect their reading. We have also provided an account of what is known more specifically about how children learn to read, summarizing, in chapter 4, the vast literature on learning to read words, but focusing, in chapter 5, on the comparatively neglected topic of reading comprehension. In chapter 6 we provided some pointers to the way that children might be taught to improve their comprehension.

One of our aims has been to draw attention to the problems of children like Nicola, who we introduced in chapter 1. Nicola can read stories out loud fluently, but she can hardly understand those stories at all. Unlike Warren, whose difficulty in identifying and saying printed words is widely recognized, Nicola's problems are in danger of going unnoticed. By focusing on comprehension, and by emphasizing that children may not realize that written language conveys information in much the same way as spoken language, we hope to have gone some way toward fulfilling this aim. Decoding and comprehension are the two main sets of abilities that skilled readers must acquire. We hope we have shown that, for both psychologists and educationalists alike, comprehension skills deserve the attention that has traditionally been reserved for decoding.

References

Ackerman, B.P. 1984: The effects of storage and processing complexity on comprehension repair in children and adults. *Journal of Experimental Child Psychology, 37*, 303-334.

Adams, M.J. 1980: Failures to comprehend and levels of processing in reading. In R.J. Spiro, B.C. Bruce, and W.F. Brewer (eds), *Theoretical Issues in Reading Comprehension*. Hillsdale, N.J.: Lawrence Erlbaum Associates.

Alvermann, D.E. 1984: Second graders' strategic preferences while reading basal stories. *Journal of Educational Research, 77*, 184-189.

Amidon, A. and Carey, P. 1972: Why five-year-olds cannot understand before and after. *Journal of Verbal Learning and Verbal Behavior, 11*, 417-423.

Anderson, T.H. 1980: Study strategies and adjunct aids. In R.J. Spiro, B.C. Bruce and W.F. Brewer (eds), *Theoretical Issues in Reading Comprehension*. Hillsdale, N.J.: Lawrence Erlbaum Associates.

Anderson, T.H. and Armbruster, B.B. 1984: Studying. In P.D. Pearson (ed.), *Handbook of Reading Research*. New York: Longman.

Anderson, R.C. and Biddle, W.B. 1975: On asking people questions about what they are reading. In G.H. Bower (ed.), *The Psychology of Learning and Motivation, vol. 9*. New York: Academic Press.

Anderson, R.C. and Freebody, P. 1983: Reading comprehension and word knowledge. In B.A. Hutson (ed.), *Advances in Reading/Language Research*. Greenwich, Conn.: JAI Press.

Anderson, R.C. and Ortony, A. 1975: On putting apples into bottles: A problem of polysemy. *Cognitive Psychology, 7*, 167-180.

Anderson, R.C. and Pichert, J.W. 1978: Recall of previously unrecallable information following a shift in perspective. *Journal of Verbal Learning and Verbal Behavior, 17*, 1-12.

Anderson, R.C., Stevens, K., Shifrin, Z. and Osborn, J.H. 1977: *Instantiation of Word Meanings in Children*. Technical Report No. 46. Urbana: University of Illinois, Center for the Study of Reading.

Anderson, R.C., Pichert, J.W., Goetz, E.T., Schallert, D.L., Stevens, K. and Trollip, S.R. 1976: Instantiation of general terms. *Journal of Verbal Learning and Verbal Behavior, 15*, 667-679.

Andre, M.E.D.A. and Anderson, T.H. 1978: The development and evaluation of a self-questioning study technique. *Reading Research Quarterly, 14*, 605-623.

Arnold, D.S. and Brooks, P.H. 1976: Influence of contextual organizing

174

material on children's listening comprehension. *Journal of Educational Psychology, 68*, 711-716.

Asch, S.E. and Nerlove, H. 1960: The development of double function terms in children: An exploratory study. In B. Kaplan and S. Wapner (eds), *Perspectives in Psychological Theory: Essays in Honour of Heinz Werner*. New York: International Humanities Press.

Au, K. 1977: Cognitive training and reading achievement. Paper presented at the meeting of the Association of the Advancement of Behavior Therapy, Atlanta, Georgia.

Austin, J.L. 1962: *How to Do Things with Words*. Oxford: Oxford University Press (edited by J.O. Urmson).

Ausubel, D.P. 1963: *The Psychology of Meaningful Verbal Learning*. New York: Grune and Stratton.

Baddeley, A.D. 1986: *Working Memory*. Oxford: Oxford University Press.

Baddeley, A.D., Logie, R., Nimmo-Smith, I. and Brereton, N. 1985: Components of fluent reading. *Journal of Memory and Language, 24*, 119-131.

Baker, L. 1984a: Spontaneous versus instructed use of multiple standards for evaluating comprehension: Effects of age, reading proficiency, and type of standard. *Journal of Experimental Child Psychology, 38*, 289-311.

Baker, L. 1984b: Children's effective use of multiple standards for evaluating their comprehension. *Journal of Educational Psychology, 76*, 588-597.

Baker, L. and Brown, A.L. 1984: Metacognitive skills and reading. In P.D. Pearson (ed.), *Handbook of Reading Research*. New York: Plenum Press.

Baker, L. and Stein, N.L. 1981: The development of prose comprehension skills. In C. Santa and B. Hayes (eds), *Children's Prose Comprehension: Research and Practice*. Newark, Del.: International Reading Association.

Baldie, B.J. 1976: The acquisition of the passive voice. *Journal of Child Language, 3*, 331-348.

Bales, R.E.J. 1984: *Induced mental imagery and the comprehension monitoring of poor readers*. Ed.D. thesis, University of Maryland.

Barr, R.C. 1972: The influence of instructional conditions on word recognition errors. *Reading Research Quarterly, 7*, 509-529.

Barr, R.C. 1974-5: The effect of instruction on pupil reading strategies. *Reading Research Quarterly, 10*, 555–582.

Barrett, T.C. 1976: Taxonomy of reading comprehension. In R. Smith and T.C. Barrett (eds), *Teaching Reading in the Middle Grades*. Reading, Mass.: Addison Wesley.

Barron, R.W. 1978: Reading skill and phonological coding in lexical access. In M.M. Gruneberg, R.N. Sykes and P.E. Morris (eds), *Proceedings of the International Conference on Practical Aspects of Memory*. London: Academic Press.

Barron, R.W. and Baron, J. 1977: How children get meaning from printed words. *Child Development, 48*, 587-594.

Bartlett, F.C. 1932: *Remembering: A Study in Experimental and Social Psychology*. Cambridge: Cambridge University Press.

Bean, T.W. and Steenwyk, F.L. 1984: The effect of three forms of summarization instruction on sixth graders' summary writing and comprehension. *Journal of Reading Behavior, 16*, 297-306.

Beaumont, C. 1982: Reading relative clauses. *Journal of Research in Reading, 5*, 29–42.

Beck, I.L. and McKeown, M.G. 1986: Instructional research in reading: A retrospective. In J. Orasanu (ed.), *Reading Comprehension: From Research to Practice*. Hillsdale, N.J.: Lawrence Erlbaum Associates.

Beck, I.L., Omanson, R.C. and McKeown, M.G. 1982: An instructional redesign of reading lessons: Effects on comprehension. *Reading Research Quarterly, 17*, 462-481.

Beck, I.L., Perfetti, C.A. and McKeown, M.G. 1982: Effects of long-term vocabulary instruction on lexical access and reading comprehension. *Journal of Educational Psychology, 74*, 506-521.

Beck, I.L., McKeown, M.G., Omanson, R.C. and Pople, M.T. 1984: Improving the comprehensibility of stories: The effects of revisions that improve coherence. *Reading Research Quarterly, 19*, 263–277.

Becker, C.A. 1979: Semantic context and word frequency effects in visual word recognition. *Journal of Experimental Psychology: Human Perception and Performance, 3*, 389-401.

Berger, N.S. 1978: Why can't John read? Perhaps he's not a good listener. *Journal of Learning Disabilities, 11*, 633-638.

Bever, T.G. 1970: The cognitive basis for linguistic structures. In J.R. Hayes (ed.), *Cognition and the Development of Language*. New York: Wiley.

Biemiller, A. 1970: The development of the use of graphic and contextual information as children learn to read. *Reading Research Quarterly, 6*, 75-96.

Bissex, G.L. 1980: *GNYS AT WRK: A Child Learns to Write and Read*. Cambridge, Mass.: Harvard University Press.

Black, J.B. and Wilensky, R. 1979: An evaluation of story grammars. *Cognitive Science, 3*, 213-230.

Blank, M. 1985: Language and school failure: Some speculations about the relationship between oral and written language. In M.M. Clark (ed.), *New Directions in the Study of Reading*. London: Falmer Press.

Bormuth, J.R., Manning, J., Carr, J. and Pearson, D. 1970: Children's comprehension of between- and within-sentence syntactic structures. *Journal of Educational Psychology, 61*, 349-357.

Bower, G.H. 1978: Experiments on story comprehension and recall. *Discourse Processes, 1*, 211-231.

Bower, G.H., Black, J.B. and Turner, T.J. 1979: Scripts in memory for text. *Cognitive Psychology, 11*, 177-220.

Bradley, L. (in press): Making connections in learning to read and spell. *Applied Cognitive Psychology*.

Bradley, L. and Bryant, P.E. 1978: Difficulties in auditory organisation as a possible cause of reading backwardness. *Nature, 271*, 746-747.

Bradley, L. and Bryant, P.E. 1983: Categorising sounds and learning to read: A causal connexion. *Nature, 301*, 419-421.

Bradley, L. and Bryant, P.E. 1985: *Rhyme and Reason in Reading and Spelling*. Ann Arbor: University of Michigan Press.

Bransford, J.D. and Johnson, M.K. 1972: Contextual prerequisites for understanding: Some investigations of comprehension and recall. *Journal of Verbal Learning and Verbal Behavior, 11*, 717-726.

Bransford, J.D., Barclay, J.R. and Franks, J.J. 1972: Sentence memory: A constructive versus interpretive approach. *Cognitive Psychology, 3*, 193–209.

Bransford, J.D. and McCarrell, N.S. 1975: A sketch of a cognitive approach to comprehension: Some thoughts about understanding what it means to comprehend. In W.B. Weimar and D.S. Palermo (eds.) *Cognition and the Symbolic Processes*. Hillsdale, NJ: Lawrence Erlbaum Associates.

Brooks, L. 1977: Visual pattern in fluent word identification. In A.S. Reber and D.L. Scarborough (eds), *Toward a Psychology of Reading*. Hillsdale, N.J.: Lawrence Erlbaum Associates.

Brown, A.L., Day, J.D. and Jones, R.S. 1983: The development of plans for summarizing texts. *Child Development, 54*, 968-979.

Brown, A.L. and Smiley, S.S. 1977: Rating the importance of structural units of prose passages: A problem of metacognitive development. *Child Development, 48*, 1-8.

Brown, A.L. and Smiley, S.S. 1978: The development of strategies for studying prose passages. *Child Development, 49*, 1076-1088.

Brown, A.L., Palincsar, A.S. and Armbruster, B.B. 1984: Instructing comprehension–fostering activities in interactive learning situations. In H. Mandl, N.L. Stein, and T. Trabasso (eds), *Learning and Comprehension of Text*. Hillsdale, N.J.: Lawrence Erlbaum Associates.

Brown, A.L., Smiley, S.S., Day, J., Townsend, H. and Lawton, S.C. 1977: Intrusion of a thematic idea in children's recall of prose. *Child Development, 48*, 1454-1466.

Bruce, D.J. 1964: The analysis of word sounds by children. *British Journal of Educational Psychology, 34*, 158-170.

Bryant, P.E. and Bradley, L. 1985: *Children's Reading Problems: Psychology and Education*. Oxford: Blackwell.

Byrne, B. 1981: Deficient syntactic control in poor readers: Is a weak phonetic memory code responsible? *Applied Psycholinguistics, 2*, 201-12.

Calfee, R.C., Arnold, R. and Drum. P.A. 1976: A review of *The Psychology of Reading* by E. Gibson and H. Levin. *Proceedings of the National Academy of Education, 3*, 1-80.

Calfee, R.C., Chapman, R. and Venezky, R. 1972: How a child needs to think to learn to read. In L.W. Gregg (ed.), *Cognition in Learning and Memory*. New York: Wiley.

Cambon, J. and Sinclair, H. 1974: Relations between syntax and semantics: Are they 'easy to see'? *British Journal of Psychology, 65*, 133-140.

Campione, J.C. and Armbruster, B.B. 1984: An analysis of the outcomes and implications of intervention research. In H. Mandl, N.L. Stein and T. Trabasso (eds), *Learning and Comprehension of Text*. Hillsdale, N.J.: Lawrence Erlbaum Asssociates.

Canney, G. and Schreiner, R. 1977: A study of the effectiveness of selected syllabication rules and phonogram patterns for word attack. *Reading Research Quarterly, 12*, 102-124.

Canney, G. and Winograd, P. 1979: *Schemata for Reading and Reading Comprehension Performance*. Technical Report No. 120, Urbana: University of Illinois, Center for the Study of Reading.

Carroll, J.B. and Walton, M. 1979: Has the reel reading prablum bin lade bear? Summary comments on the theory and practice of early reading. In L.B. Resnick and P.A. Weaver (eds), *Theory and Practice of Early Reading, vol. 3*. Hillsdale, N.J.: Lawrence Erlbaum Associates.

Case, R., Kurland, D.M. and Goldberg, J. 1982: Operational efficiency and the growth of short-term memory span. *Journal of Experimental Child Psychology, 33*, 386-404.

Chabot, R.J., Petros, T.V. and McCord, G. 1983: Developmental and reading ability differences in accessing information from semantic memory. *Journal of Experimental Child Psychology, 35*, 128-142.

Chall, J.S. 1967: *Learning to Read: The Great Debate.* New York: McGraw Hill.

Chall, J.S. 1979: The great debate: Ten years later, with a modest proposal for reading stages. In L.B. Resnick and P.A. Weaver (eds), *Theory and Practice of Early Reading, vol. 1.* Hillsdale, N.J.: Lawrence Erlbaum Associates.

Chapman, L.J. 1981: Introduction. In L.J. Chapman (ed.), *The Reader and the Text.* London: Heinemann Educational Books.

Charniak, E. 1972: *Toward a Model of Children's Story Comprehension.* Unpublished Ph.D. dissertation and Technical Report AI-TR-266. Boston, Mass.: Massachusetts Institute of Technology.

Chi, M.T.H. 1976: Short-term memory limitations in children: Capacity or processing deficits? *Memory and Cognition, 4*, 559-572.

Chiesi, H.L., Spilich, G.J. and Voss, J.F. 1979: Acquisition of domain-related information in relation to high and low domain knowledge. *Journal of Verbal Learning and Verbal Behavior, 18*, 257-274.

Chomsky, C. 1969: *The acquisition of syntax in children from five to ten.* Cambridge, Mass.: MIT Press.

Chomsky, C. 1979: Approaching reading through invented spelling. In L.B. Resnick and P.A. Weaver (eds), *Theory and Practice of Early Reading, vol. 2.* Hillsdale, N.J.: Lawrence Erlbaum Associates.

Clark, H.H. 1977: Bridging. In P.N. Johnson-Laird and P.C. Wason (eds), *Thinking: Readings in Cognitive Science.* Cambridge: Cambridge University Press.

Clark, M.M. 1976: *Young Fluent Readers.* London: Heineman Educational.

Clay, M.M. 1966: *Emergent Reading Behaviour.* Unpublished doctoral disseration. University of Auckland, New Zealand.

Clay, M.M. 1969: Reading errors and self-correction behaviour. *British Journal of Educational Psychology, 39*, 47-56.

Clay, M.M. and Imlach, R.H. 1971: Juncture, pitch, and stress as reading behavior variables. *Journal of Verbal Learning and Verbal Behavior, 10*, 133-139.

Clifton, C., Frazier, L. and Connine, C. 1984: Lexical expectations in sentence comprehension. *Journal of Verbal Learning and Verbal Behavior, 23*, 696-708.

Cohen, R. 1983: Self-generated questions as an aid to reading comprehension. *The Reading Teacher, 36*, 770-775.

Collins, A. and Smith, E.E. 1982: Teaching the process of reading comprehension. In D.K. Detterman and R.J. Sternberg (eds), *How and How Much Can Intelligence Be Increased.* Norwood, N.J.: Ablex.

Coltheart, M. 1979: When can children learn to read – and when should they be taught? In T.G. Waller and G.E. MacKinnon (eds), *Reading Research: Advances in Theory and Practice, vol. 1.* New York: Academic Press.

Coltheart, V., Laxon, V.J., Keating, G.C. and Pool, M.M. 1986: Direct access and phonological encoding processes in children's reading: Effects of word characteristics. *British Journal of Educational Psychology, 56*, 255-270.

Conrad, R. 1972: Speech and reading. In J.F. Kavanagh and I.G. Mattingly (eds), *Language by Ear and by Eye: The Relationships between Speech and Reading.* Cambridge, Mass.: MIT Press.

Corbett, A.T. and Dosher, B.A. 1978: Instrument inferences in sentence encoding. *Journal of Verbal Learning and Verbal Behavior, 17*, 479-491.

Corrigan, R. 1975: Scalogram analysis of the development of the use and comprehension of 'Because' in children. *Child Development, 46*, 195-201.

Craik, F.I.M. and ·Tulving, E. 1975: Depth of processing and the retention of words in episodic memory. *Journal of Experimental Psychology: General, 104*, 268-294.

Crain, S. and Steedman, M.J. 1985: On not being led up the garden path: The use of context by the psychological parser. In D. Dowty, L. Karttunen and A. Zwicky (eds), *Natural Language Parsing*. Cambridge: Cambridge University Press.

Cromer, R. 1970: 'Children are nice to understand': Surface structure clues for the recovery of a deep structure. *British Journal of Psychology, 61*, 397-408.

Cromer, W. 1970: The difference model: A new explanation for some reading difficulties. *Journal of Educational Psychology, 61*, 471-483.

Crowder, R.G. 1982: *The Psychology of Reading: An Introduction*. Oxford: Oxford University Press.

Cruttenden, A. 1979: *Language in Infancy and Childhood*. Manchester: Manchester University Press.

Crystal, D. 1976: *Child Language, Learning and Linguistics*. London: Edward Arnold.

Cunningham, P.M., Cunningham, J.W. and Rystrom, R.C. 1981: A new syllabication strategy and reading achievement. *Reading World, 20*, 208-214.

Curtis, M.E. 1980: Development of components of reading skill. *Journal of Educational Psychology, 72*, 656-669.

Daneman, M. and Carpenter, P.A. 1980: Individual differences in working memory and reading. *Journal of Verbal Learning and Verbal Behavior, 19*, 450-466.

Daneman, M. and Carpenter, P.A. 1983: Individual differences in integrating information between and within sentences. *Journal of Experimental Psychology: Learning, Memory and Cognition, 9*, 561-584.

Danner, F.W. 1976: Children's understanding of intersentence organization in the recall of short descriptive passages. *Journal of Educational Psychology, 68*, 174-183.

Davis, F.B. 1972: Psychometric research on comprehension in reading. *Reading Research Quarterly, 7*, 628-678.

de Villiers, J.G., Tager Flusberg, H.B., Hakuta, K. and Cohen, M. 1979: Children's comprehension of relative clauses. *Journal of Psycholinguistic Research, 8*, 499-518.

DES (Department of Education and Science) 1975: *A Language for Life*. [The Bullock Report] London: HMSO.

Deutsch, W., Koster, C. and Koster, J. 1986: What can we learn from children's errors in understanding anaphora? *Linguistics, 24*, 203-225.

van Dijk, T.A. 1972: *Some Aspects of Text Grammars*. The Hague: Mouton.

van Dijk, T.A. and Kintsch, W. 1983: *Strategies of Discourse Comprehension*. New York: Academic Press.

Doctor, E. and Coltheart, M. 1980: Phonological recoding in children's reading for meaning. *Memory and Cognition, 8*, 195-209.

Doctorow, M., Wittrock, M.C. and Marks, C. 1978: Generative processes in reading comprehension. *Journal of Educational Psychology, 70*, 109-118.

Dommes, P., Gersten, R. and Carnine, D. 1984: Instructional procedures for increasing skill-deficient fourth graders' comprehension of syntactic structures. *Educational Psychology, 4*, 155-165.

Donaldson, M. 1978: *Children's Minds.* Glasgow: Collins.

Donaldson, M. and Balfour, G. 1968: Less is more: A study of language comprehension in children. *British Journal of Psychology, 59*, 461-471.

Donaldson, M. and Reid, J. 1985: Language skills and reading: A developmental perspective. In M.M. Clark (ed.), *New Directions in the Study of Reading.* London: Falmer Press.

Dooling, D.J. and Lachman, R. 1971: Effects of comprehension on the retention of prose. *Journal of Experimental Psychology, 88*, 216-222.

Dooling, D.J. and Mullet, R.L. 1973: Locus of thematic effects in retention of prose. *Journal of Experimental Psychology, 97*, 404-406.

Downing, J. 1967: *The i.t.a. Symposium: Research Report on the British Experiment with i.t.a.* Slough: National Foundation for Educational Research.

Downing, J. 1970: Children's concepts of language in learning to read. *Educational Research, 12*, 106-112.

Downing, J. and Thackray, D.V. 1975: *Reading Readiness.* London: Hodder and Stoughton.

Drahozal, E.C. and Hanna, G.S. 1978: Reading comprehension subscores: Pretty bottles for ordinary wine. *Journal of Reading, 21*, 416-420.

Durkin, K. 1986: *Language Development in the School Years.* London: Croom Helm.

Durkin, K., Crowther, R.D. and Shire, B. 1986: Children's processing of polysemous vocabulary in school. In K. Durkin (ed.) *Language Development in the School Years.* London: Croom Helm.

Eamon, D.B. 1978-79: Selection and recall of topical information in prose by better and poorer readers. *Reading Research Quarterly, 14*, 224-257.

Ehri, L.C. 1975: Word consciousness in readers and prereaders. *Journal of Educational Psychology, 67*, 204-212.

Ehri, L.C. 1979: Linguistic insight: Threshold of reading acquisition. In T.G. Waller and G.E. MacKinnon (eds), *Reading Research: Advances in Theory and Practice, vol. 1.* New York: Academic Press.

Einstein, G.O., Morris, J. and Smith, S. 1985: Note-taking, individual differences, and memory for lecture information. *Journal of Educational Psychology, 77*, 522-532.

Elkonin, D.B. 1973: USSR. In J. Downing (ed.), *Comparative Reading: Cross-National Studies of Behavior and Processes in Reading and Writing.* New York: Macmillan.

Elliot, A. 1981: *Child Language.* Cambridge: Cambridge University Press.

Ellis, N. and Large, B. (in press) The early stages of reading: A longitudinal study. *Applied Cognitive Psychology, 2.*

Entwistle, D.R., Forsyth, D.F. and Muuss, R. 1964: The syntagmatic–paradigmatic shift in children's word associations. *Journal of Verbal Learning and Verbal Behavior, 3*, 19-29.

Erikson, D., Mattingly, I.G. and Turvey, M.T. 1973: Phonetic activity in reading: An experiment with kanji. *Haskins Laboratory Status Report on Speech Research, 33*, 137-156.

Evans, M., Taylor, N. and Blum, I. 1979: Children's written language awareness and its relation to reading acquisition. *Journal of Reading Behavior, 11*, 7-19.

Ervin, S.M. and Foster, G. 1960: The development of meaning in children's descriptive terms. *Journal of Abnormal and Social Psychology, 61*, 271-275.

Ferreira, F. and Clifton, C. 1986: The independence of syntactic processing. *Journal of Memory and Language, 25*, 348-368.

Flagg, P.W. and Reynolds, A.G. 1977: Modality of presentation and blocking in sentence recognition memory. *Memory and Cognition, 5*, 111-115.

Fleisher, L.S., Jenkins, J.R. and Pany, D. 1979: Effects on poor readers' comprehension of training in rapid decoding. *Reading Research Quarterly, 15*, 30-48.

Flores d'Arcais, G.B. 1978: The acquisition of subordinating constructions in child language. In R.N. Campbell and P.T. Smith (eds), *Language Development and Mother-Child Interaction*. New York: Plenum Press.

Flores d'Arcais, G.B. 1981: The acquisition of meaning of the connectives. In W. Deutsch (ed.), *The Child's Construction of Language*. London: Academic Press.

Forster, K.I. 1976: Accessing the mental lexicon. In R.J. Wales and E.C.T. Walker (eds), *New Approaches to Language Mechanisms*. Amsterdam: North Holland.

Fox, B. and Routh, D.K. 1975: Analyzing spoken language into words, syllables and phonemes: A developmental study. *Journal of Psycholinguistic Research, 4*, 331-342.

Frederiksen, C.H. 1979: Discourse comprehension and early reading. In L.B. Resnick and P.A. Weaver (eds), *Theory and Practice of Early Reading, vol. 1*. Hillsdale, N.J.: Lawrence Erlbaum Associates.

Frederiksen, J.R. 1978: Assessment of perceptual, decoding and lexical skills and their relation to reading proficiency. In A.M. Lesgold, J.W. Pellegrino, S.D. Fokkema and R. Glaser (eds), *Cognitive Psychology and Instruction*. New York: Plenum.

Garner, R. 1980: Monitoring of understanding: An investigation of good and poor readers' awareness of induced miscomprehension of text. *Journal of Reading Behavior, 12*, 55-63.

Garner, R. 1981: Monitoring of passage inconsistency among poor comprehenders: A preliminary test of the 'piecemeal processing' explanation. *Journal of Educational Research, 74*, 159-162.

Garner, R. 1987: *Metacognition and Reading Comprehension*. Norwood, N.J.: Ablex.

Garner, R. and Kraus, C. 1981-2: Good and poor comprehender differences in knowing and regulating reading behaviors. *Educational Research Quarterly, 6*, 5-12.

Garner, R. and Reis, R. 1981: Monitoring and resolving comprehension obstacles: An investigation of spontaneous text lookbacks among upper-grade good and poor comprehenders. *Reading Research Quarterly, 16*, 569-582.

Garnham, A. 1979: Instantiation of verbs. *Quarterly Journal of Experimental Psychology, 31*, 207-214.

Garnham, A. 1981: Mental models as representations of text. *Memory and Cognition, 9*, 560-565.

Garnham, A. 1982: Testing psychological theories about inference making. *Memory and Cognition, 10*, 341-349.

Garnham, A. 1983: What's wrong with story grammars. *Cognition, 15,* 145-154.

Garnham, A. 1985: *Psycholinguistics: Central Topics.* London: Methuen.

Garnham, A. and Oakhill, J.V. 1985: On-line resolution of anaphoric pronouns: Effects of inference making and verb semantics. *British Journal of Psychology, 76,* 385-393.

Garnham, A., Oakhill, J.V. and Johnson-Laird, P.N. 1982: Referential continuity and the coherence of discourse. *Cognition, 11,* 29-46.

Gattengo, C. 1969: *Reading with Words in Colour: A Scientific Study of the Problem of Reading.* Reading: Educational Explorers.

Gelb, I.J. 1963: *A Study of Writing* (2nd edn). Chicago: Chicago University Press.

Gibson, E.J. and Levin, H. 1975: *The Psychology of Reading.* London: MIT Press.

Gitomer, D.H., Pellegrino, J.W. and Bisanz, J. 1983: Developmental change and invariance in semantic processing. *Journal of Experimental Child Psychology, 35,* 56-80.

Goetz, E.T. 1977: *Inferences in the Comprehension of and Memory for Text.* Technical Report No. 49. Urbana: University of Illinois, Center for the Study of Reading.

Goldman, S.R. 1976: Reading skill and the minimum distance principle: A comparison of listening and reading comprehension. *Journal of Experimental Child Psychology, 22,* 123-142.

Goldman, S.R., Hogaboam, T.W., Bell, L.C. and Perfetti, C.A. 1980: Short-term retention of discourse during reading. *Journal of Educational Psychology, 72,* 647-655.

Goldstein, D.M. 1976: Cognitive–linguistic functioning and learning to read in preschoolers. *Journal of Educational Psychology, 68,* 680-688.

Golinkoff, R.M. 1975–76: A comparison of reading comprehension processes in good and poor comprehenders. *Reading Research Quarterly, 11,* 623–659.

Golinkoff, R.M. and Rosinski, R.R. 1976: Decoding, semantic processing and reading comprehension skill. *Child Development, 47,* 252-258.

Goodacre, E.J. 1971: *Children and Learning to Read.* London: Routledge & Kegan Paul.

Goodman, K.S. 1967: Reading: A psycholinguistic guessing game. *Journal of the Reading Specialist, 6,* 126-135.

Goodman, K.S. 1970: Reading: A psycholinguistic guessing game. In H. Singer and R.B. Ruddell (eds), *Theoretical Models and Processes of Reading.* Newark, Del.: International Reading Association.

Goodman, K.S. and Goodman, Y.M. 1979: Learning to read is natural. In L.B. Resnick and P.A. Weaver (eds), *Theory and Practice of Early Reading, vol. 1.* Hillsdale, N.J.: Lawrence Erlbaum Associates.

Goswami, U. 1986: Children's use of analogy in learning to read: A developmental study. *Journal of Experimental Child Psychology, 42,* 73-83.

Gough, P.B. 1972: One second of reading. In J.F. Kavanagh and I.G. Mattingly (eds), *Language by Ear and by Eye.* Cambridge, Mass.: MIT Press.

Graves, M.F., Cooke, C.L. and LaBerge, M.J. 1983: Effects of previewing difficult short stories on low ability junior high school students' comprehension, recall and attitudes. *Reading Research Quarterly, 18,* 262-276.

Graves, M.F. and Palmer, R.J. 1981: Validating previewing as a method of improving fifth and sixth grade students' comprehension of short stories. *Michigan Reading Journal, 15*, 1-3.

Gray, W.S., Monroe, M., Artley, A.S. and Arbuthnot, M.H. 1956: *Fun with Dick and Jane.* Exeter: Wheaton.

Greeno, J.G. 1973: The structure of memory and the process of solving problems. In R.L. Solso (ed.), *Contemporary Issues in Cognitive Psychology.* Washington, D.C.: Winston.

Grice, H.P. 1975: Logic and conversation. In P. Cole and J.L. Morgan (eds), *Syntax and Semantics, vol. 3: Speech Acts.* New York: Seminar Press.

Guttmann, J., Levin, J.R. and Pressley, M. 1977: Pictures, partial pictures, and young children's oral prose learning. *Journal of Educational Psychology, 69*, 473-480.

Hall, W.S., White, T.G. and Guthrie, L. 1986: Skilled reading and language development: Some key issues. In J. Orasanu (ed.), *Reading Comprehension: From Research to Practice.* Hillsdale, N.J.: Lawrence Erlbaum Associates.

Halliday, M.A.K. and Hasan, R. 1976: *Cohesion in English.* London: Longman.

Hansen, J. 1981: The effects of inference training and practice on young children's reading comprehension. *Reading Research Quarterly, 16*, 391-417.

Hansen, J. and Pearson, P.D. 1983: An instructional study: Improving the inferential comprehension of good and poor fourth-grade readers. *Journal of Educational Psychology, 75*, 821-829.

Hare, V.C. and Smith, D.C. 1982: Reading to remember: Studies of metacognitive reading skills in elementary school-aged children. *Journal of Educational Research, 75*, 157-164.

Harris. M. 1978: Noun animacy and the passive voice: A developmental approach. *Quarterly Journal of Experimental Psychology, 30*, 495–504.

Harris, P.L., Kruithof, A., Meerum Terwogt, M. and Visser, T. 1981: Children's detection and awareness of textual anomaly. *Journal of Experimental Child Psychology, 31*, 212-230.

Harris, P.L., Mandias, M., Meerum Terwogt, M. and Tjintjelaar, J. 1980: The influence of context on story recall and feelings of comprehension. *International Journal of Behavioral Development, 3*, 159-172.

Haviland, S.E. and Clark, H.H. 1974: What's new? Acquiring new information as a process in comprehension. *Journal of Verbal Learning and Verbal Behavior, 13*, 512-521.

Healy, J.M. 1982: The enigma of hyperlexia. *Reading Research Quarterly, 17*, 319-338.

Henderson, K. and Chard, J. 1978: *The child's conception of wordlikeness revealed in lexical decisions.* Paper presented at the meeting of the Psychonomic Society, San Antonio, Texas.

Hickmann, M. 1980: Creating referents in discourse: A developmental study of discourse cohesion. In J. Kreiman and A. Ojeda (eds), *Papers from the sixteenth Regional Meeting of the Chicago Linguistic Society.* Chicago: Chicago Linguistics Society.

Hickmann, M. and Schneider, P. (forthcoming): How children repair anomalies in discourse cohesion.

Hitch, G.J. and Halliday, M.S. 1983: Working memory in children. *Philosophical Transactions of the Royal Society, Series B*, 325-340.

Holden, M.H. and MacGinitie, W.H. 1972: Children's conceptions of word boundaries in speech and print. *Journal of Educational Psychology, 63,* 551-557.

Horgan, D. 1978: The development of the full passive. *Journal of Child Language, 5,* 65-80.

Huey, E. 1968: *The Psychology and Pedagogy of Reading.* Cambridge, Mass.: MIT Press (originally published 1908).

Hunt, E., Lunneborg, C. and Lewis, J. 1975: What does it mean to be high verbal? *Cognitive Psychology, 7,* 194-227.

Huttenlocher, J. 1964: Children's language: Word–phrase relationship. *Science, 143,* 264-265.

Huttenlocher, J. and Burke, C. 1976: Why does memory span increase with age? *Cognitive Psychology, 8,* 1-31.

Huttenlocher, J., Eisenberg, K. and Strauss, S. 1968: Comprehension: Relation between perceived actor and logical subject. *Journal of Verbal Learning and Verbal Behavior, 7,* 527-30.

Isakson, R.L. and Miller, J.W. 1976: Sensitivity to syntactic and semantic cues in good and poor comprehenders. *Journal of Educational Psychology, 68,* 787-792.

Jakubowicz, C. 1983: On markedness and binding principles. *Proceedings of the Northeastern Linguistics Society, 14,* 154-182.

Jarvella, R.J. 1979: Immediate memory and discourse processing. In G.H. Bower (ed.), *The Psychology of Learning and Motivation, vol. 13.* New York: Academic Press.

Jeffrey, W.E. and Samuels, S.J. 1967: Effect of method of reading training on initial learning and transfer. *Journal of Verbal Learning and Verbal Behavior, 6,* 354-358.

Jenkins, J.R. and Pany, D. 1981: Instructional variables in reading comprehension. In J. Guthrie (ed.), *Comprehension and Teaching: Research Reviews.* Newark, Del.: International Reading Association.

Jenkins, J.R., Pany, D. and Schreck, J. 1978: *Vocabulary and Reading Comprehension: Instructional Effects.* Technical Report No. 100. Urbana: University of Illinois, Center for the Study of Reading.

Johnson, D.D. and Baumann, J.F. 1984: Word identification. In P.D. Pearson (ed.), *Handbook of Reading Research.* London: Longman.

Johnson, D.D. and Pearson, P.D. 1978: *Teaching Reading Vocabulary.* New York: Holt, Rinehart and Winston.

Johnson, M.K., Bransford, J.D. and Solomon, S. 1973: Memory for tacit implications of sentences. *Journal of Experimental Psychology, 98,* 203–205.

Johnson-Laird, P.N. 1983: *Mental Models: Towards a Cognitive Science of Language, Inference, and Consciousness.* Cambridge: Cambridge University Press.

Johnson-Laird, P.N. and Bethell-Fox, C.E. 1978: Memory for questions and amount of processing. *Memory and Cognition, 6,* 496-501.

Johnston, P.H. 1983: *Reading Comprehension Assessment: A Cognitive Basis.* Newark, Del.: International Reading Association.

Johnston, P.H. 1984: The assessment of reading. In P.D. Pearson (ed.) *Handbook of Reading Research.* London: Longman.

Jorm, A.F. 1983: *The Psychology of Reading and Spelling Disabilities.* London: Routledge & Kegan Paul.

Juola, J.F., Schadler, M., Chabot, R.J. and McCaughey, M.W. 1978: The development of visual information processing skills related to reading. *Journal of Experimental Child Psychology, 25*, 459–476.

Kail, R.V., Chi, M., Ingram, A. and Danner, F. 1977: Constructive aspects of children's reading comprehension. *Child Development, 48*, 684-688.

Karmiloff-Smith, A. 1979: *A Functional Approach to Child Language: A Study of Determiners and Reference*. Cambridge: Cambridge University Press.

Karmiloff-Smith, A. 1980: Psychological processes underlying pronominalization and non-pronominalization in children's connected discourse. In J. Kreiman and A. Ojeda (eds), *Papers from the Parasession on Pronouns and Anaphora*. Chicago: Chicago Linguistics Society.

Karmiloff-Smith, A. 1981: The grammatical marking of thematic structure in the development of language production. In W. Deutsch (ed.), *The Child's Construction of Language*. London: Academic Press.

Karmiloff-Smith, A. 1985: Language and cognitive processes from a developmental perspective. *Language and Cognitive Processes, vol. 1*, 61-85.

Karmiloff-Smith, A. 1986: Some fundamental aspects of language development after five. In P. Fletcher and M. Garman (eds), *Language Acquisition* (2nd edn). Cambridge: Cambridge University Press.

Katz, E.W. and Brent, S.B. 1968: Understanding connectives. *Journal of Verbal Learning and Verbal Behavior, 7*, 501-509.

Kavale, K. and Schreiner, R. 1979: The reading processes of above average and average readers: A comparison of the use of the reasoning strategies in responding to standardized comprehension measures. *Reading Research Quarterly, 15*, 102-128.

Kennedy, D.S. and Weener, P. 1973: Visual and auditory training with the cloze procedure to improve reading and listening comprehension. *Reading Research Quarterly, 8*, 524-541.

Kessel, F.S. 1970: The role of syntax in children's comprehension from ages six to twelve. *Monographs of the Society for Research in Child Development, 35*.

Kintsch, W. 1977: On comprehending stories. In M.A. Just and P.A. Carpenter (eds), *Cognitive Processes in Comprehension*. Hillsdale, N.J.: Lawrence Erlbaum Associates.

Kintsch, W. and van Dijk, T.A. 1978: Towards a model of text comprehension and production. *Psychological Review, 85*, 363–394.

Kleiman, G.M. 1975: Speech recoding in reading. *Journal of Verbal Learning and Verbal Behavior, 14*, 323-339.

Krueger, L.E., Keen, R.H. and Rublevich, B. 1974: Letter search through words and non-words by adults and fourth-grade children. *Journal of Experimental Psychology, 102*, 845-849.

LaBerge, D. 1979: The perception of units in beginning reading. In L.B. Resnick and P.A. Weaver (eds), *Theory and Practice of Early Reading, vol. 3*. Hillsdale, N.J.: Lawrence Erlbaum Associates.

LaBerge, D. and Samuels, S.J. 1974: Toward a theory of automatic information processing in reading. *Cognitive Psychology, 6*, 293-323.

Langer, J.A. 1984: Examining background knowledge and text comprehension. *Reading Research Quarterly, 19*, 468-481.

Lavine, L.O. 1977: Differentiation of letterlike forms in prereading children. *Developmental Psychology, 13*, 89-94.

Layton, J.R. 1979: *The Psychology of Learning to Read*. London: Academic Press.

Lesgold, A.M. 1974: Variability in children's comprehension of syntactic structures. *Journal of Educational Psychology, 66*, 333-38.

Lesgold, A.M., DeGood, H. and Levin, J.R. 1977: Pictures and young children's prose learning: A supplementary report. *Journal of Reading Behavior, 9*, 353-360.

Lesgold, A.M., Resnick, L.B. and Hammond, K. 1985: Learning to read: A longitudinal study of word skill development in two curricula. In G.E. MacKinnon and T.G. Waller (eds), *Reading Research: Advances in Theory and Practice, vol. 4*. New York: Academic Press.

Lesgold, A.M., Levin, J.R., Shimron, J. and Guttmann, J. 1975: Pictures and young children's learning from oral prose. *Journal of Educational Psychology, 67*, 636–642.

Levin, H. and Kaplan, E.L. 1970: Grammatical structure and reading. In H. Levin and J.P. Williams (eds), *Basic Studies in Reading*. New York: Basic Books.

Levin, H. and Watson, J. 1963: The learning of variable grapheme–to–phoneme correspondences: Variations in the initial consonant position. In *A Basic Research Progam on Reading*, US Office of Education, Cooperative Research Project No. 639. Ithaca, N.Y.: Cornell University.

Levin, J.R. 1973: Inducing comprehension in poor readers: A test of a recent model. *Journal of Educational Psychology, 65*, 19-24.

Levin, J.R. 1981: On functions of pictures in prose. In F.J. Pirozzolo and M.C. Wittrock (eds), *Neuropsychological and Cognitive Processes in Reading*. London: Academic Press.

Levin, J.R. and Lesgold, A.M. 1978: On pictures in prose. *Educational Communication and Technology, 26*, 233-243.

Levy, B.A. 1978: Speech analysis during sentence processing: Reading vs. listening. *Visible Language, 12*, 81–101.

Liben, L.S. and Posnansky, C.J. 1977: Inferences on inference: The effects of age, transitive ability, memory load and lexical factors. *Child Development, 48*, 1490-1497.

Liberman, A.M., Cooper, F.S., Shankweiler, D. and Studdert-Kennedy, M. 1967: Perception of the speech code. *Psychological Review, 74*, 431-461.

Liberman, I.Y. and Shankweiler, D. 1979: Speech, the alphabet and teaching to read. In L.B. Resnick and P.A. Weaver (eds), *Theory and Practice of Early Reading. vol. 2*. Hillsdale, N.J.: Lawrence Erlbaum Associates.

Liberman, I.Y., Shankweiler, D., Fischer, F.W. and Carter, B. 1974: Explicit syllable and phoneme segmentation in the young child. *Journal of Experimental Child Psychology, 18*, 201-212.

Liberman, I.Y., Shankweiler, D., Liberman, A.M, Fowler, C. and Fischer, F.W. 1977: Phonetic segmentation and the beginning reader. In A.S. Reber and D.L. Scarborough (eds), *Toward a Psychology of Reading*. Hillsdale, N.J.: Lawrence Erlbaum Associates.

Linden, M. and Wittrock, M.C. 1981: The teaching of reading comprehension according to the model of generative learning. *Reading Research Quarterly, 17*, 44-57.

Loban, W.D. 1963: *The Language of Elementary School Children*. Champaign, Ill.: National Council for Teachers of English.

Lunzer, E.A. and Gardner, K. 1979: *The Effective Use of Reading*. London: Heinemann Educational Books.

McClelland, J.L. and Rumelhart, D.E. 1981: An interactive model of context effects in letter perception. Part 1: An account of basic findings. *Psychological Review, 88*, 375-407.

McClelland, J.L., Rumelhart, D.E. and Hinton, G.E. 1986: The appeal of parallel distributed processing. In D.E. Rumelhart and J.L. McClelland (eds), *Parallel Distributed Processing: Explorations in the Microstructure of Cognition, vol. 1: Foundations*. Cambridge, Mass.: MIT Press.

Mackay, D.G. 1966: To end ambiguous sentences. *Perception and Psychophysics, 1*, 426-436.

MacKay, D., Thompson, B. and Schaub, P. 1970: *Breakthrough to Literacy*. London: Longman (for the Schools Council).

McKoon, G. 1977: Organization of information in text memory. *Journal of Verbal Learning and Verbal Behavior, 16*, 247-260.

Makar, B.W. 1977: '*The Wig*' *in Primary Phonics*. Cambridge, Mass.: Educators Publishing Service.

Mann, V.A., Liberman, I.Y. and Shankweiler, D. 1980: Children's memory for sentences and word strings in relation to reading ability. *Memory and Cognition, 8*, 329-335.

Maratsos, M.P. 1974: How preschool children understand missing complement subjects. *Child Development, 45*, 700-706.

Maratsos, M.P. 1976: *The Use of Definite and Indefinite Reference in Young Children: An Experimental Study of Semantic Acquisition*. Cambridge: Cambridge University Press.

Maratsos, M.P. 1979: Learning how and when to use pronouns and determiners. In P. Fletcher and M. Garman (Eds.) *Language Acquisition: Studies in First Language Development*. Cambridge: Cambridge University Press.

Mark, L.S., Shankweiler, D., Liberman, I.Y. and Fowler, C. 1977: Phonetic recoding and reading difficulty in beginning readers. *Memory and Cognition, 5*, 623-629.

Markman, E.M. 1977: Realizing that you don't understand: A preliminary investigation. *Child Development, 48*, 986-992.

Markman, E.M. 1979: Realizing that you don't understand: Elementary school children's awareness of inconsistencies. *Child Development, 50*, 643-655.

Markman, E.M. 1981: Comprehension monitoring. In W.P. Dickson (ed) *Children's Oral Communication Skills*. London: Academic Press.

Markman, E.M. and Gorin, L. 1981: Children's ability to adjust their standards for evaluating comprehension. *Journal of Educational Psychology, 73*, 320-325.

Marr, M.B. and Gormley, K. 1982: Children's recall of familiar and unfamiliar text. *Reading Research Quarterly, 18*, 89-104.

Marsh, G., Desberg, P. and Cooper, J. 1977: Developmental changes in strategies of reading. *Journal of Reading Behavior, 9*, 391-394.

Marsh, G., Friedman, M., Welch, V. and Desberg, P. 1981: A cognitive-developmental theory of reading acquisition. In G.E. Mackinnon and T.G. Waller (eds), *Reading Research: Advances in Theory and Practice*. New York: Academic Press.

Marslen-Wilson, W.D. 1973: Linguistic structure and speech shadowing at very short latencies. *Nature, 224*, 522-523.

Marslen-Wilson, W.D. 1975: Sentence perception as an interactive parallel process. *Science, 189*, 226-228.

Mason, M. 1975: Reading ability and letter search time: Effects of orthographic structure defined by single-letter positional frequency. *Journal of Experimental Psychology: General, 104*, 146-166.

Mason, M. and Katz, L. 1976: Visual processing of nonlinguistic strings: Redundancy effects and reading ability. *Journal of Experimental Psychology: General, 105*, 338-348.

Menyuk, P. 1963: Syntactic structures in the language of children. *Child Development, 34*, 407-422.

Menyuk, P. 1964: Syntactic rules used by children from preschool through first grade. *Child Development, 35*, 533-46.

Merrill, E.C., Sperber, R.D. and McCauley, C. 1981: Differences in semantic encoding as a function of reading comprehension skill. *Memory and Cognition, 9*, 618-624.

Merritt, J. E. 1970: Learning to read: Language–experience approaches. *Where, 52*, 177-180.

Meyer, B.J. 1975: *The Organization of Prose and its Effects on Memory.* Amsterdam: North Holland.

Mickish, V. 1974: Children's perception of written word boundaries. *Journal of Reading Behavior, 6*, 19–22.

Mitchell, D.C. 1982: *The Process of Reading: A Cognitive Analysis of Fluent Reading and Learning to Read.* Chichester: Wiley.

Mitchell, D.C. and Holmes, V.M. 1985: The role of specific information about the verb in parsing sentences with local structural ambiguity. *Journal of Memory and Language, 25*, 542-559.

Morais, J., Cary, L., Alegria, J. and Bertelson, P. 1979: Does awareness of speech as a sequence of phones arise spontaneously? *Cognition, 7*, 323-331.

Morsbach, G. and Steel, P.M. 1976: 'John is easy to see' re-investigated. *Journal of Child Language, 3*, 443-447.

Morton, J. 1970: A functional model for memory. In D.A. Norman (ed.), *Models of Human Memory.* New York: Academic Press.

Morton, J. 1981: The status of information processing models of language. *Philosophical Transactions of The Royal Society of London, Series B, 295*, 387–396.

Myers, M. and Paris, S.G. 1978: Children's metacognitive knowledge about reading. *Journal of Educational Psychology, 70*, 680–690.

Neale, M.D. 1966: *The Neale Analysis of Reading Ability* (2nd edn), London: Macmillan Education.

Norris, D.G. 1986: Word recognition: Context effects without priming. *Cognition, 22*, 93-136.

Norton, D.E. and Hubert, P. 1977: *A comparison of the oral reading strategies and comprehension patterns developed by high, average, and low ability first grade students taught by two approaches – phonic emphasis and eclectic basal.* College Station: Texas A & M University.

Oakan, R., Wiener, M. and Cromer, W. 1971: Identification, organization and reading comprehension in good and poor readers. *Journal of Educational Psychology, 62*, 71-78.

Oakhill, J.V. 1981: *Children's Reading Comprehension.* Unpublished D.Phil. thesis, University of Sussex.

Oakhill, J.V. 1982: Constructive processes in skilled and less-skilled comprehenders' memory for sentences. *British Journal of Psychology, 73*, 13-20.

Oakhill, J.V. 1983: Instantiation in skilled and less-skilled comprehenders. *Quarterly Journal of Experimental Psychology, 35A*, 441-450.

Oakhill, J.V. 1984: Inferential and memory skills in children's comprehension of stories. *British Journal of Educational Psychology, 54*, 31-39.

Oakhill, J.V. and Yuill, N.M. 1986: Pronoun resolution in skilled and less-skilled comprehenders: Effects of memory load and inferential complexity. *Language and Speech, 29*, 25-37.

Oakhill, J.V., Yuill, N.M. and Parkin, A.J. 1986: On the nature of the difference between skilled and less-skilled comprehenders. *Journal of Research in Reading, 9*, 80-91.

Oakhill, J.V., Yuill, N.M. and Parkin, A.J. 1988: Memory and inference in skilled and less-skilled comprehenders. In M.M. Gruneberg, P.E. Morris, and R.N. Sykes (eds), *Practical Aspects of Memory: Current Research and Issues, vol. 2*. Chichester: Wiley.

O'Donnell, R.C., Griffin, W.J. and Norris, R.C. 1967: *Syntax of Kindergarten and Elementary School Children: A Transformational Analysis*. Champaign, Ill.: National Council of Teachers of English.

Olds, H.F. 1968: *An experimental study of syntactic factors influencing children's comprehension of certain complex relationships*. (Center for Research and Development of Educational Difficulties Report No. 4). Cambridge, Mass.: Harvard University Press.

Oliver, M.E. 1975: The development of language concepts of pre-primary Indian children. *Language Arts, 52*, 865-869.

Olshavsky, J. 1976–77: Reading as problem-solving: An investigation of strategies. *Reading Research Quarterly, 12*, 654-674.

Olson, D.R. 1984: Oral and written language and the cognitive processes of children. In A. Lock and E. Fisher (eds), *Language Development*. London: Croom Helm.

Omanson, R.C., Warren, W.H. and Trabasso, T. 1978: Goals, inferential comprehension and recall of stories by children. *Discourse Processes, 1*, 337–354.

Onmacht, D.D. 1969: *The effects of letter-knowledge on achievement in reading in the first grade*. Paper presented at the American Educational Research Association, Los Angeles.

Otto, W. and Barrett, T.C. 1968: *Two Studies of Children's Ability to Formulate and State a Literal Main Idea in reading* (Technical Report No. 57). Madison: Wisconsin Research and Development Center for Cognitive Learning.

Owings, R.A., Petersen, G.A., Bransford, J.D., Morris, D. and Stein, B.S. 1980: Spontaneous monitoring and regulation of learning : A comparison of successful and less successful fifth graders. *Journal of Educational Psychology, 72*, 250-256.

Palermo, D.S. 1973: More about less: A study of language comprehension. *Journal of Verbal Learning and Verbal Behavior, 12*, 211-221.

Palermo, D.S. and Molfese, D. 1972: Language acquisition from age five onward. *Psychological Bulletin, 78*, 409-428.

Pany, D., Jenkins, J.R. and Schreck, J. 1982: Vocabulary instruction: Effects of word knowledge and reading comprehension. *Learning Disability Quarterly, 5*, 202-215.

Paris, S.G. 1975: Integration and inference in children's comprehension and memory. In F. Restle, R.M. Shiffrin, N.J. Castellan, H.R. Lindman, and

D.B. Pisoni (eds), *Cognitive Theory, vol. 1*. Hillsdale, N.J.: Lawrence Erlbaum Associates.

Paris, S.G. 1978: The development of inference and transformation as memory operations. In P.A. Ornstein (ed.), *Memory Development in Children*. Hillsdale, N.J.: Lawrence Erlbaum Associates.

Paris, S.G. and Carter, A. 1973: Semantic and constructive aspects of sentence memory in children. *Developmental Psychology, 9*, 109-113.

Paris, S.G. and Jacobs, J.E. 1984: The benefits of informed instruction for children's reading awareness and comprehension skills. *Child Development, 55*, 2083-2093.

Paris, S.G. and Lindauer, B.K. 1976: The role of inference in children's comprehension and memory for sentences. *Cognitive Psychology, 8*, 217-227.

Paris, S.G. and Lindauer, B.K. 1978: Constructive aspects of children's comprehension and memory. In R.V. Kail and J.W. Hagen (eds), *Perspectives on the Development of Memory and Cognition*. Hillsdale, N.J.: Lawrence Erlbaum Associates.

Paris, S.G. and Mahoney, G.J. 1974: Cognitive integration in children's memory for sentences and pictures. *Child Development, 45*, 633–642.

Paris, S.G. and Myers, M. 1981: Comprehension monitoring, memory and study strategies of good and poor readers. *Journal of Reading Behavior, 13*, 5-22.

Paris, S.G. and Upton, L.R. 1976: Children's memory for inferential relationships in prose. *Child Development, 47*, 660-668.

Paris, S.G., Cross, D.R. and Lipson, M.Y. 1984: Informed strategies for learning: A program to improve children's reading awareness and comprehension. *Journal of Educational Psychology, 76*, 1239–1252.

Pearson, P.D. and Johnson, D.D. 1978: *Teaching Reading Comprehension*. New York: Holt, Rinehart and Winston.

Pearson, P.D., Hansen, J. and Gordon, C. 1979: The effect of background knowledge on young children's comprehension of explicit and implicit information. *Journal of Reading Behavior, 11*, 201-209.

Peeck, J. 1974: Retention of pictorial and verbal content of a text with illustrations. *Journal of Educational Psychology, 66*, 880-888.

Perera, K. 1985: *Children's Writing and Reading*. Oxford: Blackwell.

Perfetti, C.A. 1985: *Reading Ability*. Oxford: Oxford University Press.

Perfetti, C.A. and Goldman, S.R. 1976: Discourse memory and reading comprehension skill. *Journal of Verbal Learning and Verbal Behavior, 15*, 33–42.

Perfetti, C.A. and Hogaboam, T. 1975a: Relationship between single word decoding and reading comprehension skill. *Journal of Educational Psychology, 67*, 461-469.

Perfetti, C.A. and Hogaboam, T. 1975b: The Effects of Word Experience on Decoding Speeds of Skilled and Unskilled Readers. Paper presented at the Psychonomics Society, Denver.

Perfetti, C.A. and Lesgold, A.M. 1977: Discourse comprehension and sources of individual differences. In M. Just and P.A. Carpenter (eds), *Cognitive Processes in Comprehension*. Hillsdale, N.J.: Lawrence Erlbaum Associates.

Perfetti, C.A. and Lesgold, A.M. 1979: Coding and comprehension in skilled reading and implications for reading instruction. In L.B. Resnick and P. Weaver (eds), *Theory and Practice of Early Reading, vol. 1*. Hillsdale, N.J.: Lawrence Erlbaum Associates.

Perfetti, C.A. and McCutchen, D. 1982: Speech processes in reading. In N. Lass (ed.), *Speech and Language: Advances in Basic Research and Practice vol. 7*. New York: Academic Press.

Perfetti, C.A. and Roth, S. 1981: Some of the interactive processes in reading and their role in reading skill. In A.M. Lesgold and C.A. Perfetti (eds), *Interactive Processes in Reading*. Hillsdale, N.J.: Lawrence Erlbaum Associates.

Perfetti, C.A., Beck, I. and Hughes, C. 1981: Phonemic knowledge and learning to read. Paper presented at SRCD symposium, Boston: *Phonemic Awareness and Learning to Read: What's the Relationship?*

Perfetti, C.A., Finger, E. and Hogaboam, T. 1978: Sources of vocalization latency differences between skilled and less skilled young readers. *Journal of Educational Psychology, 70*, 730–739.

Peters, E.E., Levin, J.R., McGivern, J.E. and Pressley, M. 1985: Further comparison of representational and transformational prose-learning imagery. *Journal of Educational Psychology, 77*, 129-136.

Pichert, J.W. and Anderson, R.C. 1977: Taking different perspectives on a story. *Journal of Educational Psychology, 69*, 309-315.

Pike, R., and Olson, D.R. 1977: A question of 'More' and 'Less'. *Child Development, 48*, 579-588.

Poulsen, D., Kintsch, E., Kintsch, W. and Premack, D. 1979: Children's comprehension and memory for stories. *Journal of Experimental Child Psychology, 28*, 379-403.

Posner, M. and Snyder, C. 1975a: Attention and cognitive control. In R. Solso (ed.), *Information Processing and Cognition: The Loyola Symposium*. Hillsdale, N.J.: Lawrence Erlbaum Associates.

Posner, M. and Snyder, C. 1975b: Facilitation and inhibition in the processing of signals. In P.M.A. Rabbitt and S. Dornic (eds), *Attention and Performance, vol. V*. New York: Academic Press.

Pressley, G.M. 1976: Mental imagery helps eight-year-olds remember what they read. *Journal of Educational Psychology, 68*, 355-359.

Read, C. 1971: Pre-school children's knowledge of English phonology. *Harvard Educational Review, 41*, 1-34.

Read, C. 1973: Children's judgements of phonetic similarities in relation to English spelling. *Language Learning, 23*, 17-38.

Reicher, G.M. 1969: Perceptual recognition as a function of meaningfulness of stimulus material. *Journal of Experimental Psychology, 81*, 275-280.

Reid, J. 1966: Learning to think about reading. *Educational Research, 9*, 56-62.

Reid, J. 1970: Sentence structure in reading primers. *Research in Education, 3*, 23-37.

Reid, J. 1972: Children's comprehension of syntactic features found in some extension readers. Occasional Paper, Centre for Research in Educational Sciences, University of Edinburgh.

Reis, R. and Spekman, N. 1983: The detection of reader-based versus text-based inconsistencies and the effects of direct training of comprehension monitoring among upper-grade poor comprehenders. *Journal of Reading Behavior, 15*, 49-60.

Reitsma, P. 1984: Sound priming in beginning readers. *Child Development, 55*, 406-423.

Resnick, L.B. 1979: Theories and prescriptions for early reading instruction. In L.B. Resnick and P.A. Weaver (eds), *Theory and Practice of Early Reading, vol. 2*. Hillsdale, N.J.: Lawrence Erlbaum Associates.

Richek, M.A. 1976–77: Reading comprehension and anaphoric forms in varying linguistic contexts. *Reading Research Quarterly, 12*, 145-165.

Robertson, J.E. 1966: *An Investigation of Pupil Understanding of Connectives in Reading*. Unpublished doctoral dissertation, University of Alberta.

Rohwer, W.D. and Harris, W.J. 1975: Media effects on prose learning in two populations of children. *Journal of Educational Psychology, 67*, 651-657.

Romaine, S. 1984: *The Language of Children and Adolescents*. Oxford: Blackwell.

Rosenshine, B.V. 1980: Skill hierarchies in reading comprehension. In R.J. Spiro, B.C. Bruce and W.F. Brewer (eds), *Theoretical Issues in Reading Comprehension*. Hillsdale, N.J.: Lawrence Erlbaum Associates.

Rosinski, R.R. and Wheeler, K.E. 1972: Children's use of orthographic structure in word discrimination. *Psychonomic Science, 26*, 97-98.

Rosner, J. 1972: *The Development and Validation of an Individualized Perceptual-skills Curriculum*. University of Pittsburgh, Learning Research and Development Center.

Rosner, J. 1973: Language arts and arithmetic achievement and specifically related perceptual skills. *American Educational Research Journal, 10*, 59-68.

Rosner, J. 1974: Auditory analysis training with prereaders. *The Reading Teacher, 27*, 379-384.

Rosner, J. and Simon, D.P. 1971: The auditory analysis test: An initial report. *Journal of Learning Disabilities, 4*, 384-392.

Ross, H.S. and Killey, J.C. 1977: The effects of questioning on retention. *Child Development, 48*, 312-314.

Rothkopf, E.Z. 1982: Adjunct aids and the control of mathemagenic activities during purposeful reading. In W. Otto and S. White (eds), *Reading Expository Material*. New York: Academic Press.

Royer, J.M. and Cunningham, D.J. 1978: *On the Theory and Measurement of Reading Comprehension*. Technical Report No. 91. Urbana: University of Illinois, Center for the Study of Reading.

Rozin, P. and Gleitman, L. 1977: The structure and acquisition of reading. II: The reading process and the acquisition of the alphabetic principle. In A.S. Reber and D.L. Scarborough (eds), *Towards a Psychology of Reading*. Hillsdale, N.J.: Lawrence Erlbaum Associates.

Rozin, P., Bressman, B. and Taft, M. 1974: Do children understand the basic relationship between speech and writing? The Mow-motorcyle test. *Journal of Reading Behavior, 6*, 327-334.

Rubin, A.D. 1980: A theoretical taxonomy of the differences between oral and written language. In R.J. Spiro, B.C. Bruce and W.F. Brewer (eds), *Theoretical Issues in Reading Comprehension*. Hillsdale, N.J.: Lawrence Erlbaum Associates.

Ruch, M.D. and Levin, J.R. 1977: Pictorial organization versus verbal repetition of children's prose: Evidence for processing differences. *AV Communication Review, 25*, 269-280.

Ruddell, R.B. 1965: The effect of oral and written patterns of language structure on reading comprehension. *The Reading Teacher, 18*, 270-275.

Rumelhart, D.E. 1975: Notes on a schema for stories. In D.G. Bobrow and A.M. Collins (eds), *Representation and Understanding: Studies in Cognitive*

Science. New York: Academic Press.

Rumelhart, D.E. 1977: Toward an interactive model of reading. In S. Dornic (ed.), *Attention and Performance, vol. VI.* Hillsdale, N.J.: Lawrence Erlbaum Associates.

Rusted, J. 1984: Differential facilitation by pictures of children's retention of written texts. *Current Psychological Research and Reviews, 3,* 61-71.

Ryan, E.B., McNamara, S.R. and Kenney, M. 1977: Lexical awareness and reading performance among beginning readers. *Journal of Reading Behavior, 9,* 399-400.

Sachs, J.S. 1967: Recognition memory for syntactic and semantic aspects of connected discourse. *Perception and Psychophysics, 2,* 437-442.

Sakamoto, T. and Makita, K. 1973: Japan. In J. Downing (ed.), *Comparative Reading: Cross-national Studies of Behavior and Processes in Reading and Writing.* New York: Macmillan.

Salame, P. and Baddeley, A.D. 1982: Disruption of short-term memory by unattended speech: Implications for the structure of working memory. *Journal of Verbal Learning and Verbal Behavior, 21,* 150-164.

Samuels, S.J. 1972: The effect of letter-name knowledge on learning to read. *American Educational Research Journal, 9,* 65-74.

Schallert, D.L. 1980: The role of illustrations in reading comprehension. In R.J. Spiro, B.C. Bruce, and W.F. Brewer (eds), *Theoretical Issues in Reading Comprehension.* Hillsdale, N.J.: Lawrence Erlbaum Associates.

Schank, R.C. 1973: Identification of conceptualizations underlying natural language. In R.C. Schank and K.M. Colby (eds), *Computer Models of Thought and Language.* San Francisco: Freeman.

Schank, R.C. 1982: Reminding and memory organization: An introduction to MOPs. In W.G. Lehnert and M.H. Ringle (eds), *Strategies for Natural Language Processing.* Hillsdale, N.J.: Lawrence Erlbaum Associates.

Schank, R.C. and Abelson, R.P. 1977: *Scripts, Goals, Plans and Understanding.* Hillsdale, N.J.: Lawrence Erlbaum Associates.

Schelsinger, I.M. 1969: *Sentence Structure and the Reading Process.* New York: Humanities Press.

Schwantes, F.M. 1981: Effect of story context on children's ongoing word recognition. *Journal of Reading Behavior, 13,* 305-311.

Schwantes, F.M., Boesl, S.L. and Ritz, E.G. 1980: Children's use of context in word recogntion: A psycholinguistic guessing game. *Child Development, 51,* 730-736.

Searle, J.R. 1969: *Speech Acts: An Essay in the Philosophy of Language.* Cambridge: Cambridge University Press.

Sheldon, A. 1974: The role of parallel function in the acquisition of relative clauses in English. *Journal of Verbal Learning and Verbal Behavior, 13,* 272-281.

Shimmerlik, S.M. and Nolan, J.D. 1976: Reorganization of the recall of prose. *Journal of Educational Psychology, 68,* 779-786.

Simons, H.D. 1971: Reading comprehension: The need for a new perspective. *Reading Research Quarterly, 6,* 338-363.

Simpson, G.B., Lorsbach, T.C. and Whitehouse, D. 1983: Encoding and contextual components of word recognition in good and poor readers. *Journal of Experimental Child Psychology, 35,* 161-171.

Sinclair, H. 1967: *Langage et Opérations: Sous-systèmes Linguistiques et Opérations Concrètes.* Paris: Dunod.

Singer, H. and Ruddell, R.B. (eds), 1976: *Theoretical Models and Processes of Reading* (2nd edn). Newark, Del.: International Reading Association.

Slobin, D.I. 1966: Grammatical transformations and sentence comprehension in childhood and adulthood. *Journal of Verbal Learning and Verbal Behavior, 5,* 219-227.

Smiley, S., Oakley, D., Worthen, D., Campione, J. and Brown, A. 1977: Recall of thematically relevant material by adolescent good and poor readers as a function of written versus oral presentation. *Journal of Educational Psychology, 69,* 381-387.

Smith, F. 1971: *Understanding Reading.* New York: Holt, Rinehart and Winston.

Smith, F. 1973: *Psycholinguistics and Reading.* New York: Holt, Reinhart and Winston.

Smith, F. 1975: *Comprehension and Learning.* New York: Holt, Rinehart and Winston.

Smith, F. 1979: Conflicting approaches to reading research and instruction. In L.B. Resnick and P.A. Weaver (eds), *Theory and Practice of Early Reading, vol. 2.* Hillsdale, N.J.: Lawrence Erlbaum Associates.

Snowling, M.J. 1980: The development of grapheme–phoneme correspondence in normal and dyslexic readers. *Journal of Experimental Child Psychology, 29,* 294-305.

Sperber, D. and Wilson, D. 1986: *Relevance: Communication and Cognition.* Oxford: Blackwell.

Spilich, G.J., Vesonder, G.T., Chiesi, H.L. and Voss, J.F. 1979: Text processing of domain-related information for individuals with high and low domain knowledge. *Journal of Verbal Learning and Verbal Behavior, 18,* 275-290.

Spring, C., Blunden, D. and Gatheral, M. 1981: Effect on reading comprehension of training to automaticity in word-reading. *Perceptual and Motor Skills, 53,* 779-786.

Stanovich, K.E. 1980: Toward an interactive–compensatory model of individual differences in the development of reading fluency. *Reading Research Quarterly, 16,* 32-71.

Stanovich, K.E. 1982: Individual differences in the cognitive processes of reading. II. Text-level processes. *Journal of Learning Disabilities, 15,* 549-554.

Stanovich, K.E. 1986: Cognitive processes and reading problems of learning-disabled children: Evaluating the assumption of specificity. In J.K. Torgesen and B. Wong (eds), *Psychological and Educational Perspectives on Learning Disabilities.* New York: Academic Press.

Stanovich, K.E. and West, R.F. 1979: The effect of orthographic structure on the word search performance of good and poor readers. *Journal of Experimental Child Psychology, 28,* 258–267.

Stanovich, K.E., Cunningham, A.E. and Feeman, D.J. 1984: Relation between early reading acquisition and word decoding with and without context: A longitudinal study of first-grade children. *Journal of Educational Psychology, 76,* 668-677.

Stein, N.L. 1979: How children understand stories: A developmental analysis. In L.G. Katz (ed.), *Current Topics in Early Childhood Education, vol. 2.* Norwood, N.J.: Ablex.

Stein, N.L. and Glenn, C.G. 1979: An analysis of story comprehension in elementary school children. In R.O. Freedle (ed.), *New Directions in Discourse Processing.* Norwood, N.J.: Ablex.

Steiner, R., Wiener, M. and Cromer, W. 1971: Comprehension training and identification for poor and good readers. *Journal of Educational Psychology, 62*, 506-513.

Steingart, S.K. and Glock, M.D. 1979: Imagery and the recall of connected discourse. *Reading Research Quarterly, 15*, 62-82.

Stenning, K. and Michell, L. 1985: Learning how to tell a good story: The development of content and language in children's telling of one tale. *Discourse Processes, 8*, 261-279.

Stevenson, H.W., Parker, T., Wilkinson, A., Hegion, A. and Fish, E. 1976:

Sticht, T., Beck, L., Hauke, R., Kleiman, G. and James, J. 1974: *Auding and scholastic achievement. Journal of Educational Psychology, 68*, 377-400.

Sticht, T., Beck, L., Hauke, R., Kleiman, G. and James, J. 1974: Auding *Reading: A Developmental Model*. Alexandria, Va.: Human Resources Research Organization.

Strickland, R.G. 1962: The language of elementary school children: Its relationship to the language of reading textbooks and the quality of reading of selected children. *Bulletin of the School of Education*, Indiana University.

Swinney, D.A. 1979: Lexical access during sentence comprehension: (Re)consideration of context effects. *Journal of Verbal Learning and Verbal Behavior, 18*, 545-569.

Tatham, S.M. 1970: Reading comprehension of materials written with select oral language patterns: a study at grades two and four. *Reading Research Quarterly, 5*, 402-426.

Taylor, B.M. 1982: Text structure and children's comprehension and memory for expository material. *Journal of Educational Psychology, 74*, 323-340.

Taylor, I. and Taylor, M.M. 1983: *The Psychology of Reading*. London: Academic Press.

Theiman, T.J. and Brown, A.L. 1977: *The Effects of Semantic and Formal Similarity on Recogntion Memory for Structures in Children*. Technical Report No. 76. Urbana: University of Illinois, Center for the Study of Reading.

Thorndike, E.L. 1917: Reading as reasoning: A study of mistakes in paragraph reading. *Journal of Educational Psychology, 8*, 323-332.

Thorndike, R.L. 1973–74: Reading as reasoning. *Reading Research Quarterly, 9*, 135-147.

Tierney, R.J. and Cunningham, J.W. 1984: Research on teaching reading comprehension. In P.D. Pearson (ed.), *Handbook of Reading Research*. New York: Longman.

Torgesen, J.K. 1978–79: Performance of reading disabled children on serial memory tasks: A selective review of recent research. *Reading Research Quarterly, 14*, 57–87.

Torrey, J.W. 1979: Reading that comes naturally: The early reader. In T.G. Waller and G. MacKinnon (eds), *Reading Research: Advances in Theory and Practice, vol. 1*. New York: Academic Press.

Trabasso, T. and Nicholas, D.W. 1980: Memory and inferences in the comprehension of narratives. In F. Wilkening, J. Becker and T. Trabasso (eds), *Information Integration by Children*. Hillsdale, N.J.: Lawrence Erlbaum Associates.

Turner, E.A. and Rommetveit, R. 1967: The acquisition of sentence voice and reversibility. *Child Development, 38*, 649-660.

Underwood, G. 1985: Eye movements during the comprehension of written language. In A.W. Ellis (ed.), *Progress in the Psychology of Language*, vol. 2. London: Lawrence Erlbaum Associates.

Venezky, R.L. 1970: *The Structure of English Orthography*. The Hague: Mouton.

Venezky, R.L. 1973: The letter-sound generalizations of first, second, and third grade Finnish children. *Journal of Educational Psychology, 64*, 288-292.

Venezky, R.L. 1976: *Theoretical and Experimental Base for Teaching Reading*. The Hague: Mouton.

Vincent, D. and Cresswell, M. 1976: *Reading Tests in the Classroom*. Windsor: National Foundation for Educational Research.

Vincent, D. and de la Mare, M. 1985: *New Macmillan Reading Analysis*. London: Macmillan Education.

Vygotsky, L.S. 1962: *Thought and Language*. Cambridge, Mass.: MIT Press.

Vygotsky, L.S. 1978: *Mind in Society*. Cambridge, Mass: Harvard University Press.

Wagner, R. and Torgesen, J.K. 1987: The nature of phonological processing and its causal role in the acquisition of reading skills. *Psychological Bulletin, 101*, 192-212.

Wales, R. 1986: Deixis. In P. Fletcher and M. Garman (eds), *Language Acquisition* (2nd edn). Cambridge: Cambridge University Press.

Warburton, F.W. and Southgate, V. 1969: *ITA: An Independent Evaluation*. London: Newgate Press.

Warden, D. 1976: The influence of context on children's uses of identifying expressions and references. *British Journal of Psychology, 67*, 101-112.

Warden, D. 1981a: Learning to identify referents. *British Journal of Psychology, 72*, 93-99.

Warden, D. 1981b: Experimenting with children's language. *British Journal of Psychology, 72*, 217-222.

Warren, W.H., Nicholas, D.W. and Trabasso, T. 1979: Event chains and inferences in understanding narratives. In R.O. Freedle (ed.), *New Directions in Discourse Processing*. Norwood, N.J.: Ablex.

Waterland, L. 1985: *Read With Me: An Apprenticeship Approach to Reading*. Lockwood: The Thimble Press.

Weaver, P.A. 1979: Improving reading comprehension: Effects of sentence organization instruction. *Reading Research Quarterly, 15*, 129-146.

Weaver, P. and Shonkoff, F. 1978: *Research Within Reach: A Research-Guided Response to Concerns of Reading Educators*. St Louis: Cemrel Inc.

Weber, R. 1970: A linguistic analysis of first-grade reading errors. *Reading Research Quarterly, 5*, 427-451.

Weinstein, R. and Rabinovitch, M.S. 1971: Sentence structure and retention in good and poor readers. *Journal of Educational Psychology, 62*, 25-30.

Weintraub, S. 1968: Oral language and reading. *The Reading Teacher, 21*, 769-773.

West, R. and Stanovich, K. 1978: Automatic contextual facilitation in readers of three ages. *Child Development, 49*, 717-727.

West, R., Stanovich, K., Feeman, D. and Cunningham, A. 1983: The effect of sentence context on word recognition in second- and sixth-grade children. *Reading Research Quarterly, 19*, 6-15.

Wheeler, D.D. 1970: Processes in word recognition. *Cognitive Psychology*, *1*, 59-85.

Whimbey, A. and Lochhead, J. 1980: *Problem Solving and Comprehension: A Short Course in Analytical Reasoning*. Philadelphia: The Franklin Institute Press.

White, C.V., Pascarella, E.T. and Pflaum, S.W. 1981: Effects of training in sentence construction on the comprehension of learning disabled children. *Journal of Educational Psychology*, *73*, 697-704.

Williams, J. 1979: Reading instruction today. *American Psychologist*, *34*, 917-922.

Willows, D.M. and Ryan, E.B. 1981: Differential utilization of syntactic and semantic information by skilled and less skilled readers in the intermediate grades. *Journal of Educational Psychology*, *73*, 607-615.

Wimmer, H. 1979: Processing of script deviations by young children. *Discourse Processes*, *2*, 301-310.

Winograd, T. 1972: Understanding natural language. *Cognitive Psychology*, *3*, 1-191

Wittrock, M.C. 1981: Reading comprehension. In F.J. Pirozzolo and M.C. Wittrock (eds), *Neuropsychological and Cognitive Processes in Reading*. New York: Academic Press.

Wittrock, M.C., Marks, C., and Doctorow, M. 1975: Reading as a generative process. *Journal of Educational Psychology*, *67*, 484-489.

Wykes, T.H.M. 1978: *Inferences and Children's Comprehension of Prose*. Unpublished D.Phil. thesis, University of Sussex.

Yuill, N.M. and Joscelyne T. (in press): Effect of organisational cues and strategies on good and poor comprehenders's story understanding. *Journal of Educational Psychology*.

Yuill, N.M. and Oakhill, J.V. (in press, a): Effects on inference awareness training on poor reading comprehension. *Applied Cognitive Psychology*.

Yuill, N.M. and Oakhill, J.V. (in press, b): Understanding of anaphoric relations in skilled and less skilled comprehenders. *British Journal of Psychology*.

Yussen, S.R. 1982: Children's impressions of coherence in narratives. In B.A. Hutson (ed.), *Advances in Reading/Language Research, vol. 1*. Greenwich, Conn.: JAI Press.

Yussen, S.R., Mathews, S.R. and Hiebert, E. 1982: Metacognitive aspects of reading. In W. Otto and S. White (eds), *Reading Expository Material*. London: Academic Press.

Yussen, S.R., Mathews, S.R., Buss, R.R. and Kane, P.T. 1980: Developmental change in judging important and critical elements of stories. *Developmental Psychology*, *16*, 213-219.

Zuck, L.V. 1974: Some questions about the teaching of syllabication rules. *The Reading Teacher*, *27*, 583-588.

Index of Authors

Index of Subjects